The Protection of Property Rights Through Tort Law

This book analyses the problems caused by relying on tort law mechanisms to protect tangible property interests in the common law and suggests a new way of thinking to rectify these issues.

As English common law relies primarily on tort law for the protection of tangible property interests, property rights are protected by a group of claims that as a whole are informed by a set of concerns that have little to do with the vindication of property rights. The book demonstrates how tort law tends to focus on loss within the case law and argues that this fundamental mismatch wholly undermines the category of property rights, since the protection of property through tort is simultaneously too broad and too narrow. Discussing trespass to goods, trespass to land, private nuisance, conversion, and negligent property damage, the book advances a novel way of re-thinking about the property-protecting torts, far better suited to their unique role within the law.

Using cases throughout, the book will be of interest to students, scholars, and practitioners within the fields of property law, tort law, and private law in general.

Victoria Evans (née Ball) is a Lecturer in Private Law at the Dickson Poon School of Law at King's College London. Her research interests lie predominantly in the intersection of Property Law and Tort Law, with a specific interest on the 'Property Torts'. Prior to her appointment at KCL she completed her PhD at the University of Leicester and her LLM and LLB at the University of Birmingham.

The Protection of Property Rights Through Tort Law

Victoria Evans

Routledge
Taylor & Francis Group
LONDON AND NEW YORK

First published 2026
by Routledge
4 Park Square, Milton Park, Abingdon, Oxon OX14 4RN

and by Routledge
605 Third Avenue, New York, NY 10158

Routledge is an imprint of the Taylor & Francis Group, an informa business

British Library Cataloguing-in-Publication Data
A catalogue record for this book is available from the British Library

ISBN: 978-1-032-67712-5 (hbk)
ISBN: 978-1-032-69208-1 (pbk)
ISBN: 978-1-032-69209-8 (ebk)

DOI: 10.4324/9781032692098

Typeset in Times New Roman
by Deanta Global Publishing Services, Chennai, India

Contents

Acknowledgements

This book is based on my PhD thesis, which I completed at the University of Leicester in 2021. For the most part, the claims that are advanced and defended in this book are the same as those that I argued for in the thesis. As such, I am both indebted and grateful to my PhD supervisors, Martin George and Francois du Bois; to my examiners, Paula Giliker and Peter Jaffey; and to Leicester Law School and the wonderful PhD community therein.

Since the completion of my thesis, and throughout the process of proposing, editing, and submitting this book, I have been a lecturer at the Dickson Poon School of Law at King's College London. This book would not have been produced but for the support of the School and my wonderful colleagues (and friends). I am truly grateful to call King's my academic home. A special mention has to be made to my wonderful property law team who have given me a wonderful community and support network at KCL. Within that team, I am particularly appreciative of Jenny Russell and Kate de Contreras who have been my academic cheerleaders and kept me motivated (and even somewhat sane) during the book process.

Finally, on a personal level, I would like to thank my husband, Andy, my family, and my friends. Without their tremendous understanding and encouragement in the past few years, it would have been impossible to produce this work. Less conventionally, I would also like to thank my four-legged 'research assistant' Luna who has been by my side throughout the PhD and monograph submission process.

Table of Cases

Admiralty Commissioners v The Owners of the SS Amerika [1917] AC 38 (HL)Anchor Brewhouse Developments Ltd v Berkley House (Docklands Developments) Ltd (1988) 4 Const LJ 29
Armory v Delamire (1722) 1 Stra 505
Asher v Whitlock (1865-66) LR 1 QB 1
Beirnstein v Skyviews & General Ltd [1978] QB 479.
Blue Sky One Ltd v Blue Airways LLC [2009] EWHC 3314 (Comm)
Bryant v Macklin [2005] EWCA Civ 762
Candlewood Navigation Corp Ltd v Mitsui OSK Lines Ltd PC 1 Jul 1985, [1986] 1 AC 1
Caparo Industries PLC v Dickman [1990] UKHL 2
Cattle v Stockton Waterworks Co (1875) LR 10 QB 453
CBS Songs plc v Amstrad [1988] AC 1013
Coles v Hetherton [2013] EWCA Civ 1704, [2015] 1 WLR 160
Colonial Bank v Whinney (1886) 11 App Cas 426
Colour Quest Ltd v Total Downstream UK Plc [2010] EWCA Civ 180, [2011] QB 86
Costello v Chief Constable of Derbyshire [2001] EWCA Civ 381, [2001] 1 WLR 1437
Davies v Bridgend County Borough Council [2024] UKSC 15, [2024] 2 WLR 1237
Devenish Nutrition v Sanofi Aventis [2008] EWCA Civ 1086
Dominion Mosaics Tile Co Ltd v Trafalgar Trucking Co Ltd [1990] 2 All ER 246
Donoghue v Stevenson [1932] AC 562 (HL) 619
Dunwich (Bailiffs) v Sterry (1831) 1 B & Ad 831
Eaton Mansions (Westminster) Ltd v Stinger Compania de Inversion SA [2013] EWCA Civ 1308, [2014] CP Rep 12
Esso Petroleum Co v Southport Corporation [1956] AC 218 (HL)
Fairchild v Glenhaven Funeral Services Ltd And Others [2002] UKHL 22
Fearn v the Board of Trustees of the Tate Gallery [2020] EWCA Civ 104
Fearn v Tate Gallery [2023] UKSC 4, [2023] 2 WLR 339
Forsyth-Grant v Allen [2008] EWCA Civ 505
Fouldes v Willoughby (1841) 8 M&W 540, 151 ER 1153
García v De Aldama [2002] EWHC 2087, [2003] ECDR CN1
Hamps v Darby [1948] 2 KB 311

Hartley v Moxham (1842) 3 QB 701, 114 ER 675
High Speed Two (HS2)Ltd v Persons Unknown [2022] EWHC 2360 (KB).
Holmes v Mather (1875) LR 10 Ex 261 (Exch)
Hounslow LBC v Twickenham Garden Developments [1971] Ch 233
Howard E Perry Ltd v British Railways Board [1980] 1 WLR 1375
Hunter v Canary Wharf Ltd [1997] AC 655 (HL)
International Factors Ltd v Rodrigiez [1979] QB 351 (CA)
JA Pye (Oxford) Ltd v Graham [2002] UKHL 30, [2003] 1 AC 419
Jaggard v Sawyer [1995] 1 WLR 269
Jarvis v Williams [1955] 1 WLR 71 (CA)
Jones v Llanrwst UDC [1911] 1 Ch 393
Khorasandjian v Bush [1993] QB 727
Kirk v Gregory (1876) 1 Ex d 55
Kuwait Airways v Iraqi Airways (No 4 and 5) [2002] UKHL 19, [2002] 2 AC 883
Kuwait Airways v Iraqi Airways [1995] 1 WLR 1147
Lawrence and Another v Fen Tigers Ltd and Others [2014] UKSC 13, [2014] AC 822
Leigh and Sillavan Ltd. Appellants v Aliakmon Shipping Co. Ltd. Respondents (The Aliakmon) [1986] AC 785
Liesbosch Dredger v S.S. Edison [1933] AC 449
Livingstone v Rawyards Coal Co. (1880) 5 App Ca 25
London Borough of Southwark v Mills, Baxter v LB Camden [1999] 3 WLR 939
Manchester Airport Plc v Dutton [2000] 1 QB 133
Mayor of London v Hall [2010] EWCA Civ 817
MCC Proceeds v Lehman Bros [1998] 4 All ER 675 (CA)
Miller v Jackson [1977] QB 966
Morris-Garner v One Step (Support) Ltd [2018] UKSC 20, [2018] 2 W.L.R. 1353
National Provincial Bank v Ainsworth [1965] AC 1175
Network Rail Infrastructure Ltd v Williams [2018] EWCA Civ 1514
Newbury DC v Russell [1997] EWHC Admin 585
Nicolls v Bastard (1835) 2 CM & R 659
OBG v Allan [2007] UKHL 21 (2008) 1 AC 1
Parker v British Airways Board [1982] QB 1004
Powell v McFarlane (1977) 38 P & CR 452
Rylands v Fletcher [1868] UKHL 1
Sedleigh-Denfield v O'Callaghan [1940] AC 880
Shelfer v City of London Electric Lighting Company. Meux's Brewery Company v City of London Electric Lighting Company [1895] 1 Ch 287
Smith v Stone (1647) Sty 65
Star Energy v Bocardo [2010] UKSC 35, [2011] 1 AC 380
Sturges v Bridgman (1879) 11 Ch D 852
The Directors, etc. of the ST. Helen's Smelting Company v William Tipping (1865) XI House of Lords Cases (Clark's) 642 11 ER 1483
The Maersk Colombo [2001] EWCA Civ 717

The Manchester Shipping Canal Co v Vauxhall Motors Ltd [2019] UKSC 46, [2020] AC 1161
The Tubantia (No 2) [1924] P 78
Towers & Co Ltd v Gray [1961] 2 QB 351
Transco Plc v Stockport Metropolitan Borough Council [2003] UKHL 61
United States of America v Dollfus Meig et Cie SA [1952] AC 582
Vehicle Control Services Ltd v Revenue and Customs Commissioners [2013] EWCA Civ 186, [2013] STC 892
Victoria Park Racing & Recreation Grounds Co Ltd v Taylor (1937) 58 CLR 479
Waverley Borough Council v Fletcher [1996] QB 334 (CA)
White v Morris (1852) 11 CB 1015
Wright v Ramscot (1667) 1 Saund 84
Wrotham Park Estate Co Ltd v Parkside Homes Ltd [1974] 1 WLR 798
WWF v WWF [2006] EWHC 184 (QB)

Table of Legislation

Common Law Procedure Act 1852
County Courts Act 1984
Law of Property Act 1925
Senior Courts Act 1981
Torts (Interference with Goods) Act 1977

OTHER STATUTORY MATERIALS

RSC ORDER 113

1 Introduction

It has been argued that:

> If England had a rational system of law there would be no need for a special section on torts to chattels … It is quite true that goods get lost and stolen as well as damaged and that commercial wrongdoing is not exactly like dangerous behaviour, but the tort of negligence can perfectly well embrace cases where a person has been indirectly deprived of a physical asset and the tort of trespass can cope with the cases of forthright snatching. In a rational system this would be quite adequate, for a plaintiff who had lost goods would obtain tort damages from a defendant only if he was to blame for their loss.
>
> Two conditions would have to be fulfilled before the role of tort could be so sensibly restricted: first, the law of property must provide a means whereby the owner of goods can get them back from whoever is in possession of them without any right to retain them; secondly, the law of contract, rather than the law of tort, must regulate the right of contractors to the property they contract about. Neither condition is satisfied in England.[1]

English common law, unlike its civil law counterparts, lacks any true proprietary action, in the sense of an action that is proprietary in both substance and form[2] and instead relies primarily on tort law for the protection of land and other tangible property interests.[3] This reliance on tort law invokes criticism;[4] one powerful

1 Tony Weir, *A Casebook on Tort* (10th edn, Sweet & Maxwell 2004) 483–84.

2 The typical civil law example being *rei vindicatio* is a classical Roman law action where a claimant could go to court and make a direct assertion of his ownership. See Peter Birks, 'Personal Property: Proprietary Rights and Remedies' (2000) 11 KCLJ 1, 4. See also Michael Bridge, Louise Gullifer, Gerard McMeel, and Kevin FK Low, *The Law of Personal Property* (3rd edn, Sweet & Maxwell 2021) 1-054, which considers how actions can be proprietary in three different ways including in substance but not form.

3 See Birks (n 2) 6.

4 See, for example, Andrew Tettenborn, 'Damages in Conversion – The Exception or the Anomaly?' (1993) 52 CLJ 128; Andrew Tettenborn, 'Conversion, Tort and Restitution' in Norman Palmer and Ewan McKendrick (eds), *Interests in Goods* (2nd edn, Lloyds of London Press 1998); Alison Clarke and Paul Kohler, *Property Law: Commentary and Materials* (CUP 2005); Nick Curwen, 'The Remedy in Conversion: Confusing Property and Obligation' (2006) 26 LS 570.

DOI: 10.4324/9781032692098-1

example is detailed above. The consequence of this reliance is that property rights are protected by a group of claims rooted in an area of law that, as a whole, is informed by a set of concerns that have little to do with the vindication of property rights. This book explores the problems that relying on tort law to protect tangible property (including land), and thus fill the 'gap' in English common law, creates. Weir's argument can serve as a starting point to elucidate some of the issues, or as Weir himself labels them, the 'unfortunate consequences' that ensue, further examined herein:

> The first is to introduce an area of liability without fault: this is unavoidable, because however innocent a person may be in acquiring possession of a thing he must deliver it up to the true owner unless he has some special right to retain it. The second consequence is to raise problems about who may sue: in a property remedy we would naturally define the plaintiff in terms of his ownership or other property right, but when the remedy is in tort one tends to regard the plaintiff's loss as a necessary and sufficient criterion of eligibility to sue. This may, thirdly, give rise to multiple plaintiffs when different people have concurrent interests in the thing. Tort has its own problems, as we have seen, when several people suffer loss as a result of injury to person or property, but these problems will be greatly extended if we make tort perform a property role as well. Fourthly, what of the plaintiff's behaviour? In tort cases his contributory negligence has a role to play in reducing the damages he obtains. This can hardly happen in a property remedy: the owner either gets his thing back or he doesn't. Fifthly, what of the defendant? In a property remedy we would insist that the defendant be in actual possession of the thing: after all, an owner who wants his thing back must sue the person who actually has it. In a tort suit we would be more interested in the defendant's past behaviour – what did he do with the thing? – than in his present position or possession. Sixthly, if the owner, not being bound to sue the present possessor, can sue all those through whose hands the goods have passed, there will be grave problems of multiple defendants. We have seen what happens in proper tort cases – the victim may sue any or all of the tortfeasors until he has been paid off and then those who have paid more than their fair share can claim contribution from those who have paid less … but one cannot simply apply this solution to litigation about lost property. Finally, what order is the judge to make? In tort cases he orders the defendant to pay monetary compensation, but in a property remedy he may have to order specific restitution, and if that is impossible he will be tempted to order the defendant to pay the value of the thing even if that differs from the sum which he would award as compensation. These are the problems which arise when tort takes on the role of property law.[5]

5 Weir (n 1) 483–84.

This quote, while aimed at critiquing the chattel torts,[6] and conversion specifically, gives rise to implications that flow further than merely the protection of personal property through tort law. Rather, the quote evokes important questions about the status of property rights, the role of tort law, the suitability of eligibility to sue criteria, and the remedies provided for invasions of property rights. These questions apply more broadly and are applicable across *all* of the 'property torts' that protect real and tangible property.[7] 'Property torts' here are defined as tortious mechanisms which serve to protect 'property', or the use or enjoyment of 'property'.[8] These actions include conversion, trespass to goods, negligence (as far as it relates to property damage), private nuisance (including *Rylands v Fletcher*), and trespass to land.[9]

Research exploring the full group of these property torts (including actions that protect both real and tangible personal property) is relatively impoverished. Rather, most previous research focuses either on the real property torts,[10] such as private nuisance,[11] or focuses on the personal property torts either individually[12] or as a collective,[13] with little cross-over between the real/personal property divide. This book plugs that gap, but also shows that consideration of the actions in isolation hides wider synergies in how the actions operate, the problems affecting them, and potential solutions.

This book, in exploring the implications of relying on tortious mechanisms to protect property, adopts a structure which allows the four key issues (questions relating to property, the role of tort, bringing a claim, and remedies) to be addressed. The core argument being that *because* the actions explored in this book are classified and thought of as tortious mechanisms, the underlying view of tort law (as, for example, focused on a loss-based model) has implications for how these actions develop through the case law. These decisions often move the actions

6 Weir includes conversion (detinue – now subsumed by conversion), trespass to goods, and, to some extent, negligence within this.

7 As opposed to just the chattel torts as originally raised by Weir.

8 This is an inclusive rather than an exclusive definition; that is, the definition is satisfied whenever a tort can be used to protect property, or its use and enjoyment, including when the tort can also serve to protect other rights/interests.

9 These torts will be discussed in Chapter 3 and their inclusion justified and explained there.

10 See, for example, David Elvin and Jonathan Karas, *Unlawful Interference with Land* (2nd edn, Sweet & Maxwell 2002).

11 See, for example, John Murphy, *The Law of Nuisance* (OUP 2010); Donal Nolan, 'A Tort Against Land: Private Nuisance as a Property Tort' in Donal Nolan and Andrew Robertson (eds), *Rights and Private Law* (Hart 2012); Allan Beever, *The Law of Private Nuisance* (Hart 2013).

12 See, for example, Tettenborn, 'Damages in Conversion' (n 4); Sarah Green and John Randall, *The Tort of Conversion* (1st edn, Hart 2009); Simon Douglas, 'The Nature of Conversion' (2009) 68 CLJ 198.

13 See, for example, Andrew Bell, *Modern Law of Personal Property in England and Ireland* (Butterworths 1989); Sarah Green, 'Understanding the Wrongful Interference Actions' (2010) 1 Conv 15; Simon Douglas, *Liability for Wrongful Interferences with Chattels* (1st edn, Hart 2011); Bridge and others, *The Law of Personal Property* (n 2); Michael Bridge, *Personal Property Law* (4th edn, OUP 2015).

away from their property roots and ignore the importance these actions have to property law. The tortious nature of these actions also has implications for how well these actions remedy interferences with property.

The solution offered is that there needs to be a greater recognition given to the special place that these actions occupy, as they have a unique role spanning both property and tort law. If this is done, and in conjunction we think of tort law in a way that respects the underlying rights that tort law focuses on, property can be better respected and protected by these actions. The proposals in Chapter 7 advocate such a two-pronged approach and argues that both elements are required as these two prongs are interrelated, co-dependant, and facilitative. Focusing on the right protected through a rights-based or corrective justice approach facilitates paying attention to the nature of the right, which, in the case of a property tort is a property right; hence, encouraging a focus on their dual nature and the importance of property law.

Structure and Overview of the Book

This book is structured into three core parts. Part I (The Foundations of the Tortious Protection of Property) is made up of two chapters that explore the theoretical and practical questions that underlie using tort law to protect property; the first chapter deals with property, and the second deals with torts. This part serves as a foundation for the critique and the proposals suggested in the remainder of the book.

The two core themes explored in the property chapter are (i) definitional issues in relation to property, and (ii) the overarching question of what 'property' tort law *should* protect. In considering these themes a series of sub-questions are answered, the first being what it means for something to be a property right. To answer this the chapter identifies the common characteristics of property and property rights. These are then used to answer the second sub-question, which is whether possession can be considered proprietary. The next sub-question explores what is important about property, looking at the importance of the object and the importance of the right and contrasting the different ideas. It concludes that the importance of property lies with the second, namely, the importance of the right *per se*. This also tells us something about how property needs to be protected, which is the final sub-question explored in this chapter. The things discussed in this chapter are necessary preliminary questions as the torts that protect property *should* rely on proprietary concepts, and as such, these proprietary concepts need to be made clear at the outset.

The tort chapter, Chapter 3, starts by introducing the key conceptions and theories of tort law. The analytical approach taken in this book focuses on the underlying role of tort law and the implication of having an action classified as tortious as both a problem and a possible solution; as such, this chapter provides a foundation for the critique and the proposals suggested therein. Finally, this chapter introduces the five property torts that will be considered in this work: namely, conversion, trespass to goods, trespass to land, private nuisance (including *Rylands v Fletcher*), and negligence (as far as it relates to property damage). It discusses their scope, how they operate and briefly deals with any controversial and important aspects of the torts. The complexities and intricacies of the torts are further dealt with in the following chapters.

The second part of this book (Part II: The Implications of Relying on Tort Law to Protect Property) is also made up of two chapters and broadly considers the implications of relying on tort law to protect property. There is much criticism of using tort law to protect property and this part of the book considers some of these core critiques, applying and questioning the applicability of the critique across the whole property tort grouping. In particular, it focuses on two distinct problems that arise from using tort law to protect property. The first is, who is able to bring an action in the property torts and whether this has been unduly influenced by an emphasis on loss caused by the tort law classification of these actions. This is explored in Chapter 4 by looking at the standing rules across the torts on paper and also how they have worked in key cases. It argues that while the standing rules *on paper* are based on some property right, in practice, extensions and exceptions have been created that mean, in many circumstances, the court allows those that have suffered some 'loss' to bring an action, even if that is not backed up by the relevant right. It argues that this has happened because of the tort law classification of these actions and because of the corresponding prominence of loss-based thinking within tort law caused by the prominence of the tort of negligence. As they are classified and seen as tortious, tort law thinking about the importance of loss has infiltrated the actions and influenced the case law and entitlement-to-sue criterion. This often creates a situation where the 'propertiness' of the actions is ignored or forgotten and a greater range of people are allowed to bring an action.

The second problem, explored in Chapter 5, concerns the remedies available in the torts and questions whether they adequately protect property. In doing so, attention is paid to what was found to be important about property in Chapter 2, as well as to different conceptions of tort law. It argues that compensatory damages are often not adequate remedies as they fail to fully compensate what is lost when property is interfered with or taken. This is because they focus on the value of the object, rather than the right (especially when twinned with a conception of tort law that is loss-based as opposed to rights-based). Property rights are important because they give people freedom and control over their environment. To properly compensate for any interference, the loss of control or autonomy needs to be compensated for and not just the loss of the object. It is argued that negotiating damages may do this better. The chapter also considers the availability of return and specific performance remedies, which are often discussed as a core critique in the literature and argues that the difficulty of getting return in the personal property torts suggests a problem with prioritisation that should be revisited.

The first two parts are then coalesced in the third and final part of this book (Part III: A New Solution for the Tortious Protection of Property), which is dedicated to finding a solution to the problems identified. It is made up of two chapters. Chapter 6 argues that the analysis in the preceding chapters suggests that there are problems caused by relying on tort law to protect property: because the property torts are classified and thought of as tortious, this leads to a lack of protection and a lack of respect for the property aspects and nature of these types of actions. The property element of these torts is often ignored, and judicial decisions move the actions away from their property roots. Furthermore, the remedies available do not focus on what is important about 'property'. Together, this leads to a failure to properly protect property rights. This chapter considers whether previous suggestions from the literature made to rectify some of the problems with the property torts (which seeks to introduce a *rei vindicatio*-style property remedy into the common law) could be successful. It ultimately argues that it cannot.

The final chapter puts forward a new suggestion for reform, based around radically rethinking the group of the property torts. These actions are fundamentally part of both property law and tort law, and if we can ensure that the actions are thought of as such, then the incremental changes that move the torts away from property and lead to a lack of protection can be halted and reversed. It advocates a rethinking of the classification of the property tort grouping.

The chapter also considers how thinking of tort law from a rights-based or corrective justice approach would help stop the 'slide into loss-based thinking', which previous chapters show to be a risk resulting from the use of tort to protect property. A rights-based or corrective justice approach highlights the importance of the right underlying the action, which in the case of the property torts is a property right. This approach then helps bring to light, and maintain, a focus on the importance of property law ideals and a 'property law analysis' within questions and decisions in the property torts. The proposals include both the noted 'prongs' – a rights-based or corrective justice approach when analysing and applying the property torts, as well as attention to the character and needs of property law – which work together to ensure that property ideas are respected within the property torts. This is a workable solution to the problems identified and has been shown to be effective in some recent Court of Appeal nuisance cases. The chapter seeks to demonstrate how this would work across other torts with reference to some previous case law explored earlier in this work.

PART I

The Foundations of the Tortious Protection of Property

2 Property

What is the 'Property' that Needs Protecting through Tort Law

Introduction

Consideration of the property torts necessitates some prior discussion of 'property'. In fact, any exploration of the property torts without first considering and understanding the concept of 'property' would be lacking.[1] This is because the role of these tortious mechanisms is, or at least *should be*, the protection of property rights.[2] The torts focus on 'property' and interferences with it. They are 'parasitic' on property law[3] – they borrow ideas from property in order to perform their role – the rights and interests which make up property serve as the foundation of these torts; the law of property consists of 'constitutive rules which establish proprietary rights, and the law of tort (in this case) protects these interests through 'protective rules'. Property law defines who owns what, and then tort law protects those owners against interference.[4] An understanding and recognition of this is fundamental (and something that this work argues is lacking in practice).

It is, however, difficult (if not impossible) to adequately discuss all that property entails within a single chapter. Property is rightly the subject of many stand-alone works and producing a fully comprehensive analysis of property is a feat that is often unattainable within these full-length books, let alone within a single chapter. The approach in this chapter is to develop and use questions which flow from the quoted segment in the introduction by Tony Weir as a base to focus a discussion on property. This is a device employed throughout this work as the quote provides useful starting points for analysis and raises numerous issues that apply to the property torts. This approach allows a discussion of property which touches *only* upon the necessary and relevant debates specific to a consideration of the property

1 Simon Douglas made a similar claim in the introductory section of his book. See Simon Douglas, *Liability for Wrongful Interferences with Chattels* (1st edn, Hart 2011).

2 This is true under the rights-protection model of tort law. Under this conception, tort is said to involve the infringement of a right, or more accurately, the breach of the legal duty not to infringe that right. See, for example, Robert Stevens, *Torts and Rights* (OUP 2007) 284. There are, however, other conceptions of tort law, and these are discussed in Chapter 3.

3 Peter Birks, 'Personal Property: Proprietary Rights and Remedies' (2000) 11 KCLJ 1, 7.

4 Peter Cane, *The Anatomy of Tort Law* (Hart 1997) 10.

DOI: 10.4324/9781032692098-3

torts. Such a focus (and limitation of discussion of property) is common in the work already produced on the torts that protect property.[5]

In particular, by focusing on the quote from Weir in the introduction, the chapter aims to do two core things; The first is to address some 'definitional' questions that arise from the quote (which are also necessary preparatory steps for the analysis that follow). Weir argues that:

> The second consequence is to raise problems about who may sue: in a property remedy we would naturally define the plaintiff in terms of his ownership or other property right, but when the remedy is in tort one tends to regard the plaintiff's loss as a necessary and sufficient criterion of eligibility to sue.[6]

When Weir compares the English common law approach, or an approach which relies on tort mechanisms to protect property, to an approach that uses proprietary mechanisms (more akin to *rei vindicatio*), he argues that the tort approach does not define the claimant[7] in terms of their 'ownership or other property rights' as a proprietary remedy would, but rather, the actions see '*loss as a necessary and sufficient criterion*'[8] to determine who can sue. The role of the definitional element of this chapter is to elucidate these key terms, specifically, what is ownership, what is meant by other property rights (and property rights more generally), and how possession interacts with these concepts (as possession is a core concept in the property torts, which is discussed in greater detail in the next two chapters). This is a necessary preliminary discussion to allow full consideration of the entitlement to sue criteria done in Chapter 4.

The second part of the chapter considers the broader implications and questions arising from the quote, namely, the implication that English common law has failed by not having a remedy akin to *rei vindicatio* and the questions that flow from this:

> If England had a rational system of law there would be no need for a special section on torts to chattels … Two conditions would have to be fulfilled before the role of tort could be so sensibly restricted: first, the law of property must provide a means whereby the owner of goods can get them back from whoever is in possession of them without any right to retain them.[9]

The critique implies property needs to be protected in a way that allows a person to regain possession, and if this is the case, it must be accepted that there is something special about property that needs protecting and which justifies this special protection. This section explores if that is the case. Specifically, it seeks to answer: What is the 'property' that needs protecting through tort law?; How

5 See in particular Douglas (n 1); Sarah Green and John Randall, *The Tort of Conversion* (1st edn, Hart 2009).
6 ibid.
7 This work will use the term claimant rather than plaintiff except where the term appears in a quotation.
8 Tony Weir, *A Casebook on Tort* (10th edn, Sweet & Maxwell 2004) 483–84.
9 ibid.

does this property need protecting?; What protection should it be afforded?; and, Why does 'property' need this special protection, what justifies this? This again is a necessary preliminary discussion to allow full consideration of the adequacy of the remedies available in the property torts done in Chapter 5.

'Property'

'The law of England and Wales accords great significance to property and proprietary rights', which reflects the importance within our modern society. What the law *means*, however, by property 'is nowhere comprehensively defined'.[10] 'Property', as a term, can have many different meanings and can be used in a variety of ways, with many people fluctuating between these meanings.[11]

> Both with lawyers and with laymen this term has no definite or stable connotation. Sometimes it is employed to indicate the physical object to which various legal rights, privileges, etc. relate; then again – with far greater discrimination and accuracy – the word is used to denote the legal interest (or aggregate of legal relations) appertaining to such physical object. Frequently there is a rapid and fallacious shift from the one meaning to the other.[12]

'Property' can be used to mean an actual thing or object, for example, 'this car is my property', 'this house is my property', 'this book is my property'. This is often associated with lay usage and some authors suggest that using property in this way is 'unreflective' and 'meaningless'.[13] When referring to objects of a property relationship like a car or a house, this book will use terms such as 'thing' or 'object' to avoid confusion.

Another way that the term 'property' can be used is to describe the relationship that a person has with a thing. When talking about property in this way, it is accurate to say that you have property *in a* thing. This indicates that you have, and can assert, a 'strategically important degree of control over that resource'.[14] Taking one of the examples just given, instead of remarking that 'this car is my property', under this usage, it is more accurate to say that 'I have property in this car'. That is to suggest that you have a legal relationship of control with the object; you have

10 Lord Fancourt, 'Property's Borderline' in William Day and Julius Grower (eds) *Borderlines in Private Law* (OUP 2024).

11 Weir falls into this trap in the segment quoted in the introduction (elements of which have been repeated previously), Weir, in the same paragraph, used the term property to refer to the physical item or thing in which a property right subsists and also to refer to the legal institution and set of legal rules and norms which operate around a property relationship. See Weir (n 8) 483–84.

12 Wesley Newcomb Hohfeld, 'Some Fundamental Legal Conceptions as Applied to Judicial Reasoning' (1913–1914) 23 Yale LJ 16, 21–22.

13 Kevin Gray and Susan Francis Gray, 'The Idea of Property in Land' in Susan Bright and John K Dewar (eds), *Land Law: Themes and Perspectives* (OUP 1998) 15.

14 ibid.

legal power over that resource. In this work, this is how the term property will be used.

Definitional Challenges: Property Rights, Ownership, and Possession

One of the critiques of the property torts, highlighted at the start of this chapter, raises concerns about entitlement to sue and how much the torts rely (or do not rely) on property rights, and specifically ownership, to restrict those able to bring a claim. To enable consideration of this in Chapter 4, the concepts of ownership, property rights, and possession need to be defined and understood.

Defining Property Rights

Property rights are *rights in rem*. They are rights which avail against a very large or infinite class; they bind the world.[15] *Rights in rem* are often contrasted with *rights in personam*,[16] which differ in exigibility. *Rights in personam* avail only against a specific person, or persons, and can be called personal rights.[17]

Because *rights in rem* are property rights, they are often said to be rights to, or in, a thing; *res* in Latin meaning thing.[18] However, as explained by Hohfeld, it is impossible to have a right held against a *thing;* rights can only be against, and jural relations can only be between, *people*. Thus, to his mind, '*in rem* should only be seen as determining the compass'[19] of the right – who the right is enforceable against – rather than the subject matter of the right.[20] Viewing *in rem* in this way fails to explain *why* some rights are enforceable against the world and others are not. While a right might not be *against* a 'thing', an important element of *in rem* is that it is held in relation to a 'thing'.[21] *Rights in rem* are rights, held in relation to a thing, that are enforceable against the world.

This brief discussion of the nature of *rights in rem* elucidates two fundamental features of a property right: (i) the exigibility of the right, they are binding on the

15 Michael Bridge, Louise Gullifer, Gerard McMeel, and Kevin FK Low, *The Law of Personal Property* (3rd edn, Sweet & Maxwell 2021) 1-007.

16 Douglas (n 1) 9.

17 See Arianna Pretto-Sakmann, *Boundaries of Personal Property: Shares and Sub-Shares* (Hart 2005) 90; Douglas (n 1) 10.

18 Pretto-Sakmann (n 17) 90.

19 John Austin, *Lectures on Jurisprudence or the Philosophy of Positive Law* (Robert Campbell eds, 5th edn, The Law Book Exchange 1885) Vol. I 370.

20 Wesley Newcomb Hohfeld, 'Fundamental Legal Conceptions as Applied in Judicial Reasoning' (1916–1917) 26 Yale LJ 710, 720.

21 The reason that a person has rights enforceable against the world is because the law recognises that the relationship between a person and an object of property is an important relationship that needs to be respected by all. This also accounts for the fact that the law gives rights that are binding on the world in respect of a person's bodily integrity and reputation. People have a special relationship with their body and their reputation, in the same way they have relationships with things. See Ripstein, *Private Wrongs* (Harvard University Press 2016) for a discussion of the rights the law protects in this way.

world; and (ii) the characteristic labelled by Simon Douglas and Ben McFarlane as 'thing-relatedness'.[22] This is the idea that there must be a (physical) thing in which the right can subsist. This latter aspect is somewhat controversial.

Some argue that property rights can *only* subsist in physical things; a property right needs a physical thing to which it can relate. This is sometimes said to be because the thing's/object's physical existence allows people to be aware of it and act/behave in a particular way as a result. It is easy to stay away and not interfere with a physical thing, as you are aware of its existence. This then justifies the fact that the property right is binding on everyone.[23] For example, if I own a bicycle, I expect people to stay away from the bicycle. This is easy to do. You could not *accidentally* ride or steal my bicycle. If you see a bicycle, you expect that it is owned by someone else and thus you do not interfere. Proponents of this view argue that physical things are easier to stay away from than things that are non-physical, such as contractual rights.[24]

While this might hold true for some non-physical things, including contractual rights, this is not true of all non-physical things.[25] The recent work by the Law Commission on Digital Assets supports this contrary view.[26] The Law Commission recommends that digital assets (or data objects) *should* be considered property (or could be a thing in which a property right could subsist) and has suggested law reform to allow this.[27] Sarah Green and John Randall, in their work on the tort of conversion, also refuse to recognise the importance of *physical* things in the determination of objects of property. Instead, they argue that conversion should be applicable to intangibles,[28] as intangibles (or non-physical things) are capable of being property (or at least capable of being possessed) and therefore should benefit from the tortious protection given to other types of property.

While the recent work by the Law Commission and the previous work by Green and Randall shows that the concept of property can and sometimes is taken to have a broader remit, the narrower conception of property, in line with authors such as Douglas and McFarlane, will be employed here. The focus on physical things is justified as it is only within this narrower sphere that the questions that this book seeks to answer arise as the work is focusing *only* on the torts that deal with land or tangible personal property. The recent and authoritative work by the Law Commission shows that these torts *do not* have a role to play (currently or a

22 Douglas (n 1) 12.

23 See Simon Douglas and Ben McFarlane, 'Defining Property Rights' in James Penner and Henry Smith (eds), *Philosophical Foundations of Property Law* (OUP 2013).

24 See Douglas (n 1).

25 Elsewhere I have argued that this relies on a flawed logic. Some intangible 'things', like bitcoin or other 'data objects' (using the Law Commissions terminology) have an existence that makes people aware of them, and so do have some 'thing-relatedness' although they are not a physical thing. See Victoria Evans, 'Conversion and its Future (Reflecting on the Law Commission's work on Digital Assets)' (2024) 88(3) Conv 267.

26 Law Commission, *Digital Assets: Final Report* (Law Com No 412, 2023).

27 ibid 2.52.

28 Green and Randall (n 5).

recommended one) in the protection of intangible property. The Law Commission recommendations are clear, that while these assets *could* be property, they could not be the subject of conversion (or any of the property torts) because they are incapable of being possessed.[29] This is why 'thing-relatedness' is an important part of the concept of a property right for this work.

This discussion has drawn out two distinguishing and fundamental features of property (exigitability against the world, and the importance of 'thing-relatedness'). It is useful, for the purposes of this work, to continue to draw out and highlight these features so that they can be used as criteria to assess whether certain rights, namely, possession, share these features sufficiently to be considered property rights. This is because the classification of possession as proprietary is not universally agreed.[30] To do this, it is useful to explore other articulations of the features of property rights from both the judiciary and academics.[31]

The best known judicial articulation of the features of property rights comes from Lord Wilberforce in *National Provincial Bank v Ainsworth*[32] where it was suggested that, '[b]efore a right or an interest can be admitted into the category of property, or of a right affecting property, it must be definable, identifiable by third parties, capable in its nature of assumption by third parties, and have some degree of permanence or stability'.[33] While this definition has been critiqued for being circular, it does show important other features of property rights, namely, exigibility, excludability, and persistence.[34]

Baroness Hale (as she was) in *OBG v Allan*[35] suggested that the essential feature of a property right is its independence from a particular person; 'it can be bought and sold, given and received, bequeathed and inherited, pledged or seized to secure debts, acquired (in the olden days) by a husband on marrying its owner'.[36] The question of whether something should be considered property, in her opinion, centred on transferability. This has been subsequently supported by Green and Randall who argue that the determinative quality of objects that can be the subject of property rights is that they are transferable.[37]

A similar concept is also at the heart of Peter Jaffey's concept of property where he has suggested that property is made up of two primary rights; (i) the first he labelled as the 'right to benefit' and (ii) the second, 'the right to exclusion or non-interference'. For him, property is really about the former, 'the right to benefit',

29 Law Commission (n 26) 9.66. This is not the place for discussions of whether that is the correct decision. I have given my thoughts on this in Evans (n 25).

30 See, for example, Douglas (n 1). This will be discussed further at 2.

31 This has been pointed out by Douglas (n 1) 16.

32 [1965] AC 1175.

33 *National Provincial Bank v Ainsworth* [1965] AC 1175, 1247–48.

34 The circular nature of this test has already been noted in the literature, see Gray K and Gray S, Elements of Land Law, 5th ed (2009), 97; Martin Dixon, *Modern Land Law* (11th edn, Routledge 2018) 6. While I acknowledge this, it is outside the scope of this work to discuss this at length.

35 [2007] UKHL 21, (2008) 1 AC 1.

36 ibid [309].

37 Green and Randall (n 5) 130–31.

as this is what people would consider valuable about having property. The importance of property is the *uses* that one can put it to, the things people can do with the objects of the property relationship; for example, using it, selling it, and gifting it. As such, this conception recognises the importance and fundamental status of transferability as a defining feature of property rights.

In *Personal Property Law*, the authors sought to draw out a range of different 'suggested characteristics' of property. This list included alienability (or transferability) and exigibility, as noted earlier.[38] They further identified excludability as a feature. A feature also expressed by Jaffey in his work. This feature can be defined as a general duty on the rest of the world not to interfere and to stay away from and exclude themselves.[39] The duty, in Hohfeldian terms, is correlated with a right that the owner, or possessor, holds which is the right to exclude (although it is sometimes called the right to possess).[40] This interest plays an important part in the debate concerning the core of property and whether property relationships should be seen as a bundle of rights, or whether instead the core of property should, and can, be boiled down into one important element or interest. Both conceptions of property, however, show respect and give value to the right to exclude.[41]

The former, namely, the bundle of rights theory of property, is commonly thought of as the combination of the ideas of Antony Honoré[42] and Hohfeld. Hohfeld laid the intellectual foundations for the theory with his jural correlatives and jural opposites and his explanation of the rights, privileges, powers, and immunities.[43] When these ideas are combined, it gives a notion of property as a bundle, or a collection, of rights *vis-á-vis* other people, rather than being focused on a thing or an object.[44] One of the sticks in the bundle is the right to possess, which is the right to be put in control of the thing and remain there. This is the correlative of the duty on the rest of the world to stay away or to exclude themselves.

Those theorists who have sought to move away from the bundle of rights conception of property have often (though not always) focused their attention on the negative incidents. This includes the right to possession, often articulated as the right to exclude, and this has been labelled as the core of property. One advocate of the right of exclusion as the core of property is James Penner, who articulates an exclusionary theory of property. Instead of accepting that property is an aggregate

38 Bridge and others, *The Law of Personal Property* (n 15) 1-004–1-007.

39 Douglas and McFarlane (n 23) 240.

40 This can be defined as being synonymous with exclusive physical control and involving two elements. The first being that the right to be put into control of something, and the latter being the right to remain in control of it – taken from Honoré's articulation of the incidents of ownership. See Antony Honoré, 'Ownership' in Anthony Guest (eds), *Oxford Essays in Jurisprudence* (OUP 1961).

41 As such, it is unnecessary to decide which of these two is the correct view for the purposes of this work.

42 Honoré (n 40).

43 See Hohfeld (n 12) and (n 20).

44 Denise R Johnson, 'Reflections on the Bundle of Rights' (2007) 32 Vermont LR 247, 249.

of different elements, or a bundle of rights, he suggests that property is actually simpler. To him, property is what the average citizen would believe it to be, a right to a thing.[45] This leads him to adopt a new definition of property, where property is not a bundle of rights, but instead

> [I]t is the right to determine the use or disposition of a thing in so far as that can be achieved or aided by others excluding themselves from it, and includes the rights to abandon it, to share it, to license it to others (either exclusively or not), and to give it to others in its entirety.[46]

This he labels as the right of exclusive use. It is a variant of the right to exclude but grounded in the interest that the owner of a thing has in using it.[47]

This view, that exclusion is the focus of the law, is also suggested by Henry Smith.[48] As a law and economics theorist, he suggests that this is because exclusion is a cost-effective way of serving use.[49] The importance of the right to exclude is also argued by Felix Cohen, who maintains that private property must involve the right to exclude;[50] and Thomas Merrill, who has said that to give someone the right to exclude is to give them property.[51]

Other authors, however, argue that the core of property is not the negative aspect of the right to exclude but instead the positive aspects such as the right or liberty to use. Alison Clarke, for example, suggests that it is misleading to focus on the negative right to exclude as it diminishes what is important about owning something and having property rights in things. 'On the whole, the importance to me of book-owning is that it gives me free use of the book – I can read it whenever I want, or put it on the shelf to admire it'.[52] This, to some extent, mirrors the point made by Jaffey earlier.

However, these two rights are not inconsistent, and the latter is not really a right in the true sense; in Hohfeldian terms it is a liberty. It is not a true right (or a claim right, as Hohfeld terms them) because we should only label things as rights if they are correlated with duties. A liberty or privilege arises when the other party does not have a right to do anything to stop the action; I have a privilege to fish if you have no right to stop me fishing. The right of exclusion helps protect this liberty to use by ensuring people stay away so you can do what you want with your thing. The law, at least to some extent, and the torts which protect property, focus on this negative right of exclusion to allow use.[53]

45 James Penner, *The Idea of Property in Law* (OUP 2003) 2.
46 ibid 103.
47 ibid 70–71, Penner is clear that this interest we have in using things is the interest in purposefully dealing with things rather than use in any other sense.
48 Henry Smith, 'Property as the Law of Things' (2012) 125 Harv L Rev 1691, 1692–93.
49 Henry Smith, 'Property is Not Just a Bundle of Rights' (2011) 8 Econ Journal Watch 279, 282.
50 Felix Cohen, 'Dialogue on Private Property' (1954) 9 Rutgers L Rev 357, 371.
51 Thomas Merrill, 'Property and the Right to Exclude' (1998) 77 Neb L Rev 730, 731.
52 Alison Clarke, 'Use, Time and Entitlement' (2004) 57 CLP 239, 241–42.
53 This has also been suggested by Douglas (n 1) 24.

This indicates that the right to exclude, which is the outward aspect of the right to possess, is an important and fundamental aspect of property rights that the law is seeking to protect.

Finally, it is suggested that a 'significant characteristic' of property rights is their persistence, which means that property rights continue, and can still be claimed, in bankruptcy and insolvency.[54] This is a point which has been further made by Michael Bridge, who suggests that insolvency is one of the best touchstones for establishing the proprietary nature of a right.[55]

This brief articulation shows the numerous different 'defining features' of property, namely, exigibility against the world, excludability, 'thing-relatedness', persistence, and transferability (sometimes called alienability). When combined, these features or characteristics can be used to test whether something is a property right. While individually not all the features are distinct to property, together they paint a detailed picture of what property rights are and what features they have.[56]

Different Property Rights

There exists, in property law, a *numerus clausus* of property rights; meaning that the group of property rights is limited and closed in number so that new rights cannot be added.[57] Disputes arise, however, about *exactly* which rights fall within the *numerus clausus*, and the contentious nature of this debate varies depending on whether the focus is on real property (land) or on personal property (everything else).

For personal property, it has been remarked that: (i) ownership, and (ii) possession, are the only two interests in goods (or chattels) recognised at common law.[58] These two rights, it is claimed, make up the *numerus clausus* for personal property. However, not all agree. Douglas argues that possession is *not* a property interest but rather a way to acquire an interest. This point is considered in the 'is Possession Proprietary' section that follows .

For land and real property, the list of rights is longer and includes the fee simple absolute in possession as well as 'lesser property rights', which confer some entitlement to an aspect of the benefit of the land belonging to another.[59] The former is the closest concept to ownership in the land system – it is the greatest interest that a person could possess and a person with such a right is often referred

54 Bridge and others, *The Law of Personal Property* (n 15) 1-057.

55 Michael Bridge, *Personal Property Law* (4th edn, OUP 2015) 42.

56 For example, exigibility against the world is a feature of property rights but it is also a feature of other rights, such as rights to bodily integrity. Furthermore, transferability and how it can be used, given away, or sold, etc. could also be said to be features of some types of contractual right.

57 See, for example, Douglas (n 1) 14. Although there may be rights recognised at equity, for example, the interest under a trust, but these are outside the scope of the thesis as the thesis is focusing on the protection offered by the common law.

58 Bridge and others, *The Law of Personal Property* (n 15) 2-001.

59 Peter Jaffey, *Private Law and Property Claims* (Hart 2007) 76.

to colloquially as an 'owner'. The latter, 'lesser property rights', includes rights such as a term of years absolute in possession (a leasehold), easements, restrictive covenants, mortgages, and so on. These interests are given expression in section 1 of the Law of Property Act 1925.[60]

It is useful to consider the concepts of ownership and possession in more detail as these concepts are relevant in both real and personal property. But more importantly, these concepts are relevant in the way tort law protects property and an understanding of them is fundamental.

Ownership

Ownership is the greatest right (or bundle of rights[61]) that can exist in relation to a thing.[62] While some authors have questioned the significance of ownership (in light of the property tort protection discussed in the next few chapters),[63] it has also been labelled 'the queen of property rights'; it being the greatest possible interest a person can have in relation to a thing.[64] The most influential writing on the concept of ownership comes from Honoré.

Honoré has identified the incidents of ownership. The incidents are not individually necessary, but together are sufficient for their holder to be classed as the owner (although not all may be required).[65] These incidents are: 1) the right to possess; 2) the right to use; 3) the right to manage; 4) the right to the income of the thing; 5) the right to the capital; 6) the right to security; 7) the rights or incidents of transmissibility; 8) absence of term; 9) the prohibition of harmful use; 10) liability to execute; and finally, 11) the incident of residuarity.[66]

To link this back to the concept of property rights discussed earlier, ownership clearly fulfils the requirements of a property right. It is a right that relates to a physical thing, either a chattel or a piece of land, and it is exercisable against the whole world, giving the rest of the world the duty to exclude themselves (fulfilling the exclusion requirement). It is also transferable in that it can be used, enjoyed, gifted, and sold. It has permanence and subsists in bankruptcy and insolvency.

There is a question concerning what the relationship between property rights, ownership, and possession is. One author has suggested that the relationship between property rights and ownership is the same as the relationship between genus and species. The basic principle being that while all ownership includes

60 Law of Property Act (LPA) 1925, see section 1(1) and 1(2).

61 See Honoré (n 40).

62 Andrew Bell, *Modern Law of Personal Property in England and Ireland* (Butterworths 1989) 66. Also see Honoré (n 40) 108.

63 Crossley Vaines, *Personal Property* (1st edn, Butterworths 1954) 4.

64 Ugo Mattei, *Basic Principles of Property Law: A Comparative, Legal and Economic Introduction* (Greenwood Press 2000) 78.

65 Honoré (n 40) 112–13.

66 ibid 113.

property rights, not all property rights include ownership.[67] This is because there are other interests/rights that count as property rights, the most important, in this instance, being possession.

Possession

Possession, as a concept, is of central importance to the protection of personal property in the common law.[68] In fact, in their landmark book on conversion, Green and Randall argued that 'property' was not a helpful term in relation to conversion. It was a term bound more to confuse than clarify, and instead, it was 'far better to stick to the idea of possession'[69] as conversion is 'possessory, not proprietary'.[70] The concept of possession also has a large role to play in the protection of real property rights, especially through the torts of trespass and private nuisance.[71] Despite the importance of the concept and the fact that at first glance the concept seems intuitive,[72] the authors of *The Law of Personal Property* suggest that it is nevertheless 'almost mandatory' for any discussion about possession to begin with two judicial laments.[73] First, Earl Jowitt's observation that 'in truth the English law has never worked out a completely logical and exhaustive definition of "possession"'.[74] Second, Lord Chief Justice Parker's complaint that 'the term "possession" is always giving rise to trouble'.[75]

At its most basic level, however, possession can be said to be about exclusive control,[76] and as a legal concept it is made up of two factors[77] 1) the exercise of factual control; and, 2) the intention to exclude others.[78] These can also be labelled as the manual and cognitive indicia of control respectively.[79]

The manual indicia of possession are the most readily apparent characteristics of possession – the physical control one has over an asset or land. Broadly speaking, someone in control of an object determines, as a matter of fact, 'how [an object]

67 Mattei (n 64) 78.
68 ibid.
69 Green and Randall (n 5) 96.
70 RM Goode, 'The Right to Trace and its Impact on Commercial Transactions – I' (1976) 93 LQR 360, 364.
71 See discussion of what is needed to bring a claim in these torts in Chapter 4.
72 Law Commission, *Digital Assets: Consultation Paper* (Law Com No 256, 2022) 11.18
73 Bridge and others, *The Law of Personal Property* (n 15) 11-001.
74 *United States of America v Dollfus Meig et Cie SA* [1952] AC 582, 605.
75 *Towers & Co Ltd v Gray* [1961] 2 QB 351 at 361.
76 Donald Harris, 'Concept of Possession in English Law' in Anthony Guest (eds), *Oxford Essays in Jurisprudence* (OUP 1961) 74.
77 The term possession is sometimes used to refer to the (interest-generating) factual state of affairs and sometimes to refer to the generated legal interest itself. And when it is used in the latter way, it is normally being used to indicate that the interest is something less than ownership.
78 Bridge (n 55) 33. This was also stated in the judgment of *JA Pye (Oxford) Ltd v Graham* [2002] UKHL 30, [2003] 1 AC 419 in relation to possession of land.
79 Sarah Green, 'Can a Digitized Product be the Subject of Conversion?' (2006) 4 LMCLQ 568, 572.

is kept, whether it is used and, if so, the manner in which it is used'.[80] Physical control could be evidenced by direct physical contact with the goods, or it could be through indirect controls such as having the only key to a warehouse where the goods are held, or the key to the gate which is needed to access land.[81] The control asserted need not be absolute or 'impregnable',[82] but merely *sufficient*; this can be seen in *Manchester Ship Canal* where the Supreme Court agreed that that a person in possession needs "a sufficient degree of physical custody and control" over the relevant object of property.[83]

The degree of physical control which the claimant asserts, or needs to assert, in order to be considered 'in possession', should not be considered in isolation.[84] Instead, it needs to be judged in relation to the greatest degree of control which is possible for the claimant to exercise over the particular asset,[85] considered against 'the nature of the relevant subject matter and the manner in which that subject matter is commonly enjoyed.'[86] Donald Harris uses the example of a shipwreck at the bottom of the ocean. He argues that the control that would count as possession needs to be adapted based on its characteristics and particularly that it is a large asset which is difficult to access. This can be seen in a variety of cases.

When the asset in question is land, questions concerning possession arise within the law of adverse possession. Here it is well established that the degree of possession required depends on the nature of the land and how it is commonly used.[87] In *JA Pye (Oxford)*, for example, in relation to farming land, the defendant was deemed to be in possession where he held the only key to the padlocked farming land (the other sides were enclosed by hedges) and farmed/cultivated it.[88] The requirement is to use as an owner would.[89] In relation to personal property, there is a distinction in what is required for possession based on the characteristics of the good. So while in *Parker v British Airways Board*, Parker was deemed to have a sufficient level of physical control when he found the bracelet and handed it into BA's lost property department, the rules are different when the asset in question is not able to be handled in the same way. In *The Tubantia*, the relevant object was the wreck of a Dutch steamship that had sunk to the bottom of the North Sea. This was held to be in the possession of the claimant salvage company after they placed

80 Luke Rostill, *Possession, Relative Title, and Ownership in English Law* (OUP 2021) 17.

81 *JA Pye* (n 78).

82 Rostill (n 80) 17.

83 *The Manchester Shipping Canal Co v Vauxhall Motors Ltd* [2019] UKSC 46, [2020] AC 1161, [42], [55], and [89] (emphasis added).

84 Harris (n 76) 74.

85 ibid. This was also stated in the judgment of *JA Pye* (n 78) in relation to possession of land.

86 *JA Pye* (n 78) at [41] by Lord Bingham; see also *The Tubantia (No 2)* [1924] P 78, at 89, by Sir Henry Duke.

87 *Powell v McFarlane* (1977) 38 P & CR 452 and *JA Pye* (n 78).

88 *JA Pye* (n 78) [41].

89 In his illuminating recent piece, Jonas Atmaz has argued that what is required is to use as an owner would – not as an *occupying* owner would. See Jonas Atmaz Al-Sibaie, 'Possession and Using Land as an Owner Would' (2024) 2 Conv 176, 176.

buoys to mark the wreck's position and kept vessels and divers at the site of the wreck both to work upon it and to prevent any opportunistic 'new-comers' (competitors) from working on it (as the conditions stopped immediate work).[90]

Exclusive control is, however, only a necessary and not a sufficient condition for the acquisition of possession.[91] Exclusive control must be combined with the second element, the cognitive indicia of possession. This concerns the claimant's mental state regarding the chattel.[92] This intention has been referred to as the 'intention to possess'[93] or, in older authorities, as the '*animus possidendi*'.[94]

This includes their awareness of the goods as well as their active intention to exclude others. This would be satisfied by knowing that the asset exists and wanting (and actively trying) to be the only person who has access to it. As Mr Justice Slade put it in *Powell v McFarlane*,[95] '[t]he *animus possidendi* involves the intention, in one's own name and on one's own behalf, to exclude the world at large … so far as is reasonably practicable and so far as the processes of the law allow'.[96]

Is Possession Proprietary?

Many authors advocate that possession is a proprietary interest. For example, it has been said many times over that the only interests in personal property that are recognised by the common law are ownership and possession.[97] Similarly, Ugo Mattei has labelled possession as something that has protection from the legal system but to a lesser extent than ownership.[98] This view, however, is not uncontroversial, and so it is useful to revisit the distinguishing features of property rights identified previously. These features can be used to consider whether possession, in this legal sense, can be considered a proprietary right; if possession shares the features identified, it should be considered proprietary.

The distinguishing features of property rights identified were exigibility, excludability, 'thing-relatedness', transferability, and permanence. Possession, in the manual and cognitive indicia of the concept, places the exclusion of others at the forefront and so embodies the feature of excludability. It has 'thing-relatedness', relating as it does to an object, asset, or land,[99] and is also binding on the rest of the world as everyone is under a duty not to interfere with something that is in the

90 *The Tubantia* (n 86).
91 Law Commission (Consultation) (n 72) 11.40.
92 Green, 'Digitized Product' (n 79) 572.
93 *JA Pye* (n 78) [42]–[43]; Rostill, (n 80) 19.
94 *The Tubantia* (n 86) 89; *Powell* (n 87) 471; *Parker v British Airways Board* [1982] 1 QB 1004, 1019.
95 *Powell* (n 87).
96 ibid 471–72.
97 See Bridge (n 55) 9; Bridge and others, *The Law of Personal Property* (n 15) 2-001; Bell (n 62) 6.
98 Mattei (n 64) 78.
99 It has also recently been confirmed by the Law Commission that possession *does not* have a role to play in intangibles or data objects. See Law Commission (Final Report) (n 26) 9.66.

possession of another. Similarly, it is transferable and has permanence, which can be seen in Luke Rostill's writings on possession as a legal concept.[100]

Rostill suggests that possession is a proprietary interest but argues that a more appropriate label for this property right is 'general property right', rather than labelling it as a possessory interest, possession, or possessory title. This is because this interest encompasses more than simply the right to possession, as in his view it is also alienable and not possession-dependent. Case law similarly shows that a possession right, or right founded on possession, has all the features of a property right identified in this work.

Take the case of *Asher v Whitlock* as the first example.[101] In this case, Williamson had enclosed some waste land in 1842, and then in 1850 he built a cottage on that land and went into possession of the whole land from that point until 1860 when he died. He left the land in his will to his wife, until she died or remarried, and then to his daughter. Upon his death, his wife and daughter stayed there; his wife then remarried in 1861 and his daughter died in 1863 followed shortly after by the death of his wife. In 1865, the daughter's heir-at-law brought ejectment against the wife's second husband who remained there. The court held that the daughter's heirs could recover the whole property, based on her father's possession which he had passed to her through his will.

The title that the father gained was based on possession; he had no ownership of the land, instead he simply took possession and remained there. This gave him a possessory interest in the land. This interest had 'thing-relatedness', as it related to the land and the cottage that he built on it. The possession right had transferability as it was used and enjoyed by him and was also able to be gifted to his wife and then to his child. It also had persistence as it was able to be passed through a will and continued to exist after the death of the original possessor. Similarly, it gave excludability and exigibility as the right was able to be enforced against the new husband, who, following the right to recover, had to remove himself from the land. This suggests that a right founded on possession can fulfil all of the defining features of a property right.

The same can be noted regarding personal property. Take, for example, the case of *Parker v British Airways Board*,[102] discussed previously, where a person found a bracelet in the executive terminal at Heathrow Airport and handed it into security to try to find the true owner. The Airport did not find the true owner and sold the bracelet for £850. In this case, the court held that the finder had, through his possession, an interest that was binding on everyone else (exigibility against the world) and that continued to exist even after he handed the bracelet over to the Airport to find the true owner and after it was sold on (persistence). This interest related to a physical thing ('thing-relatedness') that allowed him to do things with the bracelet, not only to enjoy it but also to sell it himself (transferability) and created a duty

100 Rostill (n 80).
101 (1865–66) LR 1 QB 1.
102 [1982] QB 1004.

on everyone else to exclude themselves, a duty that the Airport failed to uphold (excludability).

Both cases show that an interest gained by possession comprises all the distinguishing features of a property right and, therefore, suggests that possession is a proprietary interest. In contrast, Douglas strongly argues that possession is *not* a proprietary interest and instead is a way of independently acquiring ownership.[103] For Douglas there can be no proprietary right of possession, which in his mind would be defined simply as a right to remain in possession, as it would be almost meaningless because it is solely contingent on continued physical control. He suggests that this would mean that if a person had possession of, or possessory title to, a car, and he left it unattended, for example by parking it, he would lose possession.

There are a series of problems with his claims. First, Douglas is wrong to suggest that the right gained through possession is a normal right of ownership. Second, he seems to have misinterpreted what the proprietary interest of possession encompasses. Finally, even if a possessory interest is possession-dependent, he has undervalued what a right to remain in possession means in practical terms. These will be addressed in turn.

Douglas maintains that possession is not a proprietary interest that a person can have in an object, suggesting instead that possession is a way of acquiring ownership of a chattel.[104] This suggestion ties in with his later claim that conversion, as a chattel tort, protects ownership, rather than possession as is often claimed.[105] He uses *Armory v Delamirie*[106] to support this assertion, trying to show that a right gained through possession is not possession-dependent and thus this right must be ownership. This claim does not hold up to scrutiny. The facts of *Armory v Delamirie* are well known, but it is useful to recite them to illustrate Douglas's point and the counterpoint made here. In *Armory*, a chimney sweep's boy found a ring and took it to a jeweller for valuation. The jeweller removed the stone/jewel from the ring and refused to return it. The claimant, the chimney sweep, was entitled to sue in trover (the forbear of conversion). Douglas suggests that this case shows 'that by simply taking possession you will acquire more than just a right to remain in possession; you will acquire ownership. Any notion of a "possessory right", therefore, proves superfluous'.[107]

It is true that by taking possession you acquire more than simply a right to remain in possession, a point discussed later, but that does not mean that just because it is *more* than a right to remain in possession that it should be considered and labelled as ownership. Ownership is (and was defined earlier as) the greatest possible right that can exist in a thing. This definition does not accord with the right

103 Douglas (n 1) 31.
104 ibid 30.
105 ibid Chapter 4.
106 (1722) 1 Stra 505.
107 Douglas (n 1) 31.

that a possessor, the chimney sweep in this scenario, would gain/have. To describe the right gained through possession as ownership in this sense would be peculiar; it is obvious that the chimney sweep has not gained such a powerful right. This is because it is clear, even in the reasoning of the case, that if the original owner came forward, the chimney sweep would be expected to hand over the jewel. The right you gain from taking possession is a property right, but it is of a lesser kind than ownership. In cases like the those just mentioned, the interest of the person who gained an interest through possession is less strong than the original owner's right. This right should be thought of and labelled as a lesser property interest gained through possession. This aligns with the thoughts and label given by Rostill.

This leads to the second point, that Douglas's view of what a possessory interest would entail is wrong. He suggests that it would simply be a right to remain in possession, which is possession-dependent, and this is untrue. Rostill's recent work is useful here. Rostill has sought to identify the different possible meanings of 'possession as title' and to determine which applies in English common law. He identifies three views. The first is the 'mere right of possession thesis', which suggests that when a person obtains possession they obtain some possession-dependent, non-alienable right to possession, which includes a right of non-interference binding on all persons.[108] This is the concept of possessory title that Douglas maintains. The second view is labelled as the 'acquisition of property thesis'. This suggests that if a person acquires possession, they gain an alienable and non-conditional interest of having possession, which includes the right to possess and the right to non-interference.[109] The final possible meaning is labelled as the 'deemed property thesis', and this suggests that if a person has possession of something they are deemed to be the owner of that thing.[110]

In his recent work, Rostill considered the case law in detail, examining cases which dealt with both chattels and land and came to the conclusion that the second concept of possession applies in modern law.[111] Possession gives rise to a proprietary interest of possession, which he labels as a 'general property interest'. This right gives rise to a right to possession and a right to non-interference binding on everyone. It is not possession-dependent and is alienable.

The accuracy of Rostill's account can be seen through an exploration of the previously discussed case of *Armory v Delamirie*. The chimney sweep's interest, based on possession, cannot be thought of in the first sense, as his interest was not possession-dependent. He was able to enforce the right against the jeweller even though he no longer had possession of the jewel (as, in fact, the jeweller had taken physical possession of it). Nor does it accord with the third concept of possession. The chimney sweep was not deemed to be the owner, as it was clear in that case that if the original owner came forward, they would have a better

108 Rostill (n 80) 28.

109 ibid 31.

110 ibid 35. This is also the view expressed by Douglas, see (n 104).

111 Rostill (n 80) 125.

right based on their ownership. This leaves the second view, which maintains that the possessor obtains a right to possession and non-interference that is binding on all, independent of continuing physical possession. This accords with the decision made, as the chimney sweep was able to claim trover without continued physical possession of the jewel.

Finally, *even if* Douglas is correct in suggesting that a possession right would simply be the right to remain in possession, he has undervalued what this would encompass. This conception of possession treats possession only as a fact, as simply physical control. But it has been established that legal possession is more than that, that it has both physical and mental elements. Harris has argued that when we talk of possession, we do not need to think about what is necessary to retain possession because, once established, a person will continue to be in possession until he loses it.[112] He does not lose possession until he abandons it or another person gains possession. If possession was *only* a right to remain in possession, it is still not meaningless but actually a valuable right which should be protected.

Possession and Relativity of Title

English property law does not have a system of identifying absolute entitlement, but rather of priority and relativity of title;[113] of establishing who, out of the parties before the court, has the better right. 'What each party has to prove is that he has a better title than the other, not that he has a better title than anyone else in the whole world'.[114] This idea of relativity of title is a fundamental and distinguishing feature of English property law.[115] The various interests one could have, for example, ownership or a right of possession, are prioritised or ranked according to the rules of priority.[116] When accepting the 'strong property thesis' as advanced by Rostill[117] (where taking possession gives the possessor a property right because of that possession, which he labelled as a 'general property right'), 'the doctrine of relative title is, in part, about the priority of competing interests of the same kind, and about the bindingness of the rights that are partly constitutive of those interest'.[118] It is argued that this concept of relativity of title applies to both real and personal property,[119] and can be seen in some of the cases discussed earlier, for example, in *Armory v Delamarie*. The court had to decide who had the best right. This was a case of relativity and priority – who, out of the two, had the better proprietary right. Here it was the chimney sweep. In a case between the chimney sweep and the original owner, priority would instead have been given to the original owner

112 Harris (n 76) 74.

113 *Waverley Borough Council v Fletcher* [1996] QB 334, 345.

114 Alison Clarke and Paul Kohler, *Property Law: Commentary and Materials* (CUP 2005) 386.

115 David Fox, 'Relativity of Title at Law and in Equity' (2006) 65(2) CLJ 330.

116 Rostill, (n 100) 34.

117 See ibid and 3.2 for discussion.

118 ibid 34.

119 Fox (n 115) 330.

whose right was better than the chimney sweep's. But relative to the jeweller, the chimney sweep's right was better. Therefore, when the better right is determined, the better right could be ownership or it could be the lesser right of possession, possibly better articulated as a general property right as suggested by Rostill (or in relation to land, one of the other lesser property rights), but both are examples of proprietary rights.

What is the 'Property' that Needs Protecting through the Law?

This volume is not seeking to rearticulate why we have a conception of property or how the institution began. Instead, the analysis starts from a position of accepting that the common law recognises the institution of property and recognises and respects that the rights people have in things are worthy of some kind of special protection. In the common law this protection comes in the form of torts, and it is these property torts that will be explored in the following chapters. The question here, however, is: What is the 'property' that needs protecting through the law of tort?

The critique highlighted at the start of the chapter implies that property needs to be protected in a way that allows a person to regain possession; and if this is the case, it must be accepted that there is something special about property that needs protecting and that justifies this special protection. This section explores if that is the case. As the torts should be 'parasitic', they should use ideas from property law (including what is considered to be important about property) to shape the protection they offer.

The Importance of 'Property'

In advocating a kind of special protection for the institution of property in English law, it is implied that there is something important and special about property that justifies this protection. But is property important because of the importance of the object of the property relationship or because of the relationship *per se*? This debate concerns whether the object of property is considered as important in itself or as the carrier of wealth/value. However, the debate goes further than how we conceive of objects of property and concerns *why* property rights have the weight and value that they are given. Therefore, this debate concerns whether it is the relationship *per se* that needs respect and weight as opposed to the value or importance of the object.

Importance of the Object

There are many differing ways that objects of property can be categorised or grouped. For example, real/personal; moveable/immoveable; or based on their function. The common law distinguishes between personal and real property because of their differing characteristics, and this distinction roughly corresponds with the distinction drawn in the civilian system between moveable and immovable property.[120] Real property, or realty, is land that includes houses and things attached to the land. Personal property encompasses all other forms of property, such as bikes, cars, and jewellery.[121] This distinction leads to different treatment and means that different legal regimes are used for their protection.

The same cannot be said for the groupings based on the function of the objects of property: Here a distinction is drawn between personal property (not in the same sense as noted earlier) and fungible property, but this does not result in any implications for the protection offered. Fungible is used to denote things that are seen purely as holders of wealth and so are easily replaceable with another of the same type or the market value. While personal in this sense means things valued for themselves, in which a person has a connection.

This categorisation and distinction, however, may be important for what remedies are considered suitable or adequate:

> A thing may be treated for itself and be possessed, used, and disposed of for its own qualities, however banal they be. In this case the legal regime applicable treats the object as unique: it is this house we own and live in, this book we sell and no other. On the other hand, everything may be treated merely as the clothing (investment) worn by a certain amount of wealth. In this case the relevant law accords it the modest role of a member of a class, perfectly replaceable and subject to an implacable regime of real subrogation.[122]

This distinction of seeing things as *things* or as *wealth* has parallels with personhood theory, which may help to explain why objects can fall into either category. Personhood theory, as it is known today, can be traced to Hegel and the discussion of property in the *Philosophy of Right*,[123] although the contemporary articulation comes from Radin.[124] The premise of which is said to underlie Radin's conception of personhood is that 'to achieve proper self-development – to be a person – an individual needs some control over resources in the external environment'.[125]

As a result of this process of 'taking control over resources', people come to possess objects which they feel are *almost* part of themselves. These objects are so bound up with the person's self and personhood that the objects constitute how they see themselves. They become *part of them*.[126] Common examples of this type of object are wedding rings, houses, and family heirlooms. With these types of

120 Although it is suggested that the common law draws this distinction for different reasons. It draws the distinction because of procedural rules in the Middle Ages. See Bell (n 62) 19. Briefly immoveable property is objects/assets such as land and movable is assets such as cars, bikes, etc. that can be moved, as the category names suggest.

121 Bridge and others, *The Law of Personal Property* (n 15) 1-013.

122 Bernard Rudden, 'Things as Thing and Things as Wealth' (1994) 14 OJLS 81, 83.

123 Georg WF Hegel, *Hegel's Philosophy of Right*, (TM Knox tr, Clarendon Press 1952). See discussion in Gregory Alexander and Eduardo Penalver, *An Introduction to Property Theory* (CUP 2012) 57.

124 ibid 66.

125 Margaret Radin, 'Property and Personhood' (1982) 34 Stan L Rev 957.

126 ibid 959.

objects, their loss causes pain which cannot be relieved by a replacement.[127] Radin suggests that the objects with which we form this kind of relationship varies from person to person and is subjective.[128] The opposite of these kinds of objects are those that can be replaced with a substitute or with the market value without causing distress or upset. These items are held purely for instrumental reasons, as Radin puts it.[129]

The problem is that the law surrounding the institution of property has to deal with a variety of different objects, and while the law varies its protection based on whether the object is real or personal, it does not vary its treatment based on whether it is personal or fungible. What we can learn from this exploration is that there are some objects which people are closely connected to and which, when lost or taken, are likely to be only truly remedied by the return of the exact thing, but these objects will vary from person to person.

Importance of the Right

A problem with Radin's approach and focus on the objects of property is that it fails to explain why, in some cases, the law attaches great weight and remedies to interference with property when the objects are not valued by the owner or possessor. The remedies for, and protection against, interferences with property rights are similar, if not the same, whether the object is valuable to the person – for example, their favourite piece of jewellery, or whether it is almost valueless – for example, an old t-shirt.[130] This indicates that the law extends its protection not because of the value of the *object*, but rather because of the value of the *right*, specifically the value and importance of the property right.

Joseph Raz explains this by arguing that it is *not just* the interest in the object that the right is protecting when there is some interference. It is also protecting the interest in *freedom*, in being able to control an element of one's environment.[131] The reason that rights attract a higher level of protection than appears necessary in light of the value of the object to the holder is because the right is not just protecting your interest in the object but your freedom to decide what happens to that object and what you want to do with it; your freedom in selling, giving away, or destroying the object of the right. Rights, and specifically property rights in this case, need protection because they enable people to have freedom and autonomy in making decisions about their own lives. This is why remedies which sufficiently protect the right and allow the person to regain possession are important; they allow the person to regain the control and freedom with regard to that aspect of their life.

127 ibid.
128 ibid 961.
129 ibid 959–60.
130 This is the example used in Joseph Raz, 'Rights and Individual Well-Being' in Joseph Raz, *Ethics in the Public Domain: Essays in the Morality of Law and Politics* (OUP 1995) Chapter 3.
131 ibid 48.

A similar understanding of the importance of property rights can be seen in Kantian ideas and specifically through the articulation of these ideas by Allan Beever and Arthur Ripstein.[132] Ripstein, for example, explains that the relationship between a person and objects of property are important because those objects represent your external means which allow you to pursue your own purposes.[133] Having property rights in external objects allows you to pursue aims and objectives that you set yourself. Because of this, the relationship with property is important and needs to be protected from interference, as having rights in things allows us to make decisions and pursue goals.

Accordingly, focusing on the value of the object of property does not explain the importance and justify the special protection that property has; the importance of property rights *per se* does, however, explain the importance and special protection that property rights have. Property needs special protection because of the important role it plays in autonomy and freedom.

What the Importance of the Right Tells Us about the Property that Needs Protecting

This, however, also tells us something about the property that needs to be protected by tort law. Property places emphasis not on the physical object that is the subject of the property relationship but on the property right *per se*. It is the property right *per se* that is important because of the implications it has for the autonomy and freedom of the holder. As such, when property is protected through tort law, emphasis needs to be placed on restoring the autonomy and freedom and compensating for the loss of that freedom as opposed to merely compensating for the loss of the physical object with its value. The property that needs protecting is more than the thing, and when thinking about property it needs to be thought of in this broad sense.

The Property that Needs Protecting: Respecting the Boundaries of Property

Respect for property and how property needs protecting also encompasses recognising the boundaries of property and when something *is not* a property right. Defining and determining what rights are property rights is important because property rights have implications for third parties, and hence, the world. If the boundaries are not protected, then the balance that property law has sought to create in determining which rights amount to, and can be considered, property rights is undermined. As property rights have implications for third parties, those rights that can be considered proprietary are closed in number; there is a *numerus clausus*. This balance struck by property law ensures that people can make use of things

132 See Arthur Ripstein, *Force and Freedom: Kant's Legal and Political Philosophy*, (Harvard University Press 2009) Chapters 3 and 4, and Allan Beever, *A Theory of Tort Liability*, (Bloomsbury 2016).

133 Ripstein (n 132) 91.

but do not have so much control over external things as to hinder other people's lives – this is why personal rights are not binding on third parties. For property to be properly protected, this boundary needs to be respected for the sake of property holders and the population at large. This might mean that the torts in this area look 'complex', but the complexity is caused by the complexity of the institution of property and the numerous social functions that the concept performs and balances.[134] Property is not well protected if protection is afforded to more people than just those with rights. This is because it undermines the balance struck and stretches the conceptions of what a property right is. The balance is struck by property law and needs to be protected by tort law when offering protection to these rights, as tort law has the ability to 'reshape' property rights. Tort law, in the mechanisms that are discussed in the next chapter, provides the correlative duties to the rights granted by property law, and therefore, shape the right by how the duties are enforced.[135]

Conclusion

This chapter, directed by the questions that arose from consideration of the introductory quote, focused on two broad themes. Those themes were 1) the definitional questions and, 2) what is the property that needs protecting through tort law. Together the answers to these themes give a conception of what property is, and this can now be used to analyse the property torts in more detail. The next chapter will briefly explain the property torts which will form the subject of the rest of the work before progressing to consider some of the criticisms and potential issues. The work done in this chapter will serve as the foundation for much of this.

134 Cane (n 4) 149.
135 Sarah Green, 'Understanding the Wrongful Interference Actions' (2010) 1 Conv 15, 15–16.

3 Tort Law

An Introduction to the Property Torts

Introduction

This chapter does two things; first, it introduces the 'property torts' and second, it considers the role of tort law in light of the critique raised by Weir in the Introduction, Chapter 1. The second element is dealt with first. The book, in the following chapters, focuses on the underlying role of tort law and the implication of having an action classified as tortious as both a problem (leading to a series of implications, or rather, being the basis of a series of implications) but also a possible solution to these problems. As such, it is necessary to unpack and explore why these actions are classified as tortious and how different views of tort law (from a theoretical perspective) affect the working and results of the actions.

Questions concerning tort law, its role, and its theoretical underpinnings flow from the quoted statement from Weir, the relevant sections of which are highlighted in the following:

> The common law has no special remedy for the owner of a thing who wishes to claim it back from the person in possession of it. This gap has therefore to be filled by a remedy in tort. Unfortunate consequences ensue.[1]
>
> Tort has its own problems, as we have seen … but these problems will be greatly extended if we make tort perform a property role as well … In tort cases his contributory negligence has a role to play in reducing the damages he obtains. This can hardly happen in a property remedy: the owner either gets his thing back or he doesn't … In a tort suit we would be more interested in the defendant's past behaviour – what did he do with the thing? – than in his present position or possession.[2]
>
> We have seen what happens in proper tort cases – the victim may sue any or all of the tortfeasors until he has been paid off and then those who have paid more than their fair share can claim contribution from those who have paid less … but one cannot simply apply this solution to litigation about lost property.[3]

1 Tony Weir, *A Casebook on Tort* (10th edn, Sweet & Maxwell 2004) 483–84.
2 ibid.
3 ibid.

DOI: 10.4324/9781032692098-4

> These are the problems which arise when tort takes on the role of property law.[4]

In this articulation of the problems of relying on tort law to 'fill the gaps' left by the failure of English common law to dedicate a proprietary action to the protection of property interests, many questions about tort law arise. For example, it is argued that the gap in property protection '... has therefore to be filled by a remedy in tort'.[5] The question is why. What makes the law of torts the appropriate place for property protection?; What is the function of tort law?; Does this function lend itself well to the protection of property interests?; Or is it just because tort is considered a 'gap filler' that these mechanisms have been given a home here?; and, Are there any implications of doing so? This latter question is the core question of this book, the rest need to be answered at the outset to allow such analysis to occur. Other segments of the quote (spotlighted earlier) imply that the author (Weir) has a specific view of tort law. Does this imply something about a possible conception of the role of tort law? Are there not alternative ways to conceptualise tort law?

These questions will all be addressed in the following sections to set the foundation of the remaining analysis in the subsequent chapters. The chapter then returns to the first aspect identified, namely, exploring the 'property torts'. This involves defining and clarifying the phrase 'property tort', defining the boundaries of that grouping and introducing the five actions which make up this grouping (as dealt with in this work).

The Role of Tort Law

Tort law has, in English common law, been given the important job of being one of the primary mechanisms for the protection of property.[6] Why tort law has this, as it is sometimes called, 'filler role',[7] or 'vacuum cleaner' role,[8] filling in for the lack of a proprietary mechanism and housing the hybrid actions that are a construction of an array of principles that belong to different legal categories, is an important question of significant controversy and debate.[9] The historical why is, however, a

4 ibid.
5 ibid.
6 Simon Douglas, *Liability for Wrongful Interferences with Chattels* (1st edn, Hart 2011) 2.
7 Weir (n 1) 483.
8 John Murphy, 'Hybrid Torts and Explanatory Tort Theory' (2018) 64(1) McGill Law Journal 1, 12.
9 Lady Carr, 'Torts Borderlines' in William Day and Julius Gower (eds) *Borderline in Private Law* (OUP 2024) 63.

less interesting question than the theoretical why[10]; because, actually, '[t]he protection of property has always been one of the prime functions of the law of tort'.[11]

Despite the protection of property always being within the remit of tort law, and arguably being one of the 'most important' functions of tort law,[12] this use of tort law for the protection of property elicits criticisms, some of which are spotlighted at the start of this chapter. However, any perceived conceptual difficulty associated with this combination of proprietary and tortious concerns depends upon an interpretation of the law of torts which does not allow, in and of itself, for the protection of property rights.[13] The focus/function of tort law is thus an important question. The role of tort law within the common law system is, however, often disputed, and there are many different explanations of the role/function/focus that tort law is said to have.[14]

Regardless of the array of different explanations which have been advocated as underlying tort law, Cane has argued that the structure of tort law has been 'fundamentally impacted' *because* the law of tort has been forced to take on this property-protecting role.[15] He argues that within tort law there exists two conceptually different orientations: (i) towards the compensation of losses and (ii) towards the protection of rights.[16] These competing notions will be the focus of the rest of the chapter, and indeed, the rest of the work. These two conceptions, identified by Cane, are also particularly prominent in the literature and can be identified in the

10 Tort law did not develop from a principle of liability which applies and knits all of the torts together. Instead, it 'grew up' without a unified structure, behind a screen of legal procedure. The torts developed from the old writs of trespass and case, which, when abolished, were replaced by causes of actions. These were essentially configurations of facts disclosing a right realisable in court, still using the old names of the forms of action. See David Nolan and John Davis, 'Torts and Equitable Wrongs' in Andrew Burrows (eds) *English Private Law* (3rd edn, OUP 2013) 17.05; John Baker, *An Introduction to English Legal History* (4th edn, Butterworths 2002) 401–65; David Ibbetson, *A Historical Introduction to the Law of Obligations* (OUP 1999) 39–70, 97–125, 153–187. See also James Goudkamp and Donal Nolan (eds) *Winfield & Jolowicz on Tort* (20th edn, Sweet & Maxwell 2020) 2-001. This is the historical answer to why the common law used tort law to protect property interests.

11 Peter Cane, *Tort Law and Economic Interests* (OUP 1991) 21.

12 Peter Cane, *The Anatomy of Tort Law* (Hart 1997) 75.

13 Sarah Green, 'Understanding the Wrongful Interference Actions' (2010) 1 Conv 15, 15–16.

14 For example, some argue that tort is best explained by the residual wrongs model. From this understanding, tort law is made up of civil wrongs which are not dealt with under any other area of law: It is the sum of the wrongs left once those wrongs which fall under contract law, or equity, are removed. See Roderick Bagshaw and Nicholas McBride, *Tort Law* (6th edn, Pearsons 2018) 13 (this is not replicated in the newer edition of this text). Many other scholars have attempted to identify the common characteristic or thread that runs through all of the torts. There are multiple different options which have been explored, the main ones being: 1) compensating harm or loss; 2) the protection of rights and doing corrective justice between the parties; or 3) deterring wrongful conduct.

15 Cane, *Tort Law and Economic Interests* (n 11) 21–22.

16 ibid 21–22.

judgements in property tort cases. They can further represent extremes in thinking that are useful when considering options for reform or ways forward.[17]

Loss Model – Compensating Harms and Loss

Modern tort law allegedly presents itself in two ways: firstly, as a long list of actions; and secondly, as part of society's response to loss.[18] Under this latter perspective, tort law is about compensating for losses; the loss caused to the claimant is the core focus of the tort and what the defendant needs to remedy. While there is nothing intrinsic in the actions themselves, which means that this interpretation is true, Beever argues that this seems to have become the accepted view over the last century.[19] Bagshaw and McBride agree that, at least historically, especially in the second half of the twentieth century (and particularly the 1970s and 1980s), this was the dominant way of thinking about tort law; tort law responds to loss.[20] The predominance and uncontested nature of this idea (historically) is often evidenced by scholars by directing attention towards dicta by Lord Bingham in *Fairchild v Glenhaven Funeral Services*[21] where he alleged 'the overall object of tort law is to define cases in which the law may justly hold one party liable to compensate another'.[22]

Even with the predominance of this idea 40 or 50 years ago (or even 20 years ago in *Fairchild*), some would argue that this idea fails to represent tort law *now*. Bagshaw and McBride, for example, argue that this account of tort law fails to explain important elements of the law of tort. Specifically, they argue, that the loss model of tort law cannot account for the fact that some torts are *actionable per se* or the availability of injunctions as a remedy for some torts. Tort law, thus, cannot be solely responding to, or allocating, loss(es). In fact, they maintain that this view of tort law is 'dangerous' as the predominance of it allows judges to justify becoming 'Loss-finder Generals and start thinking that it is their role as judges when deciding tort cases to determine when [the defendant] should "justly" be held liable to compensate [the claimant] for some loss that [the claimant] has suffered'.[23] This is something explored in the next chapter.

17 Because of the contentious nature of the question and variety of explanations given in the literature, the discussion here is merely an overview of *some* of the core explanations and is necessarily brief and tailored to the discussion and analysis completed later. It does not aim to be a comprehensive account of all of tort law theory, nor could it be in the space of half a chapter. However, the account aims to set up some of the core arguments made later in the work.

18 Allan Beever, 'What Does Tort Law Protect?' (2015) 27 SAcLJ, 626. Here Beever argues that tort law presents itself in two ways. The first is as a long list of actions, and the second is as part of society's response to loss.

19 ibid 262.

20 Nicholas McBride and Roderick Bagshaw, *Tort Law* (7th edn, Pearsons 2024) 15.

21 [2002] UKHL 22.

22 *Fairchild v Glenhaven Funeral Services Ltd and Others* [2002] UKHL 22, per Lord Bingham [9]. Beever (n 18) 626 made reference to this dicta.

23 McBride and Bagshaw, *Tort Law* (7th edn) (n 20) 15.

Despite some scholars' reluctance to admit that the loss model might still have significance in modern tort law, there remains a plethora of works that continues to advocate this model or at least talk of tort in terms of loss and compensation.[24] Regardless of whether the literature and academic work has moved on from this perspective (towards the model that is discussed further on), Cane suggests that many 'participants' in the tort process, by which he means judges, legislators, lawyers, litigants, and so on, think and talk about tort law not only in terms of righting wrongs but also in terms of 'compensation'[25] and allocating loss.

Protection of Rights and Doing 'Corrective Justice'

The other view explored here is the idea that tort law aims to protect rights and do corrective justice.[26] Although rights-based theories (e.g., the work of Robert Stevens[27]) and corrective justice theories (e.g., those put forward by Ernest Weinrib[28] and Arthur Ripstein[29]) are not identical, they share a common feature that distinguishes them from the loss model. Both are non-instrumental theories of private law that hold that the wrongfulness of a tortious act results not from the infliction of a loss as such but from the violation of a right.

This view, for example, does not deny that tort law compensates for loss, but it recognises that loss is recoverable in tort *only* because it is the result of the violation of the claimant's rights; it is the interference with (or violation of) the right, not the loss itself, with which the law is directly concerned.[30] 'Where there is a right, there is a remedy. But where there is no right, there is no remedy (in tort).'[31]

24 See, for example, Calabresi and Melamed, who argue that tort law is a matter of 'liability rules' – making people pay money for the losses caused by them acting in a particular way: Guido Calabresi and Douglas Melamed, 'Property Rules, Liability Rules, and Inalienability: One View of the Cathedral' (1972) 85 Harv L Rev 1089. This view can also be found in the writings of some economic theorists, for example, Posner, who contends that tort law is concerned with allocating losses in the most efficient way, as such there need not be any moral or other kind of judgment – the loss is the focus. See Richard Posner and William Landes, 'The Positive Economic Theory of Tort Law' (1980) 15 Ga L Rev 851, 864. The writers of *Winfield on Torts* would seemingly agree as it is suggested that, at a very general level at least, tort law is concerned with allocating responsibility for certain types of losses. See *Winfield & Jolowicz* (n 10) 1-002.

25 Peter Cane, 'The Anatomy of Private Law Theory: A 25th Anniversary Essay' (2005) 25 OJLS 203, 208.

26 The idea of correcting injustices is intimately and inescapably linked with the idea of protecting rights and thus considered together in this work. The former necessarily encompasses the latter. The injustice that is corrected can (by definition) only consist in the violation of a right and the protection of rights requires a correction of injustice and inequality.

27 See Robert Stevens, *Torts and Rights* (OUP 2007).

28 See Ernest Weinrib, 'Corrective Justice in a Nutshell' (2002) 52 UTLJ 349; Ernest Weinrib, *The Idea of Private Law* (OUP 2012).

29 See Arthur Ripstein, *Private Wrongs* (Harvard University Press 2016).

30 Beever 'What Does Tort Law Protect?' (n 18) 627.

31 Nicholas McBride, 'Rights and the Basis of Tort Law' in Andrew Robertson and Donal Nolan (eds), *Rights and Private Law* (Hart 2011) 335.

As such, if a claimant has suffered loss at the defendant's hands but the defendant has not violated the claimant's rights in causing the claimant's loss, then – on this rights-based view of tort law – the claimant has no case and cannot have a case for suing the defendant in tort.

A rights-based or corrective justice account of tort law, then, shifts the focus so that the gist of tort law is seen as an infringement of rights and about correcting the injustice that results rather than the infliction of loss.[32]

Tort Law and the Protection of Property

The view of tort law adopted has implications for *why* the protection of property should fall within the remit of tort law, and as is argued later, it also has implications for *how* property is protected. Regarding the former, these different conceptions give their own accounts of *why* this gap in property protection was filled by torts: Either because interferences with property usually result in loss (e.g., through the destruction of, or damage to, property); or because interferences with property are infringements of property rights and these rights are rights that can be protected through tort law.

Under this latter explanation of tort law, there is a substantial overlap between tort law and property law. The rights that tort seeks to protect are the product of property law. However, this is often not recognised. This is because of the desire to create clear distinctions between different areas of law that often gives the impression that rules or principles need to be either allocated to property law or to tort law and that they cannot sit in the middle or be allocated to both.[33] The reality is that tort and property overlap significantly. Tort law comes into play only after someone has acquired an interest in property, and that interest, or right, creates a duty which is then protected through tort law.[34] To put this another way, property law establishes proprietary rights and interests through what can be called constitutive rules and tort law then protects through protective rules.[35] Viewing tort law as rights-based or based on corrective justice allows this dual focus to be seen and brings the importance of both property and tort law to the forefront. This specifically, and in general the different theories of tort law, could help solve some of the problems that authors have sought to identify in the property torts.

The 'Property Torts'

Throughout this work, the actions of conversion, trespass to goods, trespass to land, private nuisance, and negligence (as far as it relates to property damage) have been, and will be, grouped and collectively labelled as the 'property torts'.

32 Stevens (n 27) 1. See also *Admiralty Commissioners v The Owners of the SS Amerika* [1917] AC 38 (HL) 55, per Lord Sumner; *Donoghue v Stevenson* [1932] AC 562 (HL) 619, per Lord Macmillan.

33 Bagshaw and McBride (6th edn) (n 14) 30.

34 ibid 30–31.

35 Cane, *Anatomy* (n 12) 10.

This adopted label of 'property torts' is used to mean tortious actions which serve to protect tangible property and land (or interests often equated with property; for example, possession), such as conversion and trespass or those which seek to protect the use and enjoyment of property, such as private nuisance. This is an inclusive rather than an exclusive definition; that is, the definition is satisfied whenever a tort can be used to protect property or its use and enjoyment, including when the tort can also serve to protect other rights or interests.

While there are other torts which might contribute to the protection of property interests, these five torts are the focus as they represent the most widely applicable actions and are considered the most important in terms of the protection of tangible property interests.[36] They are often grouped together and labelled as the property torts in work that has come before.[37] In addition, they have shared features, such as a focus on possession or property interests in determining who can sue, protecting the same interest, and similar remedies, which makes consideration of them as a group appropriate.

This work explores only the torts which deal with tangible property (and land), but in doing so it includes both the torts which deal with personal property and those that relate to real property. This grouping of actions is under-explored (if not completely unexplored), with much of the previous research focusing on individual torts[38] or the personal property torts as a group.[39]

36 See Douglas *Wrongful Interference* (n 6) 3, suggesting that conversion, negligence, and trespass to goods are the most important torts which protect property in chattels.

37 Note, however, that much of the previous research focuses either on the real property torts such as private nuisance or focuses on the personal property torts, either individually or as a collective with little cross-over between the real/personal property divide. As such, consideration of torts which span the real/personal property tort distinction is rarely done; this is something that is done in this book. See, for example, Sukhnider Panesar, 'The Importance of Possession in the Common Law Tradition' [2003] Cov LJ 1, 4–5. However, much of the work focuses either on the personal property torts or the real property torts rather than considering all of the actions as a collective. See, for example, Andrew Bell, *Modern Law of Personal Property in England and Ireland* (Butterworths 1989); Green, 'Understanding the Wrongful Interference Actions' (n 13); Douglas, *Wrongful Interference* (n 6); Michael Bridge, Louise Gullifer, Gerard McMeel, and Kevin FK Low, *The Law of Personal Property* (3rd edn, Sweet & Maxwell 2021); Michael Bridge, *Personal Property Law* (4th edn, OUP 2015) for discussion of the personal property torts. See also, David Elvin and Jonathan Karas, *Unlawful Interference with Land* (2nd edn, Sweet & Maxwell 2002) for discussion of the real property torts.

38 See, for example, John Murphy, *The Law of Nuisance* (OUP 2010); Donal Nolan, 'A Tort Against Land: Private Nuisance as a Property Tort' in Donal Nolan and Andrew Robertson (eds), *Rights and Private Law* (Hart 2012); Allan Beever, *The Law of Private Nuisance* (Hart 2013), in relation to private nuisance. See also, Andrew Tettenborn, 'Damages in Conversion – The Exception or the Anomaly?' (1993) 52 CLJ 128; Sarah Green and John Randall, *The Tort of Conversion* (1st edn, Hart 2009) 170; Simon Douglas, 'The Nature of Conversion' (2009) 68 CLJ 198, in relation to conversion.

39 See, for example, Andrew Bell, *Modern Law of Personal Property in England and Ireland* (Butterworths 1989); Green, 'Understanding the Wrongful Interference Actions' (n 13); Douglas *Wrongful Interference* (n 6); Bridge and others, *The Law of Personal Property* (n 37); Bridge (n 37).

Real property relates to land and the interests in land.[40] The main tortious actions which relate to real property are trespass to land, private nuisance, and negligence as far as it relates to property damage. Personal property is the category of property that is left behind once land has been subtracted.[41] It is a large category which encompasses everything that is not land, for example, bicycles, cars, and books. In the law of tort, personal property or chattels are protected indirectly through focusing on 'wrongful interferences'. The main actions which seek to protect against these 'wrongful interferences' are conversion, trespass to goods, and negligence (so far as it results in damage to goods or to an interest in goods).[42]

Some of the torts that protect interests in property do so only to the extent that there is loss, or damage or harm, caused; most notably this is how negligence and private nuisance functions. Other torts, however, protect against interferences even where no harm beyond the interference itself has occurred, in particular trespass claims.[43] The latter is said to reflect the very high value that the law attaches to property,[44] and specifically to misappropriation and unauthorised exploitation that endangers the economic and social functions of property in a more fundamental way (than those interferences that negligence and nuisance deal with).[45] The complexity of tort law in this area is a reflection of the complexity of the concept of property and the important social and political functions it performs.[46] In following sections, each of the property torts will be considered, analysing how they operate and function. The introduction of the torts will be brief, but the intricacies of these actions will be elucidated and developed through consideration of the issues that flow from these torts in later chapters.

Conversion

The tort of conversion plays a significant and important role in the protection of personal property. In fact, conversion provides the primary mechanism for the protection of personal property in the UK common law and is often labelled as 'the most important of the property torts'.[47] Despite its significance, conversion is also an unpopular and problematic tort. It has been described as 'misunderstood',[48]

40 Bridge and others, *The Law of Personal Property* (n 37) 1-009.
41 Bridge (n 37) 10.
42 Torts (Interference with Goods) Act 1977 (T(IWG)A), s1.
43 Cane, *Anatomy* (n 12) 90.
44 ibid 45.
45 ibid 144.
46 ibid 149.
47 Bridge and others, *The Law of Personal Property* (n 37) 33-013. See also, Peter Birks, 'Personal Property: Proprietary Rights and Remedies' KCLJ 2000, 11(1) 1, 6.
48 Sarah Green, 'To Have and to Hold? Conversion and Intangible Property' (2008) 71(1) MLR 114, 115.

'notoriously difficult to define',[49] 'daunting',[50] and one of the 'mysteries, or perhaps embarrassments of the English Law'.[51] Commentators have suggested that there is no good general definition of the tort, and one senior judge has gone as far as to say that a definition of the action is 'well nigh impossible'.[52]

At a basic level, the tort responds to scenarios when a person intentionally interferes with goods belonging to another – or, more accurately, goods in another's possession – to such an extent that they are excluded from possession of that thing. This interference needs to be so serious that it amounts to an act of dominium by the defendant.[53] This definition can be broken down into its component parts: (i) an intentional interference; (ii) with goods; (iii) in possession of the claimant; (iv) resulting in the claimant being excluded and the defendant acting in dominion.

The leading case that illustrates this last aspect is *Fouldes v Willoughby*.[54] In this case, the manager of a ferry took the claimant's horses onshore to try to entice the misbehaving owner to leave the ferry. This, it was held, was not a conversion because the defendant did not exclude the claimant from his goods, the horses. The claimant could have gone onshore to retrieve his horses and, therefore, it was not an act of true dominium; the ferry owner was not making all the decisions about the thing, in this case, the horses.

To return to the first element, there needs to be an intentional interference. All that is necessary for this is that there must be an intention to exercise dominium, or control, over the goods. This does not have to be an intention to interfere with the goods of someone else. Examples of intentional actions would be driving a car or wearing clothes, because it is impossible to *accidentally* drive a car or put on clothes. An action would be 'intentional' in this sense even if A drove the car wrongly believing it to be their own car, or believing that A had permission to drive the car, because A intended an act of dominium over that car.

This intentional interference needs to be with 'goods'. 'Goods' is defined within the Torts (Interference with Goods) Act (T(IWG)A) 1977 as, including 'all chattels personal other than things in action and money'.[55] This, as such, restricts the tort to protecting things/choses in possession, as 'all personal things are either in possession or in action' (and there is no 'no tertium quid [third thing] between the two')[56] and the latter is expressly excluded from 'goods'. This focus on 'goods' aligns with the historical origins of the tort of conversion. Conversion grew from

49 Douglas *Wrongful Interference* (n 6) 51.

50 Speaking of a 'daunting reputation' – Bridge and others, *The Law of Personal Property* (n 37) 33-013.

51 Andrew Tettenborn, 'Conversion, Tort and Restitution' in N Palmer and E McKendrick (eds), *Interests in Goods* (2nd edn, Lloyds of London Press 1998) 825.

52 *Kuwait Airways Corp v. Iraq Airways Co (Nos. 4 and 5)* [2002] 2 AC 883, 1084 per Lord Nicholls of Birkenhead [39].

53 Bridge (n 37) 88.

54 (1841) 8 M & W 540, 151 ER 1153.

55 Section 14 Torts (Interference with Goods) Act (T(IWG)A) 1977.

56 *Colonial Bank v Whinney* (1886) 11 App Cas 426 (HL) Per Fry LJ at 285.

its forebearers of trover and detinue. Trover was pleaded on the basis of a fictitious losing and finding. To succeed in a claim, the claimant would need to allege: 1) that they were in possession of some specific good as the rightful owner; 2) that they 'casually lost' that item from their possession; 3) that the defendant then found the item and took it into their control/possession; 4) that the defendant then failed to return or deliver the goods back to the claimant upon their request; and 5) that the defendant converted them to their own use.[57] This allegation of losing and finding was in almost all cases a mere fiction used to explain how the good changed hands, and the pleading was abolished in the Common Law Procedure Act 1852. Regardless, the fiction of losing and finding lives on in conversion's focus on tangible goods, as it is only tangible items that would be able to be both lost and found.

This element of the action has recently (and not as recently) been questioned as debates continue about how (and whether) conversion fits in with, or could adapt to fit, the modern world and new types of property. This occurred in 2007 in the House of Lords decision in *OBG v Allan*,[58] which considered whether contractual rights could be converted and recently arose again in light of the Law Commission's work on digital assets. While the Law Commission suggested that *some* digital assets should be considered 'property', they suggested that conversion should not be extended to protect them; instead a new action should be developed, modelled on, or inspired by conversion to protect this type of 'property'.[59] While this is not the place to discuss this further, it is important to (i) recognise the debate currently happening in this area and (ii) note that conversion and the other property torts discussed in this work have been restricted (or at least not extended) by the Law Commission's suggestions and continue to only protect tangible personal property.[60]

The final requirement is that the interference needs to be with the claimant's possession of some good. As a tortious action, conversion focuses on a possessory right. In fact, some have described the action as possessory, not proprietary.[61] As such, it is not necessary to prove ownership of the good in order to make a claim in conversion. Instead, the claimant in a case needs only to show that he had possession immediately before the conversion or that he has an immediate right to possess.[62] Ownership, not coupled with possession, is not enough. So, while the

57 Fifoot, *History and Sources of the Common Law: Tort and Contract* (Stevens & Sons 1949) at 104, recounting collection by Rastell in Rastell, *Collections of Entries* (R Tottell, 1566) at Detinue of charters 204.

58 [2007] UKHL 21, [2008] 1 AC 1.

59 I have given my opinions on this in Victoria Evans, 'Conversion and its Future (Reflecting on the Law Commission's work on Digital Assets)' (2024) 88(3) Conv 267.

60 Reference was made to trespass to good as well as conversion in the Law Commission recommendations. Though much of the discussion concerned conversion. See, Law Commission, *Digital Assets: Final Report* (Law Com No 412, 2023).

61 RM Goode, 'The Right to Trace and its Impact on Commercial Transactions – I' (1976) 93 LQR 360, 364.

62 Andrew Tettenborn (eds) *Clerk & Lindsell on Torts* (24th edn, Sweet & Maxwell 2024) 16–43.

essence of the conversion may well be the protection of property interests,[63] it achieves this by focusing on a superior possessory interest, not the proprietary interest of ownership. It will be seen that this is a common theme in the property torts.[64]

There are numerous ways that a conversion can take place, including: 1) when property is wrongfully taken or received by someone not entitled to do so;[65] 2) when it is wrongfully parted with, usually through a wrongful transfer; 3) when it is lost by a bailee in breach of his duty;[66] 4) when it is wrongfully sold; 5) when it is wrongfully retained or detained;[67] 6) when it is wrongfully misused or destroyed; and 7) when the defendant, without physically interfering with it, wrongfully denies access to it to the claimant.[68]

The remedies for conversion, and the other torts that protect personal property, are governed by T(IWG)A. In practice, an award of damages is the most common relief granted in response to a claim in conversion.[69] The alternative relief, under the T(IWG)A is an order for delivery of the goods or an order for delivery with the option to pay damages in the alternative.[70] These are discussed at greater length in Chapter 5.

Trespass to Goods

Unlike conversion, the definition (or general description) of the tort of trespass to goods is not that controversial. It is generally agreed that the tort is committed when there is a direct, immediate, and unjustified interference with the claimant's possession of a chattel.[71] Alongside this, some authors would argue that there needs to be some mental element, such as intention or at least that the tort could not be founded on some accidental interference of a non-negligent nature.[72] This definition serves as a starting point, and like with conversion noted earlier, it can be broken down into its component parts of (i) a direct, (ii) immediate, and (iii) unjustified interference (iv) with the claimant's possession of a chattel and some level of (v) intention.

63 Sarah Green, 'To Have and to Hold? Conversion and Intangible Property' (2008) 71 MLR 114, 115.

64 This will be discussed at length in Chapter 4.

65 This can be seen in the case of *Kuwait Airways Corp v Iraqi Airways Co* [1995] 1 WLR 1147. In this case, although the actions were covered by state immunity, the action of expropriating a number of Kuwaiti airliners and having pilots ferry them from Kuwait to Iraq was always assumed to amount to a conversion.

66 This is explicitly stated in s2(2) of the T(IWG)A 1977.

67 This can be seen in *Howard E. Perry v British Railways Board* [1980] 1 W.L.R. 1375 (Ch) which stated that detention alone could be a conversion.

68 *Clerk & Lindsell* (n 62) 16-08.

69 Sarah Green and John Randall, *The Tort of Conversion* (1st edn, Hart 2009) 168.

70 Section 3(2) T(IWG)A 1977.

71 See, for example, *Clerk & Lindsell* (n 62) 16–133; Bridge and others (n 37) 3-003; Bridge (n 37).

72 *Clerk & Lindsell* (n 62) 16–135.

An action can be described as direct if there is some kind of physical contact or damage, and without this contact there can be no trespass to goods.[73] This requirement of directness in the tort of trespass is a feature of its development and the historical distinction between the actions of trespass and case.[74] The directness requirement ensured that only the most serious actions were brought before the court, and the requirement remains one of the key requirements in trespass cases. The directness requirement is best shown through examples. The one often used to illustrate this point in the literature involves feeding a dog poison. If a person were to lay down poisonous food for a dog to find, and then eat, this would be indirect. However, if a person were to physically feed the dog the poison, then it would be classified as direct.[75] It is only the latter that could constitute trespass. There are numerous well-established forms of direct interference.[76] Examples include touching a chattel (as in physically making contact with the chattel with your hands),[77] striking/hitting it,[78] handling it,[79] and in shooting it.[80]

In Douglas's work on the chattel torts, he has suggested that the law has 'moved on' from requiring directness in trespass cases (which was only introduced as an administrative tool) and that the tort should instead be assimilated with the other chattel torts which focus on intentional interferences.[81] It is agreed that intention, or at least wilful conduct, is a requirement for trespass to goods; and this has already been included as an element of the definition. However, it is argued that intentional conduct has not *overtaken* the directness criterion, rather the tort requires both. Even in the few cases cited by Douglas where there is a focus on intention, many still cited directness as a requirement,[82] and much of the modern literature and discussion still suggests that an action needs to be direct to allow a claimant to sue in trespass to goods.[83]

Additionally, this direct contact needs to be the immediate result of the conduct of the defendant. An act is said to be immediate when it follows 'so immediately upon the act of the defendant that it might be termed part of the act'.[84] In *Esso Petroleum Co v Southport Corporation*,[85] an oil tanker released oil into an estuary

73 *Hartley v Moxham* (1842) 3 QB 701, 114 ER 675.
74 Douglas *Wrongful Interference* (n 6) 98.
75 Bridge (n 37) 80.
76 Douglas (n 6) 100.
77 In *Hartley v Moxham* (1842) 3 QB 701, 114 ER 675 scratching a car panel was held to be a trespass.
78 *Wright v Ramscot* (1667) 1 Saund 84.
79 *Kirk v Gregory* (1876) 1 Ex d 55.
80 *Hamps v Darby* [1948] 2 KB 311.
81 Douglas (n 6) Ch 6.
82 See *Holmes v Mather* (1875) LR 10 Ex 261 (Exch) where Lord Bramwell, although suggesting the need for intention, continued to acknowledge the importance of the directness requirement.
83 See, for example, *Clerk & Lindsell* (n 62) 16–133; Bridge and others, *The Law of Personal Property* (n 37) 33-004.
84 Anthony Hudson, 'Trespass to Goods' in Norman Palmer and Ewan McKendrick (eds), *Interests in Goods* (2nd edn, Lloyds of London Press 1998) 809.
85 [1956] AC 218 (HL).

that was then carried to the foreshore. There was no immediacy in this case because the oil took over a day to reach the shore and it was only because of the influence of the wind and waves that it reached the foreshore. Because of this, the damage to the foreshore could not be said to be the immediate result of the defendant's conduct.

This interference also needs to be unjustified. An action is unjustified in trespass if it does not fall under one of the defences. It has been suggested that trespass has defences of consent, both implied and express, and of reasonable necessity.[86]

Finally, like conversion, this tort focuses on possession, and so there needs to be an interference with the claimant's possession of the good. The remedies are also similarly governed by the Torts (Interference with Goods) Act, although the remedies available prior to the implementation of T(IWG)A remain available to a claimant.

Negligence (as far as it Relates to Property Damage)

Something needs to be said at the outset about the inclusion of negligence as a property tort, as this might appear somewhat contentious.[87] Negligence, as a tort, is different in kind to the other torts considered in this work. Unlike the other torts included, negligence is not limited to the protection of one particular kind of interest (e.g., property through the protection of possession or use and enjoyment), but instead, because its focus is on the defendant's behaviour,[88] it can protect a variety of interests. That being so, it still has an important role in the protection of property, which justifies its inclusion here despite these differences,[89] and in fact, a

86 Bridge and others, *The Law of Personal Property* (n 37) 33-009.

87 Note also that property tort is not a term of art. It does not have a recognised and strict meaning and is often used interchangeably with other phrases like land-based torts or chattel torts. It can also be used with a narrower or wider meaning. At the outset (and above) 'property torts' were defined as 'tortious mechanisms which serve to protect "property", or the use or enjoyment of "property"'. This is a broad conception of property torts, which focuses on torts that serve to protect property. It is also an inclusive rather than an exclusive definition; that is, the definition is satisfied whenever a tort can be used to protect property or its use and enjoyment, including when the tort can also serve to protect other rights or interests. Negligence, therefore, falls into this classification.

88 *Clerk & Lindsell* (n 62) 7-01.

89 This is also justified because negligence (as far as it relates to property damage) has been included as a property tort in work that has come before. See, for example, Dolan Nolan, 'A Tort Against Land: Private Nuisance as a Property Tort' in Dolan Nolan and Andrew Robertson (ed), *Rights and Private Law* (Hart 2011) 473. Here Nolan talks about the 'other property torts' in the context of claiming that nuisance is a property tort and cites trespass to land, conversion, and 'indeed – property damage claims in negligence' as property torts. Further, Luke Rostill considers the protection of possession and property through torts and lists these actions, including 'property damage resulting from negligence', alongside the other actions considered in this work; he later labels these as the property torts. See Luke Rostill, *Possession, Relative Title, and Ownership in English Law* (OUP 2021) 14–15. See also Green 'Understanding the Wrongful Interference Actions' (n 13) 15; Douglas *Wrongful Interference* (n 6).

consideration of the torts that protect property without the inclusion of negligence would be lacking.[90]

Indeed, Green argued that 'any evaluation of the wrongful interference actions ought always to take into account *all* of the available protection',[91] and this includes negligence as the Torts (Interference with Goods) Act 1977 is clear that negligence is a 'wrongful interference action'.[92] Despite this, negligence is often forgotten about in this regard, or sometimes purposely left out, leaving the protection of property 'incompletely analysed, and consequently insufficiently understood'.[93] This work aims to avoid this common pitfall and instead creates a full and comprehensive picture of the tortious protection of tangible property in the common law.

Green has argued that when the personal property torts (including conversion, trespass to goods, and negligence) are considered as a group of actions, each with its own specific role within the programme of protection, they are 'rigorous and comprehensive'.[94] Conversion and trespass to goods protects property that is interfered with in a direct way, while negligence is concerned with indirect and negligent interferences which nonetheless 'harm' property or a right that someone has in property. Together these torts ensure that property is fully protected. As such, failure to include negligence in this work would mean that the book would provide only part of the picture of the tortious protection of property interests.

A claimant may be able to bring a negligence claim whenever the defendant has acted unreasonably and as a result the claimant has suffered some harm. This is the case if the defendant owed him, and breached, a duty to take care.[95] For this purpose, the focus is only on negligence that results in harm or damage to property. This tort works alongside the other torts in the protection of property by catching non-voluntary behaviour which nevertheless interferes with, or damages, the objects of property or the interests which subsist in property relationships.[96]

To make a successful claim, a claimant will need to satisfy the standard negligence requirements, namely, that a duty of care exists[97]; that it has been breached; that there was a causal link between that breach and the actionable damage suffered; and that this actionable damage should have been reasonably foreseeable by

90 Something similar is said by Douglas in relation to the chattel torts. See Douglas, *Wrongful Interference* (n 6).

91 Green, 'Understanding the Wrongful Interference Actions' (n 13) 16. Emphasis original authors.

92 Torts (Interference with Goods) Act 1977, s1.

93 Green, 'Understanding the Wrongful Interference Actions' (n 13) 17.

94 ibid 15.

95 *Clerk & Lindsell* (n 62) 7-04.

96 Green, 'Understanding the Wrongful Interference Actions' (n 13) 25. Conversion and trespass to goods both focus on voluntary or intentional behaviour.

97 The issue of a duty of care arises comparatively rarely in day-to-day business of the courts, and there is generally a duty of care in physical damage cases. *Winfield & Jolowicz on Tort* (n 10) 5-014. Lord Oliver, for example, in *Caparo* said that in relation to physical damage caused directly by the defendant, 'the existence of the nexus [of duty] between the careless defendant and the injured claimant can rarely give rise to any difficulty' – *Caparo Industries PLC v Dickman* [1990] UKHL 2, 633.

the defendant.[98] Damage is the gist of the tort of negligence, and without it there is no tort.[99] In many cases the question of damage will not be difficult; destroying or damaging (for example, by scratching or denting) an item will amount, obviously, to inflicting damage. *Hunter v Canary Wharf* explained that property will be considered to have been damaged if it undergoes 'a physical change which renders [it] less useful or less valuable'.[100]

To bring a claim in negligence for property damage, it was generally thought that the claimant would have to show that they have an interest in the property that has been damaged or that they were in possession of it, as can be seen in the case of the *Aliakmon*.[101] However, this appears to have been altered by the Court of Appeal decision in *Colour Quest Ltd v Total Downstream*,[102] where a beneficial owner was able to sue for physical loss of pipes as well as foreseeable consequences thereof, provided they joined the legal owner in the proceedings. The interest, therefore, does not seem to have to be a legal interest; an equitable interest may do.

As a 'wrongful interference' under the Torts (Interference with Goods) Act,[103] the remedies available are primarily damages, although there are alternatives of an order for delivery of the goods or an order for delivery with the option to pay damages in substitute (although it is questionable how much these may apply in trespass to goods and negligence cases).[104] As with trespass to goods, remedies available for negligence prior to the enactment of T(IWG)A remain available, and these will also be used in relation to negligence claims relating to land.

Trespass to Land

Trespass to land is the real property equivalent of trespass to goods, as such, there are analogies in the definitions of the two torts. Trespass to land is an 'unjustified interference with the possession of land belonging to (or in possession of) another'.[105] This definition can be broken into its component parts: (i) unjustified interference, (ii) with land, (iii) in possession of another. Some authors would add 'direct' to this definition, and there are often comparisons between trespass to land and private nuisance, the two torts which protect real property. The distinction between these torts is often said to be that while a nuisance action protects against

98 Green, 'Understanding the Wrongful Interference Actions' (n 13) 26.

99 *Clerk & Lindsell* (n 62) 7-06. Douglas, in contrast, has argued that the need for damage should be replaced with the need for an interference to align better with the other chattel torts. However, damage is a fundamental and well-established criterion and reinterpreting this as interference on the basis of a few rogue decisions seems like a rather drastic and radical change in the tort despite the claims of Douglas. See Douglas *Wrongful Interference* (n 6) 151 for this discussion.

100 *Hunter v Canary Wharf Ltd* [1997] AC 655, 676.

101 *Leigh & Sillavan Ltd v Aliakmon Shipping Ltd, The Aliakmon* [1986] AC 785.

102 *Colour Quest Ltd v Total Downstream UK Plc* [2010] EWCA Civ 180, [2011] QB 86.

103 T(IWG)A s1.

104 T(IWG)A s3(2).

105 *Star Energy v Bocardo* [2010] UKSC 35, [2011] 1 AC 380, Per Lord Hope at [6].

indirect action, trespass is concerned with direct actions.[106] This requirement can be shown through the case of *Smith v Stone*.[107] In this case, the defendant pleaded that they had been carried across the boundary onto the claimant's land. The judge found that the defendant had not committed the tort of trespass in this scenario as the trespass was not the direct result of the defendant's actions. The inclusion of direct, also mirrors the definition of trespass to goods discussed earlier.

An interference with land will be deemed unjustified if no defence is applicable. Defences are available if the party had been granted a licence, if the intrusion was necessary, or if it was otherwise justified by law.[108] While the action needs to be unjustified, the action need not, however, be intentional in that the defendant does not need to know that he is trespassing. The defendant would still be guilty of trespass even if he honestly believed that the land he was walking on was his or that he had permission to be there.[109]

This unjustified interference needs to be with 'land'. In this regard, the legal definition of 'land' is employed and so this includes more than simply the surface. Land includes the airspace (up to a height as is reasonably necessary for the ordinary use and enjoyment of land and the structures upon it),[110] it includes below the surface (until it reaches absurdity[111]), and includes interference with the rights held in land such as easements and profits (although claims for the interference with these rights are more appropriately brought in nuisance, considered next).[112]

As trespass seeks to protect the interest of the person in possession of land, one needs to be in possession in order to bring a claim in trespass. Although, as discussed in Chapter 4, there have been cases which have doubted (or gone against this proposition).[113]

Trespass to land is actionable *per se* (unlike private nuisance discussed next where there must be proof of damage to bring a claim), this means that a claimant can bring an action regardless of the extent of the intrusion and without showing any injury or damage to the claimant.[114] Even the slightest crossing of a boundary will be sufficient for a claim.[115] Though they may be restricted in the remedies they receive for minimal interferences. Trespass to land can be remedied by damages, or through awarding an injunction. The latter is particularly useful where the trespass is ongoing because damages will not normally adequately compensate for future

106 *Clerk & Lindsell* (n 62) 18-08.
107 (1647) Sty 65.
108 *Clerk & Lindsell* (n 62) 18–32.
109 Bagshaw and McBride, *Tort Law* (7th edn) (n 20) 276.
110 *Bernstein v Skyviews* [1978] QB 479.
111 *Star Energy* (n 105).
112 See, for example, *Network Rail Infrastructure Ltd v Williams* [2018] EWCA Civ 1514 [40].
113 *Manchester Airport v Dutton* [2000] 1 QB 133.
114 There is a fundamental right to object to a trespass as said in *Newbury DC v Russell* [1997] EWHC Admin 585 per Rattee J.
115 *Clerk & Lindsell* (n 62) 18-01.

trespasses.[116] Damages can be substantial, or if there is no physical harm, they can be nominal.[117]

Private Nuisance

Private nuisance[118] has been accepted, by both academics and judges, as a property tort or a tort against land.[119] It is a tort which protects real property, land, and deals with violations of the rights (or interests) held in it. More specifically, a nuisance action seeks to protect the claimant's use and enjoyment of land,[120] or possibly more accurately, the usability of land.[121] This latter expression is useful as it better elucidates the idea that the focus of the action, as a property tort, is on interferences with the utility and amenity value of the land *itself*, as opposed to interferences with the specific and individual uses people occupying the land might have put to it or their personal discomforts.[122]

The tort of nuisance was recently clarified, or rather 'transformed',[123] by the Supreme Court decision in *Fearn v Trustees of the Tate Gallery*.[124] This landmark decision questioned whether private nuisance could protect privacy or visual intrusion. The claimants were long leaseholders of flats in a luxury development (Neo Bankside) opposite the new extension of Tate Modern (the Blavatnik), which included a viewing gallery on the top floor that gave panoramic views over London. As well as panoramic views of London, the viewing gallery gave an unobstructed view to the almost half-a-million visitors a year into the claimants' flats via the apartments' floor-to-ceiling glass windows, and it was claimed that despite notices asking visitors to respect the privacy of the Tate's neighbours, a significant number of visitors took photos/videos, peered into the flats, and even waved to the occupants. The claimants argued that this constituted a nuisance and the Supreme Court, by majority, found both that visual intrusion *can* amount to a private nuisance and that on the facts it *did* amount to a nuisance. More interesting than this

116 Kevin Gray and Susan Gray, *Land Law* (7th edn, OUP 2011) 10-012.

117 *Clerk & Lindsell* (n 62) 18–65. Although, there is an alternative way of quantifying damages based on a hypothetical negotiation between the parties or a licence fee calculation. This will be discussed in Chapter 6.

118 In this work, any reference to 'nuisance' will mean 'private nuisance'. I will primarily use the former for ease of language.

119 See, for example, Donal Nolan, 'A Tort Against Land: Private Nuisance as a Property Tort' in Donal Nolan and Andrew Robertson (eds), *Rights and Private Law* (Hart 2012); Donal Nolan, 'The Essence of Private Nuisance' in Ben McFarlane and Sinead Agnew (eds) *Modern Studies in Property Law, Volume 10* (Bloomsbury 2019). This has also been reiterated in core cases including *Fearn v Tate Gallery* [2023] UKSC 4, *Network Rail Infrastructure Ltd v Williams* [2018] EWCA Civ 1514, *Hunter v Canary Wharf* [1997] AC 655.

120 Paula Giliker, Tort (8th edn, Sweet & Maxwell 2023) 10-03

121 Nolan, 'The Essence of Private Nuisance' (n 119).

122 *Fearn* (n 119) [11].

123 James Lee, 'Different Views of Nuisance' (2023) 139 LQR 535, 536.

124 [2023] UKSC 4.

specific conclusion, though, was the significant ramifications for the *scope* of nuisance and changes made to the *approach* taken in nuisance claims which flow from the core principles of nuisance set out by Lord Leggatt.[125] This case, thus, now serves as the basis for understanding the tort.

The essence of nuisance, post-*Fearn*, is a *substantial interference with the claimant's ordinary use of their land*.[126] This is the core enquiry in a nuisance action, and it is worth breaking it down. The finding of a substantial interference is an objective test; the focus is on the ability of the land to be used or enjoyed or the 'usability' of the land, as opposed to specific uses that those occupying wish to make. 'Substantial' was used here to mean that this interference must exceed a minimum level – this was compared to terms such as 'real', 'substantial', 'material', and 'significant', which have all been used in previous decisions.[127] Further made clear in the judgment is that this substantial interference can be caused by any means; there is no conceptual or *a priori* limit to what can constitute a nuisance.[128] In particular, Lord Leggatt made clear that nuisance does not have to be caused by emanations.[129] This puts an end to the physical invasion view of nuisance, which was made popular by scholars such as Simon Douglas and Ben McFarlane.

The physical invasion view of nuisance tried (or tries) to reformulate nuisance as a mini-trespass-like tort and argue that nuisance is a tort that deals with boundary crossing by 'intangible things' like smells and noises which would not otherwise be a trespass.[130] The underlying reason for these scholars arguing the physical invasion view of nuisance was a desire to maintain that the right protected (in Hohfeldian terms) by nuisance is the right to exclude, which is the element of a property right that has implications on third parties and which the other property torts protect.

The implication of the acceptance that emanations do not underlie the tort is that nuisance is *not* protecting the right of exclusion. While the other property torts help show the boundaries of property in terms of the hard and fast lines about exclusion, for example, with trespass to land helping to demark what is and is not land through the application of its strict rule and enforcement of the right to exclude,[131] nuisance adds colour to the picture. Nuisance, instead, is about the balancing of rights of neighbours – 'about the terms on which owners can relate to one another and to others, about what would be fair and reasonable for an owner to ask others

125 As argued in Victoria Ball, 'The "Property" in [Tate] Modern Nuisance: Case Comment on *Fearn v Trustees of the Tate Gallery*'. (2023) 87(2) Conv 205, 205. Here Lord Leggatt framed this as re-articulating the core principles of the tort that already existed, but it has been widely commentated in the literature that this amounts to a reframing and new account. See, for example, Lee (n 123) 536 and also Ball (n 125) 205.

126 *Fearn* (n 119) [21].

127 ibid [22–23].

128 ibid [12].

129 ibid [13].

130 Simon Douglas and Ben McFarlane, 'Defining Property Rghts' in Penner J and Smith H (eds), *Philosophical Foundations of Property Law* (OUP 2013).

131 See, for example, *Star Energy* (n 105)

to bear'.[132] It highlights the uses of property and the powers and limits of owners to do things on their own land when others could be unfairly affected.

The second aspect of this core enquiry is the priority afforded to the general and ordinary use of land over more particular and uncommon uses,[133] which Lord Leggatt emphasised as being fundamental to the common law.[134] He went on to say there are two aspects to this. The first is that the occupier cannot complain if the use interfered with is not an ordinary use[135] – recall *Robinson v Kilvert*[136] here: The brown paper stored, that was particularly sensitive to heat, was not a usual or ordinary use of the claimant's land. The second aspect of this priority is that, '[e]ven where the defendant's activity substantially interferes with the ordinary use and enjoyment of the claimant's land, it will not give rise to liability if the activity is itself no more than an ordinary use of the defendant's own land'.[137] This stops normal uses of land e.g., living in a house without adequate soundproofing from being a nuisance,[138] but fumes which damage crops and trees[139] and noise and vibrations which affect your business[140] will be considered a nuisance. The aim being to balance the interests of the defendant to use their land in any way legally permitted, with the conflicting interest of the claimant to have the quiet enjoyment of their land.

The 'new' articulation of the role of 'ordinary and common use' subsumes discussions of 'reasonable user' and the ideas of 'give and take' or reciprocity between neighbours, all of which were said to underlie the priority given to ordinary uses of land. It is within this 'common and ordinary' use test that other factors such as locality, malice, etc. can be considered, as they previously were under 'reasonable user'. Public benefit, and the fact that the activity causing the nuisance was carried out for the public benefit, however, is not relevant within this element of the framework. Lord Leggatt did suggest that this would be relevant in determining the appropriate remedy. The standard remedies available in nuisance are an injunction or damages, although the award of the former is discretionary.[141]

The result of this new articulation is that all the claimant has to show is a substantial interference. Once this is found, attention then turns to the defendant. If a defendant can show that the use of their land was 'common and ordinary', then this will be sufficient for it not to be deemed an actionable nuisance. This is because of

132 Christopher Essert, 'Nuisance and the Normative Boundaries of Ownership' (2016) 52 Tulsa Law Review 85, 88.
133 *Fearn* (n 119) [24].
134 ibid.
135 ibid [25].
136 (1889) 41 Ch D 88.
137 *Fearn* (n 119) [27].
138 *London Borough of Southwark v Mills*, *Baxter v LB Camden* [1999] 3 WLR 939.
139 *The Directors, etc. of the St. Helen's Smelting Company v William Tipping* (1865) XI House of Lords Cases (Clark's) 642 11 E.R. 1483.
140 *Sturges v Bridgman* (1879) 11 Ch D 852.
141 Allan Beever, *The Law of Private Nuisance* (Hart 2013) 145.

the priority that nuisance *now* accords to the general and ordinary use of land over more 'particular and uncommon uses'.[142]

Like the other torts already discussed, the claimant in a nuisance action needs to have exclusive possession, or an interest in land, to bring a claim. This is because it is a tort which protects land and thus protects only those that have an interest in the land or are deemed to be the owner.[143] This has elicited criticisms in the past, and is discussed in Chapter 4, but flows from the idea that as a property tort, the action is seeking to protect the land itself as opposed to the comfort of the individuals occupying, something once again reiterated in *Fearn*.

Rylands v Fletcher

There remains a question about the inclusion of the tort commonly referred to as the *rule in Rylands v Fletcher*.[144] Ever since its conception, this tort has been controversial.[145] Historically, there has been some debate about the nature and classification of the *rule in Rylands v Fletcher*.[146] This disagreement was 'resolved'[147] by the decision in *Transco Plc v Stockport MBC*, which contains a confirmation by the highest court that the rule in *Rylands v Fletcher* is, in fact, a sub-species of nuisance.[148]

Lord Bingham in *Transco* summed up the modern-day rule of *Rylands v Fletcher* as follows:

> An occupier of land who can show that another occupier of land has brought or kept on his land an exceptionally dangerous or mischievous thing in extraordinary or unusual circumstances is in my opinion entitled to recover compensation from that occupier for any damage caused to his property interest by the escape of that thing, subject to defences of act of God or of a stranger, without the need to prove negligence.[149]

142 *Fearn* (n 119) [24].

143 *Clerk & Lindsell* (n 62) 19–60.

144 [1868] UKHL 1.

145 Donal Nolan, 'The Distinctiveness of *Rylands v Fletcher*' (2005) 121 LQR 421, 421.

146 Some authors have argued that *Rylands v Fletcher* is a subset of nuisance; see, for example, *Clerk & Lindsell* (n 62) 19–41. Other authors have disagreed, arguing that it is a distinct and different kind of action, See, for example, Percy Winfield, 'Nuisance as a Tort' [1931] CLJ 189, 195; John Eekelaar, 'Nuisance and Strict Liability' (1973) 8 IJ 191, 196. Finally, there is a further category of academics who have argued that it is impossible to decide between the two options because of the incoherence of nuisance. See, for example Beever (n 141) 108. Suggesting on page 107 that even the courts have taken a 'cop-out' position in *Transco Plc v Stockport Metropolitan Borough Council* [2003] UKHL 61.

147 Quote marks are used here to recognise that not all authors think this debate has been resolved. See Nolan, 'The Distinctiveness of *Rylands v Fletcher*' (n 145), arguing that this assimilation is bad for nuisance and bad for *Rylands v Fletcher* at 422.

148 *Transco Plc v Stockport MBC* [2003] UKHL 61; [2004] 2 AC 1, [9].

149 ibid [11].

The result of this is that *Rylands v Fletcher*, as an offshoot of the law of private nuisance, is concerned with the protection of land[150] and covers the division of risk between different owners of the land.[151] As a sub-species of nuisance, *Rylands v Fletcher* belongs to the category of property torts. But, on the authority of *Transco*, it is merely a 'sub-species' of nuisance and all important cases or elements will be considered as part of the analysis of private nuisance (as opposed to giving separate).[152]

150 *Winfield & Jolowicz on Tort* (n 10) [16-004].

151 *Transco* (n 148) [52].

152 This is also justified as the role of *Rylands v Fletcher* in the protection of property is very minimal in practice. The authors of *Winfield on Torts*, for example, have said that 'the tort has rarely been the basis of a successful claim in the English courts since 1900'. See *Winfield & Jolowicz* (n 10) [16-004].

PART II

The Implications of Relying on Tort Law to Protect Property

4 Bringing a Claim

The Influence of 'Loss-Thinking'

Introduction

This chapter and the next engage with some of the 'unfortunate consequences' raised by Weir in the introductory quote to show some of the implications (or problems) caused by relying on tort law to protect property. The focus of this chapter is on the entitlement to sue criteria in the property torts and what is needed to bring a claim in these torts. This was one of the first critiques raised in the introductory quote, Weir argued that:

> The second consequence is to raise problems about who may sue: in a property remedy we would naturally define the plaintiff in terms of his ownership or other property right, but when the remedy is in tort one tends to regard the plaintiff's loss as a necessary and sufficient criterion of eligibility to sue.[1]

This quote suggests that unlike a 'property remedy', tort remedies (or actions) do not define the claimant[2] in terms of their 'ownership or other property right', but instead use 'loss as a necessary and sufficient criterion' to determine who can sue.[3] In the property torts, the criteria to sue *on paper* are not focused on 'loss' but rather on proprietary rights. The argument, nonetheless, is, and must be, that regardless of the criteria *on paper*, there is a tension between the preoccupation of tort law with loss and the need for a remedy designed to properly protect property, and this has resulted in an infiltration of 'loss-thinking' where there is a more significant focus on the presence or absence of loss as opposed to the proprietary rights at play.

To put another way, due to the tortious classification of these actions, 'normal tortious thinking', influenced by the modern dominance of negligence,[4] about the importance of loss (widely defined) informs (consciously or unconsciously) the development of the case law, and as a result the actions themselves, often creating a move away from property protection and rules. The wider argument here is that the protection of property is compromised because these actions are classified as,

1 Tony Weir, *A Casebook on Tort* (10th edn, Sweet & Maxwell 2004) 483–84.

2 In this work, I will use the term claimant rather than plaintiff except where the term appears in a quotation.

3 Tony Weir, *A Casebook on Tort* (10th edn, Sweet & Maxwell 2004) 483–84.

4 Andrew Tettenborn (eds), *Clerk & Lindsell on Torts* (Sweet & Maxwell, 24th edn 2024) 1–15.

DOI: 10.4324/9781032692098-6

and property is protected through, mechanisms that are tortious, and thus rooted in an area of law that as a whole is informed by a set of concerns that have little to do with the vindication of property rights.

However, this emphasis on loss is not inescapable. Recent decisions by the Court of Appeal (to some extent retreated from by the Supreme Court) in *Network Rail Infrastructure Ltd v Williams*[5] and *Fearn v the Board of Trustees of the Tate Gallery*,[6] both private nuisance cases, show how strong dicta on the property-protecting role and nature of the property torts can stop the over-extension of a property tort that results from such a slide into loss-focused thinking. This focus on the dual role of the property torts and the importance of property law to these actions is aided by a theoretical conception of tort law that focuses on rights. This is because a rights-based model directs attention to the underlying right that is being protected, which in the case of these torts (including negligence when it is being used to protect a property interest) is a property right.

The structure and content of this chapter is guided by the introductory quote. Specifically, it seeks to answer two core questions which arise from the quoted statement: i) how is entitlement to sue defined *on paper* in the property torts?, and ii) how does the idea of 'loss as a necessary and sufficient criterion' fit or interact with the criteria for bringing a claim in the torts? Essentially, how is eligibility to sue determined *in practice*? This chapter will explore these questions by first considering the importance of 'loss' in tort law. It will go on to examine the different entitlement to sue rules and relevant cases in each of the torts, exploring how claims are brought both *on paper* and *in practice*. In doing so, specific attention will be paid to the influence of loss-thinking within these decisions and whether such thinking is avoided.

'[L]oss as a Necessary and Sufficient Criterion'

It was claimed that because the torts (specifically conversion in the introductory quote) are tortious, there is a tendency 'to regard the plaintiff's loss as a necessary and sufficient criterion of eligibility to sue'. It is difficult to deny the obvious, i.e. that the torts base entitlement to sue on some kind of property right – at least on the face of it. As such, the problem is based on something other than the standing rules *on paper*. Rather, the concern is that due to the tortious classification of these actions, the loss-based conception of tortious liability (which has been made predominant by the modern dominance of the tort of negligence) informs the development of the case law and as a result, the actions themselves. This view features in the introductory quote, but can also be found in other writing; for example, Green argued, in relation to conversion, that *because* conversion is tortious, it is more focused on what has been lost as opposed to what the claimant is entitled

5 [2018] EWCA Civ 1514, [2018] 3 WLR 1105.
6 [2020] EWCA Civ 104, [2020] 2 WLR 1081.

to.[7] Implying a focus on loss, as opposed to proprietary entitlement. If correct, this suggests that actions classified as tortious could never rid themselves of loss-focused tort thinking and focus instead purely on the proprietary interest at stake. This is because it is the theoretical ideas underlying tort law that causes and creates a difference in treatment because of the primary focus of that area of law and the conception of what that area of law should do. Cane observed a similar trend. He argued that because tort law has been given a significant role in the protection of property, this has (fundamentally) impacted the structure of tort law. Within tort law there exists two distinct conceptual orientations; one towards compensating loss and the other towards protecting rights.[8] The latter should be the focus of the actions which protect property. However, the influence of negligence has created a tendency to see tort *only* as the former.

However, this critique reaches beyond the initial focus on entitlement to sue; the issue is not just that loss-thinking informs who is entitled to sue, but that it influences the whole action and determines when a claim is likely to be successful (because loss-thinking interacts and informs the decision-making of the judges and results of cases). As such, while the primary focus in this chapter will remain on the entitlement to sue criteria, the discussion will range more widely where appropriate to fully consider the influence of loss-thinking in tort law. For example, where relevant, in what follows there will be consideration of how loss-thinking interacts and influences the substantive application of the property torts.

To consider this fully, it is first useful to consider whether and how loss is viewed as an important part of tort law.

Loss and Tort Law – Classification

In law there is a tendency to classify actions into discrete categories, to subdivide things into areas such as tort law, contract law, constitutional law, for instance.[9] Classification in this sense involves forming, from the mass of legal claims,

7 Sarah Green, 'Can a Digitized Product be the Subject of Conversion?' (2006) 4 LMCLQ 568, 570.

8 Peter Cane, *Tort Law and Economic Interests* (OUP 1991).

9 Eveline Ramaekers, 'What is Property Law' (2017) 37 OJLS 588, 589. It should be noted, however, that there are some proponents who argue that classification is meaningless and unhelpful. See, for example, Andrew Scott, 'The Scope of Non-Contractual Obligations' in John Ahern and William Binchy (eds) *The Rome II Regulation on the Law Applicable to Non-Contractual Obligations: A New International Litigation Regime* (Brill 2009) and Andrew Scott and Adam Rushworth, 'Rome II Regulation: Choice of Law for Non-contractual Obligations' [2008] LMCLQ 274. Talking from a conflict of law background, he argues that the process of classification or characterisation of laws into discreet categories is unhelpful and pointless because to classify an action, a person would have already had to make some judgment about where that law is to be classified, to then consider the grouping in more detail to see if it fits. As such there seems to be a two-stage test where classification is predetermined before we truly consider the classification question.

groupings on the basis that they share such common features as to make them suitable for collective categorisation.[10]

Charlie Webb advocates that there are two possible objectives for a classificatory scheme. The first is simply to present the law in a more simple and accessible way.[11] This is in line with the idea that classification makes the teaching of law more coherent – teaching is easier if the law is structured and classified in a convenient way. The alternative approach is that classificatory schemes can be used to contribute to the development of the law.[12] In this sense, classification can be used to shape or influence judicial and legislative decision-making beyond simply providing a neatly ordered account of what the cases and statutes have previously decided or declared.[13] Classificatory schemes are to be *followed* – they provide direction when deciding novel points of law and give a standard against which existing law is to be judged.[14] As has been recently alluded to by Lord Sales in his chapter in *Borderlines in Private Law*:

> Law is complex. You see only a part of the forest in one case, and it is easy to make a misstep. So taxonomy is important when considering the guidance function of a judge, particularly at the level of an apex court providing strategic guidance for the legal system as a whole. We need to be able to fit our rulings into the existing framework in a coherent way, or to be able to give good reasons when we choose to modify it.[15]

Taxonomy and classification guide judges. This latter objective of classification can be labelled as dispositive, in contrast to the former, which is expository.[16]

Despite the importance and unavoidability of this idea of classification, it is widely accepted that it is an illusion to try to draw hard and fast lines between the different categories, as they connect,[17] and interact, and in reality are only 'relatively' independent from each other.[18] The creation of distinct categories of law can be analogised with the slicing of a cake – the law can be divided in many different ways, in the same way a cake can be sliced in different ways.[19] Despite this,

10 Charlie Webb, 'Treating Like Cases Alike: Principle and Classification in Private Law' in Andrew Robertson and Hang Wu Tang (eds) *Goals of Private Law* (Hart 2009) 215.

11 ibid 216.

12 ibid 216–17.

13 ibid.

14 ibid.

15 Lord Sales, 'Borderline in Private Law: An Introduction' in William Day and Julius Gower (eds) *Borderlines in Private Law* (OUP 2024) 2.

16 ibid using the terminology adopted by Cane. See Cane, *The Anatomy of Tort Law* (Hart 1997) 200–202.

17 Ramaekers (n 9) 589. See also Roderick Bagshaw and Nicholas McBride, *Tort Law* (6th edn, Pearsons 2018) 30, suggesting that 'One unfortunate side effect of this need to divide up the law is that it creates the impression that there is a clear-cut division between these different areas of law'. This, they suggest, is incorrect. This statement is not replicated in newer versions of this text.

18 James Penner, *The Idea of Property in Law* (OUP 2000) 37.

19 This is an analogy used by Stevens. See Robert Stevens, *Torts and Rights* (OUP 2007) 284.

the classifying of an action into one group can have implications for how that area develops and grows. This is especially true if classification is seen as dispositive. This can be regarded as a problem if the classification does not seem to be fully appropriate or the best place for the actions to sit in the classification system.[20] If, for example, the property torts are classified and thought of as purely tortious, judges' use of this classification could influence and shape their decisions. This can lead to the property element of the action being ignored, and this is how 'loss' or tort law thinking more generally can infiltrate the torts.

Loss as a Central Concept in Tort Law

Within tort law there is a distinction commonly drawn between property torts and personal torts.[21] The actions considered in this work fall into the former group, for example, conversion, nuisance, and trespass to land and goods. Negligence is the exception here as it appears to straddle both groups, with property damage negligence claims falling into the former category and other negligence cases falling into the second group. Along with personal injury negligence cases, actions such as defamation and trespass to the person make up the latter group. Despite this distinction between the two groupings of torts, it has been argued that the modern dominance of negligence has caused an emphasis on loss and compensation as the primary role or the core of tort law.[22] This emphasis on loss has spread across both groupings and as such informs the development of all of the torts.[23]

Weir advocated such an opinion in his chapter entitled the 'Staggering March of Negligence'.[24] Here he argued that there has been an 'infiltration of negligence' and that negligence-thinking has started to take the space and influence the decision in other areas of tort law.[25] He suggested that the influence of negligence thinking across the tort spectrum had been varied but 'far from negligible'[26] and that the 'pull of the negligence principle … is immensely strong'.[27] Since Weir

20 This is especially true if we compare the classification of the property torts (conversion, trespass to land, and private nuisance) to their civil law equivalent. In civil law traditions *rei vindicatio*, often seen as a true proprietary action, and similarly the possessory interdicts and nuisance, are seen as being part of property law as opposed to part of tort law.

21 Paula Giliker, 'The Relationship between Property Law and Tort Law' in Alistair Hudson (eds) *New Perspectives on Property Law: Obligations and Restitution* (Taylor and Francis 2003) 69.

22 *Clerk & Lindsell on Torts* (n 4) 1–15.

23 Giliker 'The Relationship between Property Law and Tort Law' (n 21) 71 – suggesting that 'the influence of negligence-based reasoning in the 20th century has extended beyond such 'personal' torts, and, combined with concerns as to distributive justice, has made some impact on the development of the property torts'.

24 Weir, 'Staggering March of Negligence' in Peter Cane and Jane Stapleton (eds) *The Law of Obligations: Essays in Celebration of John Fleming* (OUP 1998).

25 ibid 112. Mentions it taking the space that used to be reserved for trespass to the person and influencing and causing discussions about whether conversion has been influenced or affected by 'thinking more characteristic of tort', 114.

26 ibid 137.

27 ibid.

made this statement twenty-two years ago, the pull of negligence has only gotten stronger, as has the loss-thinking underlying this 'negligence thinking'.

The different theories of tort law were discussed in the previous chapter. These varying explanations of tort law appear to disguise the influence that loss-thinking has in practice. Some of these theories do not appear to focus on the concept of loss; yet, in practice, loss has a great influence on case law. For example, loss clearly has an influence under the loss-model of tort law and still plays a role under the rights-based or corrective justice approach where our conception of loss influences our thinking about the rights that require protection.[28]

Despite the myriad of differing explanations of tort law, it is submitted that the modern dominance of negligence in tort law has, at least in the eyes of some authors and judges, caused an emphasis on loss and compensation as the primary role or focus of tort law.[29] Cane suggests that many 'participants' in the tort process (by which he means judges, legislators, lawyers, litigants, and so on), think and talk about tort law not only in terms of righting wrongs but also in terms of 'compensation'.[30]

Beever has claimed that the dismantling of the loss-based model, in favour of the rights-based approach, while attempted, has been incomplete.[31] This is because even with a move to a focus on rights, tort law, and the rights that we see as important, are influenced by a person's understanding of what tort law is, or should, be doing, and because of the dominance of negligence within modern tort law, the focus still remains on loss. Therefore, if people tend to think about tort law as loss-based, those rights will be intimately linked with loss. This, Beever argues, can be seen in the case of defamation; defamation is thought of as protecting a right to reputation, but this is because reputation is usually what is lost in these kind of actions.[32] A similar thing can be said to occur in property-based torts. The focus is traditionally on what was lost, which, for example, was the possession of the land or good. This, then, influences the rights that we think the torts protect – the right to possession – but when we think about this right, we subconsciously focus on physically losing something. This causes extensions to the torts and this can be seen in the cases, for example, the exceptions in conversion and the contractual right to possession, discussed shortly. This argument suggests that even if the law has moved on from seeing loss as fundamental to tort law, the history of this account still bears heavily on the way we think about the individual torts, even if this is now done through the guise of a rights-based

28 Allan Beever, 'What Does Tort Law Protect' (2015) 27 SAcLJ 627, suggesting that the dismantling of the loss model remains incomplete and so this influences our perceptions of what rights need to be protected.

29 *Clerk & Lindsell* (n 4) 1–15.

30 Peter Cane, 'The Anatomy of Private Law Theory: A 25th Anniversary Essay' (2005) 25 OJLS 203, 208.

31 Beever (n 28) 627.

32 ibid, 628.

approach. This appears to suggest that efforts to re-analyse and re-emphasise the role of the torts, and specifically the role of the property torts, will not be totally effective, as tort law (and the actors involved in tort law) seem unwilling to forget or move on from loss-based thinking (even if they think they already have or are doing so).

This dominance of negligence and the idea of loss arguably informs the development of all of the torts, and this will be explored in the following sections. The differing explanations, however, are useful as they articulate that loss does not have to have this primary role, or even if important, it need not be the complete focus. Tort law can be viewed in different ways. This could help alleviate the criticism or implications of the property torts.

The Property Torts, Entitlement to Sue, and the Concept of Loss 'as a Necessary and Sufficient Criterion'

The starting point is that the tortious actions do use proprietary concepts to determine who is entitled to bring an action. They use either the concept of possession (which is proprietary [see Chapter 2] and a simple and effective concept to use in the determination of entitlement to sue) or the actions focus on other property rights (such as having title/ownership), which can be seen in nuisance and negligence. The standing rules on paper thus obscure the interaction of loss-thinking in the torts and in their eligibility to sue criterion. This section argues that loss-focused thinking permeates the actions so that judges and cases focus on repairing or compensating losses, be that physical or normative, even when this causes extensions to the actions and those entitled to bring a claim. This undermines 'property' and the limits of property rights.

Use of Possession – Conversion and Trespass to Goods

An important similarity between the actions is that many of the property torts rely on the concept of possession, at least to some extent, to determine who is entitled to bring a claim in the tort. This is especially true of conversion, trespass to goods, and trespass to land (nuisance sometimes uses possession, although only exclusive possession, to determine who can bring an action). However, possession does not necessarily mean the same thing in each of the torts, and they all draw the boundaries of possession in a slightly different way (at least superficially) so there are subtle differences between the torts.

In conversion, the claimant needs to show that she had possession immediately before the conversion or that she has an immediate right to possess to be able to bring a claim.[33] A possessor, and thus someone entitled to bring a claim, could be

33 *Clerk & Lindsell* (n 4) 16-043.

an owner, but they could also be a thief – someone who had illegitimately gained possession,[34] or they could be a finder of the good/item.[35]

With regards to the right to immediate possession, it has been suggested that this right needs to be (or at least theoretically should be) a proprietary right, rather than a merely contractual right (although this does not seem to be the case).[36] This original proposition is in line with the case of *Jarvis v Williams*,[37] which concerned the sale of bathroom fittings. The court in this case held that the property had already passed to the purchaser and the contractual arrangement for re-collection held by the claimant was not enough to alter that finding. The result was that the claimant had no immediate right to possess, which was proprietary in nature sufficient to bring a claim in detinue (a forebearer to conversion[38]).[39] This case has since been relied on to suggest that the immediate right to possession necessary to bring a claim in conversion needs to be proprietary rather than contractual,[40] but not all of the case law and commentary surrounding this area of law supports this proposition. For example, in *MCC Proceeds v Lehman Bros*,[41] the court sought to explain the previous decision of *International Factors Ltd v Rodrigiez*.[42] They suggested that the right to sue in that case was based on the contractual right to possession that derived from the factoring agreement; the right to possess need not always be proprietary.

Green has sought to provide an alternative interpretation of *Jarvis*, arguing that the reason the contractual rights were not sufficient in that case was because they were not contractual rights which gave them a right to possession.[43] Contractual rights to immediate possession may be sufficient if they are actually such rights – this is in line with the Eighteenth Report of the Law Reform Committee which asserted that 'in conversion an immediate right to possession, however arising, is sufficient'.[44] This suggests that the immediate right to possession criterion has been interpreted in case law as allowing those with a contractual *or* proprietary immediate right to possession to bring an action.

34 *Costello v Chief Constable of Derbyshire* [2001] EWCA Civ 381, [2001] 1 WLR 1437.

35 *Armory v Delamarie* (1722) 1 Stra 505.

36 *Clerk & Lindsell* (n 4) 16-062. A proprietary right to immediate possession would be a property right; in contrast, a contractual right to possession would not be proprietary.

37 [1955] 1 WLR 71 (CA).

38 An action that was previously separate to conversion but which now falls under conversion and can no longer be brought as a separate action as per the Torts (Interference with Goods Act) 1977.

39 *Jarvis* (n 37).

40 See Andrew Tettenborn, 'Trust Property and Conversion: An Equitable Confusion' [1996] CLJ 36, 37; *Clerk & Lindsell* (n 4) 16–62; *International Factors Ltd v Rodrigiez* [1979] QB 351 (CA), per Sir David Cairns at 357. A contractual right to possession does not give right to a proprietary interest – a proprietary right to immediate possession does.

41 [1998] 4 All ER 675 (CA).

42 [1979] QB 351 (CA).

43 Sarah Green and John Randall, *The Tort of Conversion* (1st edn, Hart 2009) 98.

44 The Eighteenth Report of The Law Reform Committee (Conversion and Detinue) Cmnd. 4774, 1971, Para 9(1).

Like conversion, trespass to goods protects possession; only someone in possession of the goods at the time of the alleged trespass is entitled to sue.[45] It could be argued, however, that trespass to goods is more restrictive than conversion in its focus on possession – only actual possession prior to the trespass will be sufficient (rather than also allowing those with an immediate right to possession to claim).[46] Notwithstanding this, there are numerous exceptions to this rule. Firstly, a trustee not in possession can sue any third party in trespass even if the chattels are in the hands of the beneficiary.[47] Secondly, an executor or administrator may also sue anyone interfering with the chattels of the deceased before probate or letters of administration are granted in trespass. The owner of a franchise (for example, to take wreck or treasure trove) can sue in trespass anyone taking the goods before he could seize them.[48] And finally, where a bailment is determinable at will,[49] the bailor retains sufficient possession to entitle him to sue third parties.[50] This has led some authors to suggest that while it is established that only those in possession of the chattel at the time of the interference can sue, possession has been defined in such a way as to blur the distinction between actual possession and an immediate right to possession.[51] Bridge, for example, argues that this means that the same interest is needed to sue in either conversion or trespass to goods, though articulated in a slightly different way.

It is unclear whether these are *exactly* the same type of interests. There are similarities between the exceptions in trespass and the rule in conversion. For example, the bailment at will example depends on the bailor having some immediate right to possession that is exercisable by notice to the bailee. Likewise, the franchise example relies on the idea that the owner of the franchise has some right to possession that allows him to bring such an action. As such, the trespass exceptions and conversion rules are comparable, and both seem to be based on the idea or concept of a right to possession. The rule in conversion, however, is wider than the exceptions listed for trespass to goods. For example, it is possible to think of some cases where title to sue in conversion would be found on the basis of their immediate right to possession, but there would be no entitlement in trespass falling under one of the exceptions. In *International Factors Ltd v Rodrigiez*, the claimants had an immediate right to possession under the factoring agreement, which would not fall under the exceptions in trespass. The entitlement to sue in conversion, therefore, is broader than in trespass despite the exceptions extending the scope.

Generally, both trespass to goods and conversion use proprietary rights to determine entitlement to sue. However, the fact that in conversion a non-proprietary

45 *Clerk & Lindsell* (n 4) 16–139.

46 ibid.

47 *White v Morris* (1852) 11 CB 1015; *Barker v Furlong* [1891] 2 Ch 172.

48 *Dunwich (Bailiffs) v Sterry* (1831) 1 B & Ad 831.

49 *Nicolls v Bastard* (1835) 2 CM & R 659.

50 *Clerk & Lindsell* (n 4) 16–139.

51 Michael Bridge, *Personal Property Law* (4th edn, OUP 2015) 84.

immediate right to possession entitles someone to bring a claim might also suggest that the torts do not always rely on proprietary concepts.

While these exceptions and extensions do not fully align with the concept of loss as a purely factual concept, the courts do seem to be focusing on loss, just in the normative sense, as a loss of entitlement features in these cases. Due to the tortious classification of these actions, 'tort-based thinking' concerning the importance of loss and remedying loss influences the property torts. As such, the torts do not have a focus on property but instead on remedying any loss, even if this means extending the parties entitled to sue, as we saw in *Jarvis* and *Rodriguez*. By allowing those with either a proprietary or contractual right to immediate possession, the law is moving away from a proprietary focus and instead ensuring that any party who has suffered some loss of entitlement is compensated.

It is interesting to note that under a rights-based or corrective justice approach, these decisions, which allow someone with merely a contractual right to possess to make a claim, would appear to be wrong. This is not to deny that tort law can be used to protect personal or non-proprietary rights under the rights model, but rather when employing a rights-based or corrective justice model in the property torts, that the rights should be proprietary to ensure correlativity. Weinrib, for example, makes it clear in his articulation of corrective justice that rights need to underlie the action to ensure correlativity between the claimant and the defendant. He explains that 'if the loss of which the plaintiff is complaining is not the subject matter of a right or if the defendant's conduct is not wrongful with respect to that right, then the defendant is not under a duty of care to the plaintiff'.[52] In this scenario, the right that the claimant may have or is claiming is a contractual right and that would not create a correlative duty on the defendant; to make a claim in tort, a claimant must show that they have (or had) a right, exercisable against the defendant, that has been infringed.[53] The claimant here, while possessing a right, does not have a right exercisable against the defendant as it is not a property right (which is exercisable against the world), rather it is contractual and thus exercisable against only the other contracting party. Therefore, this decision is wrong from this perspective. Ripstein makes a similar point; he argues that a person can only wrong another by interfering with something to which the other party has a right, or as he articulates it, something which they already have, being your body or property. As such, interfering with property that is not yours but in which you merely have a contractual interest would not suffice. He suggests that there are many ways in which another can 'do something to another', and many of these are characterised as losses caused by some action, but they can only truthfully be classified as wrongs if they have interfered with something that you had.[54] This does not appear to be the case with a contractual right to possess. This is because in reality, the claim is not that your

52 Ernest Weinrib, *Corrective Justice* (OUP 2012) 51.

53 Robert Stevens, 'Rights and Other Things' in Andrew Robertson and Donal Nolan (eds) *Rights and Private Law* (Hart 2011) 120.

54 Ripstein, *Private Wrongs* (Harvard University Press 2016) 29.

right, your contractual right, was interfered with but rather that the thing was interfered with, and you do not have the thing (or any right in it) but merely the contractual right related to the thing in some way.

This shows that while in these cases there appears to be a focus on rights and entitlement, akin to the rights-based or corrective justice approach, it is still an extension of the standing rules in line with loss thinking as it forgets the property element of these actions and is influenced by this broad concept of loss.

The Use of Possession – Trespass to Land

In terms of entitlement to sue, trespass to land operates in a similar way to both trespass to goods and conversion. It protects property through the protection of the person in possession. 'Trespass is, in essence, a remedy for the infringement of possession'[55] and because of this a claimant must show that they were in actual possession at the time of the infringement or be deemed to have been in possession by relation back.[56] This is very similar to conversion, with the 'possession by relation back' having parallels with allowing someone with a right to immediate possession to bring a claim.

Possession by relation back allows someone who has only a right to possession at a later point (for example, after the trespass had begun), to enter into possession of that land, and as a result gain lawful possession. The courts have treated this actual entry as relating back to the date when the owner became entitled to possession, allowing a person to bring a claim in trespass, which (technically) occurred when they only had a right to possession and were not, in fact, in possession. This allows, at least in limited circumstances, a person who merely has a right to possess to take steps to gain access to this remedy, like in conversion, but in this action it is achieved through the use of a legal fiction.

More recently, the courts have held that merely having the right to possess, or more accurately a right to occupy, even if this is contractual rather than proprietary, can give you the standing to sue, as per the reasoning in *Manchester Airport Plc v Dutton*.[57] This decision concerned not a claim in trespass to land but rather a claim for an order of possession. It has since been confirmed that the reasoning behind *Dutton* applies to trespass to land in *Vehicle Control Services Ltd v Revenue and Customs Commissioners*[58] and more recently in *High Speed Two (HS2) Ltd v Persons Unknown*,[59] a claim often made in the scholarly literature in the aftermath

55 David Elvin and Jonathan Karas, *Unlawful Interference with Land* (2nd edn, Sweet & Maxwell 2002) 1-003.
56 ibid.
57 [2000] QB 133, [1999] 3 WLR 524.
58 [2013] EWCA Civ 186, [2013] STC 892.
59 [2022] EWHC 2360 (KB).

of *Dutton*.[60] These cases seem to have made it possible for those out of possession to sue in trespass.

In *Dutton*, the claimant, Manchester Airport, was granted a licence to 'enter and occupy' a woodland (Arthur's Woodland) for the purpose of carrying out works (felling trees) that were needed for the construction of a new runway at the airport. Before the works could begin, the defendants, who were not in favour of the works, entered the woodland in order to make it difficult for the claimant to fell the trees. The claimant sought an order for possession, which was granted by the district judge and ultimately upheld by the Court of Appeal. The defendant's objection was that the claimant did not have a sufficient possessory interest to bring such a claim; they were only granted a licence and did not have exclusive possession. Chadwick J, in his dissenting opinion, agreed. The majority of the Court of Appeal, however, in their judgment said that neither exclusive possession nor an estate in land were necessary in order to bring an action for possession, although a licensee's right was limited to the enforcement of the grant/rights granted in the licence.[61] The court, in particular Laws LJ, explained that a person in exclusive possession but also a party in actual occupation (for example, under a licence), would be able to bring a claim.[62] Laws LJ suggested that there is a logical mistake in holding that someone who has been granted a licence but has not yet entered physical possession is left without a remedy. The court sought to remedy this by allowing them to pursue the action 'if that is a necessary remedy to vindicate and give effect to such rights of occupation as by contract with his licensor he enjoys'.[63]

This decision was reaffirmed in *Mayor of London v Hall*.[64] Here Lord Neuberger argued that the modern law relating to possession claims should not be 'shackled by the arcane and archaic rules relating to ejectment.'[65] The law, in his opinion, should accommodate anyone 'entitled to use and control, effectively amounting to physical possession, of the land in question – along the lines of the views expressed by Laws LJ in Dutton's case'.[66] It was later confirmed, in *Vehicle Control Services Ltd v Revenue and Customs Commissioners*, that the principle derived from *Dutton* that a person with a mere licence has standing to bring a claim for an order of possession, equally applies to trespass to land.[67] The case concerned the management and operations of parking enforcement on private car parks and whether the income was outside of VAT as it was paid as damages in lieu of trespass. *Dutton* was relevant to decide whether Vehicle Control Services had sufficient standing to

60 This is something I argued in Victoria Ball, 'Looking Back on *Dutton*: The Precedent Set, the Accounts Given and the Problems Caused'. (2023) 87(2) Conv 181. See also, *Clerk & Lindsell on Torts* (n 4) 18–24.

61 *Manchester Airport* (n 57).

62 ibid per Laws LJ 147.

63 ibid per Laws LJ 149.

64 [2010] EWCA Civ 817.

65 ibid per Lord Neuberger at [22].

66 ibid per Lord Neuberger at [27].

67 *Vehicle Control Services Ltd* (n 58) [at [33]–[35].

sue in trespass as a licensee to make the claim that the money received was damages in lieu of trespass a viable argument. While the argument did not work before the first-instance or upper-tribunal, the Court of Appeal found that the principles derived from *Dutton* applied in trespass to land cases and gave a more extensive view of *Dutton*. This was recently reaffirmed in *High Speed Two (HS2) Ltd v Persons Unknown*, a case concerning protests relating to HS2, where it was said that:

> [a]ctual occupation or possession of land is not required [to bring a claim in trespass to land], as *Dutton* shows (see in particular Laws LJ's judgment at p151); the legal right to occupy or possess land, without more, is sufficient to maintain an action for trespass against those not so entitled.[68]

The decision made in *Dutton* and the extension of that principle in *Hall* and *Vehicle Control Services* have been (rightly) criticised heavily by property lawyers.[69] They further seem at odds with the leading case on standing in nuisance, *Hunter v Canary Wharf*.[70] In *Hunter*, the House of Lords, after an extensive analysis,[71] held that those with a mere licence could not sue in nuisance as they had no interest in the land affected. It was thought that this approach would equally apply in other land-related causes of action.[72] This does not seem to be the case.

Even before the cases of *Dutton* and *Hall*, however, it had been held that a licensee already in *de facto* possession could maintain an action for trespass, at least in some cases, against subsequent intruders.[73] This was because of their *de facto* possession; not on the basis of the licence alone, i.e. not on his title.[74] The result is that those in factual possession or occupancy as opposed to those who can satisfy the legal concept of possession are able to bring an action.[75] This is a similar position to that found in conversion, although it provides less stringent requirements than those contained in a nuisance action.[76]

The extensions caused by cases like *Dutton* and *Hall* seem to also align with the concern about the influence of loss-thinking. While this might appear to be an

68 *High Speed Two (HS2) Ltd* (n 59) at [77].

69 Andrew Dobbs, 'Possession and Occupation – Two Sides of the Same Coin?' (1999) 10 KCLJ 226; Ewan Paton and Gwen Seabourne, 'Unchained Remedy: Recovery of Land by Licensees' [1999] Conv 535; William Swadling, 'Opening the Numerus Clausus' (2000) 116 LQR 354; Emma Lochery, 'Pushing the Boundaries of *Dutton*?' (2011) Conv 74. I have also made this argument previously in Victoria Ball, 'Looking Back on *Dutton*: The Precedent Set, the Accounts Given and the Problems Caused'. (2023) 87(2) Conv 181.

70 [1997] AC 655 (HL), [1997] 2 WLR 684.

71 Seabourne (n 69) 535.

72 ibid 535.

73 See *National Provincial Bank v Ainsworth* [1965] 3 WLR 1; *Hounslow LBC v Twickenham Garden Developments* [1971] Ch 233.

74 Seabourne (n 69) 535.

75 Factual possession here meaning merely occupancy, while legal possession gives rise to a property right.

76 *Hunter v Canary Wharf Ltd* (n 70).

isolated case, recent research has highlighted that *Dutton* remains fairly regularly cited, with a recent flurry of cases, especially in cases which have similarities to the original facts (specifically protest scenarios).[77] As such, this type of extension represents an ongoing problem for property law. The claimants in *Dutton*, for example, had merely licences and were out of possession, and as such they had no property interest on which their entitlement to sue could be based. Instead, the court fashioned a remedy and entitlement to sue based on the idea that they had suffered a loss (albeit a normative loss), which, from a property perspective, is wrong.

While this decision sits in line with the loss conception of tort, and the idea that tort law requires remedying loss, it flies in the face of the rights-protection model of tort (or a conception based on corrective justice). Under the rights-protection or corrective justice account of tort law, to have a claim in tort a person, 'A', must show that they have (or had) a right, exercisable against the defendant, that has been infringed. Stevens has said that if the wrong committed is in relation to a thing, the claimant must show that they have a right in relation to the thing that is exigible against the defendant in order to have standing to bring a claim.[78] He goes on to stress that if instead we allow all those who suffer loss as a result of damage to any property to have a claim based in tort, we would live in a legal system where all of us had rights in relation to all things.[79] These cases show at least a move towards this position through the abandonment of requiring possession or a property interest. The law, being so concerned or preoccupied with remedying loss, which here is a normative loss, or a loss of entitlement, notwithstanding one which is not enforceable against the parties claimed against, is, in effect, giving parties rights exercisable against people who they otherwise would not be exercisable against. While the licensees have rights, these rights are personal[80] and would not be binding on the parties who the trespass actions were claimed against. They are extending contractual rights beyond their remit in a bid to remedy some kind of loss or infringement of entitlement. As such, this focus on loss-thinking is extending the protection of the law, and in doing so it is creating rights where they otherwise would not exist. The preoccupation with loss-thinking in these cases also creates a situation where we 'forget' or 'ignore' the proprietary nature of the actions and the implication for property law that these decisions have. As suggested, this extends 'property rights', or at least rights which bind third parties, beyond their current existence.

77 Victoria Ball, 'Looking Back on *Dutton*: The Precedent Set, the Accounts Given and the Problems Caused.' (2023) 87(2) Conv 181.

78 Stevens (n 53) 120.

79 ibid.

80 Talking here about the distinction between personal and property rights – the former being exigible only against those who are party to the agreement, and the latter being exigible against the world.

Protecting Property Rights – Private Nuisance

Nuisance focuses primarily on an interest in land and exclusive possession (which is an interest in land as it is a proprietary interest). This can be seen in the dicta from *Hunter v Canary Wharf*, which is the leading case on standing in nuisance. Lord Goff stated that the general rule in private nuisance is that:

> [A]n action in private nuisance will only lie at the suit of a person who has a right to the land affected. Ordinarily, such a person can only sue if he has the right to exclusive possession of the land, such as a freeholder or tenant in possession, or even a licensee with exclusive possession.[81]

This shows that nuisance, at least in its standing rules, has a strong focus on property and property rights. However, this has been controversial. There are disagreements in academic commentary[82] and to some extent in the judgments of our highest courts, regarding the standing rules and the need for a claimant to have an interest in land. This disagreement was heightened by the decision in *Khorasandjian v Bush*.[83] In this case, which concerned harassing phone calls to a young lady living in her parents' house, the court decided that a nuisance claim could be brought without a proprietary right or interest in the house, going against the general rule in the tort.[84]

Hunter v Canary Wharf Ltd later reaffirmed the original position, confirming that nuisance was a tort against land[85] and thus the requirement of an interest in land was essential.[86] Lord Cooke of Thornton strongly dissented, suggesting instead that the right to sue should be extended to all those who occupy the property as a home – those who have a substantial link with the property.[87] This would change the position of lodgers or dependants (children living with their parents) who do not have a property interest[88] but would seem to fall under this requirement of a substantial link.

81 *Hunter* (n 70) per Lord Goff at 692.

82 See Peter Cane, 'What a Nuisance!' (1997) LQR 515; Maria Lee, 'What is Private Nuisance?' (2003) LQR 298; Giliker 'The Relationship between Property Law and Tort Law' (n 21); John Murphy, *The Law of Nuisance* (OUP 2010); Allan Beever, *The Law of Private Nuisance* (Hart 2013).

83 [1993] QB 727 at 735.

84 This was criticised in *Hunter*, Lord Goff maintained that the complaint in *Khorasandjian v Bush* was not that the defendant was committing a nuisance, which meant that the claimant was unable to use and enjoy the land, but instead the complaint was that she did not want to be harassed – as such, nuisance was not the appropriate tort for this type of claim. See *Hunter* (n 70) 691–92.

85 *Hunter* (n 70) per Lord Goff at 687.

86 ibid per Lord Hoffmann at 702.

87 ibid per Lord Cooke at 718.

88 This can be seen through using the test of a property right developed in Chapter 2. These 'interests' would not fall under the conception of property right and any inclusion of these type of interests in the standing rules would be moving the law away from property-based determination of who can sue.

The distinction between these two cases (or at least between the majority in *Hunter*) could be said to be the difference between choosing the traditional approach or a more interventionist approach to the property torts.[89] The former has been said to import into tort law the relative certainty of proprietary interests, recognising that (at least part of) the role of this type of action is the protection of property interests. As such, this is sometimes also referred to as the 'property-based approach'.[90] The latter approach in contrast advocates that tort should move away from its roots and respond to more modern social needs[91] and, therefore, focuses on the 'obligation-style approach' that seeks to compensate the victim.[92] The tort of private nuisance is a tort which concerns interferences with the claimant's use and enjoyment of her land,[93] or possibly more accurately interferences with the usability of land more generally (focusing on the ability of the land itself to be used and enjoyed as opposed to the specific uses that a claimant might want to put to it).[94] Changing the standing rule would mean moving away from the function and the history of the action as well as arguably threatening the coherence of the action itself.[95]

This discussion, however, highlights the impact of changing contemporary attitudes to the development of English tort law and makes us question whether the 'property torts', or in this context specifically nuisance, should alter their essential character to meet modern social and political needs. At their core they are concerned with the protection of proprietary interests, but it has been argued that this does not necessarily indicate that in the twenty-first century they should continue to be focused on this.[96] Such a move away from property concepts, however, loses sight of the fact that as property torts they are part of the wider law of property.[97] This leads to decisions which fit badly with the principle's underlying property. This can be seen clearly in *Dutton* and *Hall.*

In nuisance cases, this divergence from the concerns of property law can also be seen in the influence of negligence-based thinking in some cases outside the sphere of negligence. The influence of negligence-based thinking can be seen specifically in *Sedleigh-Denfield v O'Callaghan*[98] and the line of cases following it on the liability of occupiers for adopting and continuing a nuisance. Here nuisance liability was held to turn on the fault of the occupier. This influence of fault-based

89 Terminology borrowed from Giliker, see Giliker, 'The Relationship between Property Law and Tort Law' (n 21) 74.
90 Giliker 'The Relationship between Property Law and Tort Law' (n 21) 74.
91 ibid 75.
92 ibid 74.
93 Beever, *The Law of Private Nuisance* (n 82) 104.
94 Donal Nolan, 'The Essence of Private Nuisance' in Ben McFarlane and Sinead Agnew (eds) *Modern Studies in Property Law, Volume 10* (Bloomsbury 2019) 74–75.
95 Donal Nolan 'A Tort Against Land': Private Nuisance as a Property Tort' in Donal Nolan and Andrew Robertson (eds) *Rights and Private Law* (Hart 2012) 475.
96 Giliker (n 21) 72.
97 Nolan (n 95) 475.
98 [1940] AC 880, [1940] 3 All ER 349.

liability has been described as motivated by a mixture of loss and responsibility ideas[99] – allocating the loss suffered to the most appropriate party. Understood in this way, the *Sedleigh-Denfield* approach is another example of how the desire to compensate loss is shaping the property torts in ways that would not be appropriate from the perspective of property law. Another example of this influence of negligence ideas and reasoning can be found in the recent Supreme Court case of *Davies v Bridgend County Borough Council*.[100] The case concerned the encroachment onto the claimant's land of Japanese knotweed. This encroachment happened some time 'before 2004', which was before the now publicly available information about the risks of damage and loss of amenity caused by Japanese knotweed was widely known. Before the case began, the encroachment had already been 'treated' and so the claim was framed as seeking to recover residual diminution in the value of his land that was said to still exist despite the treatment for Japanese knotweed, which was no longer actively growing on his land.[101] Despite the potential for claiming that the previous encroachment had reduced the amenity of the land by restricting the ability of the claimant to use the land in any way that might disturb the Japanese knotweed rhizomes (which do stay in the soil), meaning that gardening or construction was more difficult or expensive (a synonymous claim to that which succeeded in *Williams* discussed shortly), the claimants framed the claim as a reduction in value based on the stigma from the previous encroachment.[102] The Supreme Court ultimately held that the claim based on diminution in market value is not recoverable as the claimant cannot show that 'but for' the wrongdoing of the defendant, which was held to take place between 2013–2018 (when they should have been aware of the risk of encroachment and damage but failed to rectify) but significantly after the actual encroachment 'before 2004' was the cause or materially contributed to the diminution in value.[103] As such, the diminution in value had occurred prior to and was not caused by the defendant's breach of duty.[104] This is another clear example of the importation of normal negligence ideas to claims in nuisance. Causation and breach were relevant because this was a claim for common law damages in private nuisance.[105] Within that discussion, Lord Burrows, in his concurring judgment, drew a distinction between cases relating to damages only, where causation and breach were relevant as it was more of a tort claim proper, and cases where the claimants were seeking an injunction or damages in lieu.[106] In the latter, the implication was that, where there was a continuing nuisance, there

99 Paula Giliker, 'Marking the Boundary: The Relationship between Private Nuisance, Negligence and Fault' in John Lowry and Rod Edmunds (eds) *Environmental Protection and the Common Law* (Hart 2000) 177.
100 [2024] UKSC 15, [2024] 2 WLR 1237.
101 ibid [3].
102 ibid.
103 ibid [70].
104 ibid [71].
105 ibid [79].
106 ibid [78]–[79].

would not be a causation question. This discussion shows the dual or hybrid nature of the property torts and how different ideals of the underlying law can pull in different directions.

However, recent Court of Appeal decisions on nuisance (to some extent moved on from by the Supreme Court decision in *Fearn*) show how a strong dicta on the position of these actions as 'property torts' can restrict the influence of loss-thinking and the need to provide a remedy whenever some harm or loss has been suffered, just as it did in *Hunter*. The first is *Network Rail Infrastructure Ltd v Williams*[107] and the second is *Fearn v the Board of Trustees of the Tate Gallery*, which recently went to the Supreme Court.[108] Although the Supreme Court decision in *Fearn* changed the landscape of nuisance significantly, it is worth starting at the beginning, as the Court of Appeal decisions, show well how a focus on the rights underlying nuisance can help stop a slide into negligence and loss thinking. Something that the Supreme Court appears to fail to recognise and actually is a trap that they fall into themselves.

The first case, as with *Davies* mentioned earlier, concerned the encroachment of Japanese knotweed and specifically whether this encroachment, without physical damage, was sufficient for an actionable nuisance; or in the alternative, whether the presence of knotweed interfered with the quiet enjoyment and amenity value of the land by affecting the market value. At first instance, the recorder held that the second element of the claim succeeded. On appeal, however, the Court of Appeal held that the amenity of the property in nuisance does not include the right to realise the value of the property. In contrast, the court held that the mere presence of the knotweed interfered with amenity without the need for physical damage. This is because it imposed an immediate burden in terms of an increased difficulty to develop and cost of developing. As such, the court held that in this case nuisance had been made out. This is the type of claim that it was suggested that the claimants in *Davies* could, and should, have made. In its judgment, the Court of Appeal made strong reference to the purpose of private nuisance and the role that it has in the protection of real property rights. Sir Terence Etherton MR stated in the decision that:

> private nuisance is a violation of real property rights. That means that it involves either interference with the legal rights of an owner of land … or interference with the amenity of the land, that is to say the right to use and enjoy it, which is an inherent facet of a right of exclusive possession.[109]

107 [2018] EWCA Civ 1514, [2018] 3 WLR 1105.

108 Court of Appeal citation: [2020] EWCA Civ 104, [2020] 2 WLR 1081. Citation in the Supreme Court [2023] UKSC 4, [2023] 2 WLR 339.

109 *Williams* (n 107) para 40.

The Master of the Rolls also remarked that 'it has been described as a property tort'.[110] This strong judicial focus on the property element of the tort stopped a potential slide into loss-thinking. The Court of Appeal held that:

> [T]he recorder's conclusion that the presence of knotweed on [National Rail's] land within seven metres of the claimants' properties was an actionable nuisance simply because it diminished the market value of the claimants' respective properties, because of lender caution in such situations, was wrong in principle.[111]

This is because, according to the Court, the purpose of nuisance is not to protect the value of property as an investment or a financial asset but to protect the owner of land and their use and enjoyment, which is a facet of ownership or exclusive possession.[112] The Court of Appeal, therefore, stated that the decision of the recorder would have extended nuisance to a claim for pure economic loss, which they held was an unacceptable development that would be a 'radical reformulation of the purpose and scope of the tort'.[113] The slight reformulation of the action that would have occurred if the recorder's findings were to be left standing is once again a stretching of the actions and a move away from the rights that should be protected in nuisance and the property torts. The Court of Appeal's conclusions respect the rights and the role of the action more, focusing on what a property right should give an owner and possessor.

A similar focus on the classification of nuisance as a property tort in the Court of Appeal decision in *Fearn* once again stopped a slippage into loss-thinking prevalent in other torts and tort law in general. *Fearn* was a case concerning whether nuisance could lie for an invasion of privacy and was already briefly introduced in the previous chapter, as the Supreme Court decision radically changed nuisance as a whole. The core question in the case was whether a nuisance could be founded on the basis of invasions of privacy and whether visitors of the viewing gallery looking into the neighbouring flats interfered with their quiet enjoyment of land enough to constitute a claim in nuisance. At first instance, Mann J held that invasions of privacy could amount to a nuisance. However, on the facts it did not amount to an actionable nuisance because of the sensitivity of the claimants and the additional (available and reasonable) measures that were open to the claimants to reduce the interference. The Court of Appeal decided, however, that invasions of privacy were not capable of amounting to a nuisance.[114] This decision was based on the lack of any previous authority to suggest that an invasion of privacy, or overlooking,

110 ibid. Reference to Nolan, 'A Tort Against Land' (n 95).

111 *Williams* (n 107) [46].

112 ibid [48].

113 ibid.

114 They also said that the claimants were not particularly sensitive that it would not stop a nuisance case if invasion was capable of amounting to a nuisance.

could amount to an actionable nuisance.[115] Sir Terence Etherton MR, Lord Justice Lewison, and Lady Justice Rose DBE, in their joint judgment, gave prevalence to the decision of the majority in *Victoria Park Racing*[116] (in contrast, Mann J expressed his preference for the minority judgment). For example, they cited, with approval, dicta from Dixon J explaining that 'English law is, rightly or wrongly, clear that the natural rights of an occupier do not include freedom from the view and inspection of neighbouring occupiers or of other persons.'[117] The 'overwhelming weight of judicial authority' suggests that overlooking is not capable of giving rise to a nuisance action, as such the court held that there was no actionable nuisance in this case or this type of case. In coming to that conclusion, the court once again repeated that nuisance was a property tort and a violation of real property rights, citing *Williams*. The court also made a point, previously stated in *Hunter*, that 'even in modern times the law does not always provide a remedy for every annoyance to a neighbour, however considerable that annoyance may be'.[118] In *Hunter* there was: 1) no claim without a sufficient right in the property; but also, 2) there was no claim for interference caused by tall buildings stopping television signals because, as a general principle in common law, anyone may build whatever they like on their land and so there has been no infringement of their legal rights.[119]

This last point is of vital importance and goes to the core of the argument here. All the property torts should be focusing on the underlying property rights and not on any loss or harm that has been caused. By focusing strongly on the affected rights, *and* on their character as property rights, the 'property tort' nature of these actions can be brought to the fore and over-extensions of the torts as a result of the loss-thinking prevalent in tort law can be avoided. It is the combination of a rights perspective and attention to the property character of the rights that encourages reasoning and decisions which ensure that the property torts remain focused on property and interferences with property. The rights-based or corrective justice perspective produces a focus on entitlements and normative losses, but as cases like *Dutton* and the conversion exceptions discussed previously show, this does not automatically result in due recognition that property torts serve to protect property rights. The influence of loss-based thinking in tort law sometimes tends to pull the courts towards correcting other normative losses, for example, the intervention of personal rights such as privacy. Nevertheless, a strict rights-based or corrective justice approach as elucidated by Weinrib, Stevens, or Ripstein facilitates such recognition by directing the courts' attention to the rights at stake in the dispute between the parties and thus to the question whether these rights are such that they are apt for protection by the relevant property tort. This can be seen in *Williams*. But to achieve this outcome, the second step – attention to whether the right is a

115 *Fearn* CA (n 108) [53].

116 *Victoria Park Racing & Recreation Grounds Co Ltd v Taylor* (1937) 58 CLR 479.

117 ibid per Dixon J at 507.

118 *Fearn* CA (n 108) [79].

119 *Hunter* (n 70) Per Lord Lloyd at 669.

property right or not – is essential. This means that tort law theory is not sufficient by itself to bring about the necessary focus on the underlying property rights. It needs to be supplemented by property theory so that the characteristics of property rights and the concerns of property law are also reflected in a court's reasoning. *Williams*, again, provides a good illustration.

The decision of Mann J, while not necessarily going the whole way to opening up the tort, as he decided that it was not a nuisance in this case, leaves open the idea that nuisance can be available for privacy invasions even though this does not relate to any right but just the idea that harm or loss has been suffered. The decision would be a starting point in, once again, opening the actions to respond to loss and forgetting the importance to property that these actions have, and, in fact, forgetting the role of tort (if tort is understood from a rights-based or corrective justice approach). The Supreme Court, in their decision in *Fearn*, seem to have done this.

In a surprising decision, the judges in both the majority (the judgment being delivered by Lord Leggatt with whom Lord Reed and Lord Lloyd-Jones agreed) and the minority (the judgment being delivered by Lord Sales with whom Lord Kitchen agreed) of the Supreme Court found that visual intrusions were *capable* of amounting to a nuisance. The majority further held that on the facts an actionable nuisance had been made out, describing the case as a *straightforward case of nuisance*.[120] In doing so, however, the court continued to emphasise the 'property-tort' nature of nuisance; showing that words alone are not enough to maintain a focus on the property underlying the decision, and the sentiment behind those words needs to be followed through. The result was that while the majority attempted to some extent to recognise the property tort nature of the action, they did so in a limited way, and in words only; which allowed the actual decision to, in fact, undermine the property dimension of the case and instead be influenced by compensating loss. This is because they accepted that the action still relates to interests in land but now can be founded on the basis of visual intrusion. This reshaped the concept of property so that the protection from visual intrusion is now part of a property right that the law protects. And this is a significant change in the scope of nuisance, but also potentially significant *beyond that* for 'property'. And this latter aspect of the discussion is often forgotten, but this is the implication of the dual nature of the property torts. This decision, once again, shows how a preoccupation with tort law ideals about the need to compensate loss (in a broad interpretation of this term) can lead to decisions which are questionable from a property perspective.

120 *Fearn* (SC) (n 108) [7]. He opined that the unwillingness of the previous courts to find a nuisance was because of a reluctance to decide that the private rights of a few wealthy property owners should prevent the general public from enjoying an unrestricted view of London and a major national museum from providing public access to such a view. I do not, respectfully, think that there is any evidence that this was at the heart of either the first instance or Court of Appeal decision.

This concern has parallels and fits with the concerns regarding the influence of loss-thinking and the move away from property concepts. These actions are (or should be) fundamentally part of property law, and as such, the torts are not free to establish their own standing rules but instead have some prior independent method for defining and recognising the property rights which they protect from property law.[121] The issue is that while recognised as part of property law, they are classified and labelled as tortious actions. Thus, tortious thinking concerning the significance of loss permeates the decisions of the cases and the way the torts develop. As such there is a move from the concept of property to tortious concepts such as loss (whether factual or normative). Due to this, judges as well as academics want to remedy loss or remedy any interference with entitlement, and this thinking influences the decisions such as the one in *Khorasandjian v Bush* and the academic commentary surrounding it. Along these lines Beever has claimed that, 'If the law of nuisance did not exist, we would have to invent it. If the law continues its slide into negligence, we will have to reinvent it. It would be easier just to understand it better'.[122] This comment about a slide into negligence aligns with the loss concern, although here I associate the tort-based thinking with a concern for loss or tort law thinking more generally rather than articulating it as a 'slide into negligence'.

However, there exists another argument. Rather than the judges being stuck between seeing the property torts as part of property law or part of tort law, it could be argued that instead the judges and different academics are simply disagreeing about what tort law does or should be doing. The disagreement suggests that the judges were viewing the function of tort law in different ways – with the majority in *Hunter* and the Court of Appeal in *Williams* and *Fearn*, for example, focusing on tort law's rights-protection or corrective justice role, while the minority in *Hunter*, the judges in *Khorasandjian*, and those at first instance in *Williams* and the first instance and Supreme Court in *Fearn* focusing on wrong-correction and loss. Weir fits in with the latter approach and sees tort law as purely loss focused, hence, a focus on how these actions need to be reclassified as this is the only way to rid them of loss-thinking.

The discussions found in *Hunter*, *Williams*, and *Fearn*, as well as the cases that led to them, are interesting because of the line of case law and the academic and judicial commentary surrounding it really gets to the nub of the argument concerning the influence of loss and loss-thinking and the importance of remembering the property tort nature of the torts. In decisions such as *Khorasandjian v Bush*, the harm caused was seen as enough to allow a claim even though the party did not have any proprietary interest; and similarly in *Fearn*, the Supreme Court found a nuisance despite no property right protecting privacy and visual intrusions. This idea that loss is what is important continues to influence academic commentary and once again can be seen in the dissenting opinions in *Hunter*, and the first instance

121 Richard Epstein 'Nuisance Law: Corrective Justice and its Utilitarian Constraints' (1979) 8 JLS 49, 52.

122 Beever, *The Law of Private Nuisance* (n 82) 106.

decision and Supreme Court decision in *Fearn*. The actual decision in *Hunter* and the Court of Appeal decisions in *Fearn* and *Williams*, however, suggests that this focus on loss does not necessarily force the outcome of cases as the majority/Court of Appeal pushed back and didn't allow this type of argument to inform the decision, instead focusing on the property interest that needed to be found. This is because they saw the role of tort law as being rights-based rather than loss-based and because they also recognise the property torts as part of the wider law of property. Regardless, this suggests that while the classification of these actions as tortious might impact on the development of the cases, the law and the protection offered, they do not have to. This might suggest that these actions could remain classed as tortious but need a greater understanding of their focus and their specific role as property torts to ensure the dominant thinking on tort law and loss does not engulf these torts and limit the protection offered to property and property interests. This relates to the ideas of Cane and his view of tort law. Cane is clear that tort law is actually the law of torts,[123] pointing out that the title of 'torts' actually encompasses a wide range of differing actions which could be seen as a bit of a 'ragbag'.[124] He sees tort law as based on a number of different theories.[125] Following on from the ideas of Cane, even if loss and harm underlie some tort actions and is even seen by some as the primary purpose, this does not stop the property torts being explained under a different theory and conception, such as suggesting that they are rights-based instead. But the Supreme Court decision in *Fearn* also tells us that more than mere words are needed to respect the dual nature of the property torts. Here the court recognised the dual nature of the action but still disregarded the importance to property that decisions in nuisance can have.

The issue is that the minority in *Hunter*, and the Supreme Court in *Fearn* were still influenced enough by loss-based thinking to lead them to the conclusion that the actions should be successful due to the loss. This demonstrates that this type of thinking and influence of loss is still prominent and important to consider, just as it is with conversion, trespass to goods, and trespass to land.

Protecting Property Rights – Negligence

Negligence (considering it here, only as far as it relates to the protection of property and thus property damage) uses property rights to decide eligibility to sue. To succeed in a claim in negligence for property damage, it was generally thought that the claimant would have to show that they have an interest in the property (using this term here to mean a thing) that has been damaged or that they were in possession of it (thus having possessory title). This can be seen in the case of the *Aliakmon*.[126] In this case, the court reaffirmed the long established principle that for a claimant

123 Peter Cane, *Key Ideas in Law: Tort Law* (Hart 2017) 13.

124 ibid.

125 Peter Cane, 'Justice and Justifications for Tort Liability' (1982) 2 OJLS 30, 30.

126 *Leigh & Sillavan Ltd v Aliakmon Shipping Ltd, The Aliakmon* [1986] AC 785.

to have a right to claim in negligence for loss caused to him by reason of loss of, or damage to, property, he had to have had either the legal ownership, a property interest, or a possessory title to the property at the time when the loss or damage occurred.[127] The claimants in this case had merely contractual rights to the goods on board a ship, and it was held that this was insufficient to bring a claim.

This was assumed to be the correct position but has since been doubted and the original position altered somewhat by the Court of Appeal decision in *Colour Quest Ltd v Total Downstream*.[128] However, this case was settled before it was appealed to the Supreme Court so there remains a question about whether the position might have changed on appeal or at least the reasoning questioned. In the case, a beneficial owner was able to recover damages for physical loss of pipes as well as foreseeable consequences of such, provided they joined the legal owner in the proceedings. The proceedings were a result of the explosion at the Buncefield oil terminal, which caused damage to the pipelines and other storage equipment. The legal ownership of these were held by two companies which were bare trustees who held the pipelines and storage tanks on trust for the claimant, Shell. Commentators have argued that while the reasoning is conceptually flawed, it is hard to argue against the decision based on the result reached.[129] The reasoning has conflated and merged two exceptions to the general rule to allow the beneficiary in this case to sue,[130] but it seems correct that someone who has a property right, albeit a property right gained through equity, is entitled to bring a claim when they are the most suitable party to do so.

A similar exception applies for reversioners in some of the torts to ensure those who have a property right and are the most appropriate party can bring an action. Although seemingly justified, this decision, again, supports the assertion that loss-thinking might be extending the class of parties entitled to bring a claim and influencing the cases and decisions. In this case, the court extended and adapted the original rules to ensure that a party who has suffered some normative loss and that otherwise would not be compensated was entitled and allowed to bring a claim. This decision seems to dispense of the need for a (legal) property entitlement but does not dispense altogether the need for a rights violation in line with the idea that tort law responds to infringements with loss and entitlements.

Standing of Those with a Reversionary Interest

One implication of the fact that most of the torts require possession to enable a person to sue is that reversioners are unable to bring a claim successfully, or at

127 This principle can be seen in previous cases such as *Cattle v Stockton Waterworks Co (1875) LR 10 QB 453* and further affirmed in the privy council in *Candlewood Navigation Corp Ltd v Mitsui OSK Lines Ltd* PC 1 Jul 1985.

128 *Colour Quest Ltd v Total Downstream UK Plc* [2010] EWCA Civ 180, [2011] QB 86.

129 Nicholas Macklam, 'Colour Quest Ltd v Total Downstream UK Plc: The Nature of A Beneficiary's Interest Under a Trust' [2010] Conv 265, 268.

130 See, for example, ibid; and, Andrew Scott, 'Total Chaos?' [2010] LMCLQ 536.

least this is the case in the personal property torts (trespass to goods and conversion). This is not the case, however, in nuisance and trespass to land where, exceptionally at least, reversioners can succeed in their claim. This applies if, and only if, a person's reversionary interest is affected by the nuisance[131] or trespass.[132] A reversioner can sue, therefore, if the value of the property will be diminished when they come back into possession of it.[133] For a claim in nuisance, this may happen if vibrations affect the structure of the property, but they will be unable to sue when the property is interfered with by smoke or smells which are necessarily temporary in nature (and so they are unlikely to still be causing a nuisance at the time when the reversioner takes back the property).[134] In trespass, if the landlord can prove damage, he may be able to obtain an injunction stopping the behaviour.[135] Although this exception is not considered a proper trespass claim. This is because the claim concerns an injury to the reversion rather than a claim of unlawful entry and thus is properly categorised as a nuisance action.[136]

This exception allows some people who have an important interest in the property to be able to bring a claim, but this is not mirrored in the personal property torts for those with a reversionary interest. Arguably, however, the extensions allowing those with a right to possession to sue in conversion and the exceptions in trespass try to plug this gap.

This appears to be another example of tort law thinking extending the actions in response to some loss of entitlement.

The Influence of Loss Thinking

On paper, and generally at least, the property torts do use proprietary interests to limit and define the scope of the action and the parties entitled to sue. But loss and a concern with remedying loss permeates the torts and the decisions in cases. As such, many cases, and thus the development of the torts, show a tendency towards remedying loss even if this can only occur through extensions of the current law that move away from property considerations and are often deemed as 'wrong' or 'worrying' decisions from a property perspective (though not all do).

These types of decisions and developments move the torts away from property-based thinking and, as such, many commentators and judges forget or ignore the inherent 'propertiness' of this type of claim. This does not, however, always have to happen – the decisions in *Hunter*, *Williams*, and the Court of Appeal decision in *Fearn* are good examples of this. The commentary and decisions leading up to *Hunter* show how loss-thinking permeates and causes commentators to suggest greater extensions, seemingly forgetting or ignoring the property aspect of the tort.

131 *Hunter* (n 70) per Lord Goff at 692.
132 *Clerk & Lindsell* (n 4) 19–62.
133 *Jones v Llanrwst UDC* [1911] 1 Ch 393, 404.
134 Paula Giliker, Tort (8th edn, Sweet & Maxwell 2023) 10-016.
135 *Jones* (n 133).
136 Elvin and Karas (n 55) 1-010.

The decision, and specifically the majority reasoning in *Hunter*, however, push back against this type of thinking and reasoning, making it very clear that nuisance is a tort against land and emphasising its position between property and tort law. A similar thing can be seen in the more recent Court of Appeal decisions of *Williams* and *Fearn*. In the first instance decisions, some elements of the tort seem to have been extended to allow a possible remedy, despite the lack of a property right underpinning such an extension. Despite this, the Court of Appeal had a strong property tort rhetoric that helped to push back this type of extension and focused the decision on the real property rights that nuisance seeks to protect. The Supreme Court decision in *Fearn*, nonetheless, shows the importance of truly focusing on the right underlying these actions and not just paying 'lip-service' to the property tort nature of these actions.

Some of these decisions thus go against the concern that loss will be considered as the necessary and sufficient criterion causing extensions and moving away from property type concerns in these torts as elucidated by Weir. These cases show very much that this does not have to be the case. However, the influence of loss was only halted in this situation by a very strong judicial statement on the tort, its role, and its position, and sometimes even this was not enough.

If this type of thinking could be mirrored for all the property torts and the sentiment behind the words truly focused on, the slippage into loss-based thinking could possibly be stopped. To diminish this influence of loss, we need to think about these actions not just as torts but as property torts that have a special role sitting between tort law and property law. The actions are underpinned by property rights and by thinking about the actions as property torts and the role of tort law as rights-based, we can stop the influence of loss.

Even if the torts do gravitate towards loss, there is a question of whether this is necessarily an issue. When explored from a slightly different perspective, it might show that remedying and focusing on loss (whether physical or normative loss) does, at least, indirectly protect the rights underlying the torts that are defined by property law. For example, think about compensatory damages: The primary function of these damages is to compensate the claimant's loss but in so doing one is inevitably vindicating the rights infringed. The same can be said to be true in other types of remedy and damage awards. While the primary function of restitutionary damages is to reverse the gain made by the wrongdoer, in so doing, one is also vindicating the underlying right that the claimant had. Similarly, in an order of specific performance, while the action or remedy is primarily concerned with compelling performance of a positive obligation, it also inevitably vindicates the right infringed.[137] By analogy, even actions that focus or tend to think merely in terms of loss (and as the claimant needing to suffer loss) indirectly at least protect property rights. The desire to remedy the loss of a physical object also necessarily vindicates or protects the right that the person has in that physical object. This

137 Andrew Burrows, 'Damages and Rights' in Donal Nolan and Andrew Robertson (eds), *Rights and Private Law* (Hart 2012).

is especially true as the loss that we have been exploring has been construed very widely to incorporate any harm or wrongdoing on the part of the defendant – even if that wrongdoing is, in effect, the breach of a right held by the claimant.

While this may not result in a lack of protection for the rights that need to be protected, there remain issues. The first has already been suggested. This results in extensions to the actions. Extensions to the rights which bind third parties, as can be seen in *Dutton* and in *Fearn*, undermines the balance that property law has sought to create in determining what rights amount to and what can be considered property rights. As property rights have implications for third parties, those rights that can be considered proprietary are closed in number, there is a *numerus clausus*. This balance struck by property law ensures that people can make use of things, but that people do not have so much control over external things to hinder other people's lives – this is why personal rights are not binding on third parties. The balance that the law has sought to achieve limits those affected by such rights; cases like *Dutton* and *Fearn* change this balance by allowing these rights to bind third parties. The implications of this will be discussed more in Chapter 6 when the implications of using tort law to protect property are more fully examined. Likewise, it also moves the focus of the actions away from what they should be focused on. This, therefore, compromises the protection of property – it creates a deficiency. The compromise or deficiency is created because the theoretical ideas underlying tort law causes and creates a difference in treatment because of the primary focus of that area of law. The focus in tort law on remedying loss is different from the primary focus in property law, which is the protection of property interests.

The next chapter will consider another criticism waged by Weir in the introductory quote concerning remedies and damages.

5 Remedying an Interference with Property

Introduction

While the previous chapter considered the 'consequences' flowing from bringing a claim and the influence of 'loss' in that regard, this chapter concerns those 'consequences' relating to the remedies available and given in the property torts. In particular, Weir argued:

> If England had a rational system of law there would be no need for a special section on torts to chattels ... Two conditions would have to be fulfilled before the role of tort could be so sensibly restricted: first, the law of property must provide a means whereby the owner of goods can get them back from whoever is in possession of them without any right to retain them.[1]
>
> The common law has no special remedy for the owner of a thing who wishes to claim it back from the person in possession of it. This gap has therefore to be filled by a remedy in tort. Unfortunate consequences ensue.[2]
>
> Finally, what order is the judge to make? In tort cases he orders the defendant to pay monetary compensation, but in a property remedy he may have to order specific restitution, and if that is impossible he will be tempted to order the defendant to pay the value of the thing even if that differs from the sum which he would award as compensation. These are the problems which arise when tort takes on the role of property law.[3]

Weir's arguments, once again, generate a series of underlying questions; this time relating to the meaning of remedies, what a remedy *should* be doing when property is interfered with, and whether proprietary or tortious ideals or conceptions will alter this perspective.

The remedies available in the torts, particularly in conversion, have attracted the attention of several other authors alongside Weir[4] and, as with the discussion in the previous chapter, the issues discussed raise wider questions about the tortious

1 Tony Weir, *A Casebook on Tort* (10th edn, Sweet & Maxwell 2004) 483–84.
2 ibid.
3 ibid.
4 See, for example, Nick Curwen, 'The Remedy in Conversion: Confusing Property and Obligation' (2006) 26 LS 570; Andrew Tettenborn 'Conversion, Tort and Restitution' in N Palmer and E McK-

DOI: 10.4324/9781032692098-7

classification of these actions and the implications of this for the protection of property rights. In particular, this chapter argues that because of the tortious classification of these actions, the emphasis of the existing remedies for the property torts largely ignores or fails to reflect property or proprietary matters. They are focused purely on tort law concerns (on what tort law should do) and on trying to align these actions with normal tort law principles and rules. However, this does not seem to fully acknowledge the importance of these actions to property law or the dual/proprietary nature of these actions and does not respect the importance of the property right at play or what these actions, from a property law perspective, at least, should be protecting.

The chapter will start with a general discussion of remedies as this is a prerequisite of any discussion of the actual remedies available and their technicalities. It will then go on to discuss the different remedies available for interferences with property. To avoid repetition, and to allow for the similarities and differences between the protection of real and personal property to be seen, the discussion will focus on the different remedies available and then signal the tort which favours this remedy, rather than dealing with the question tort by tort. This discussion will include a consideration of damages, injunctions, and the specific rules under the Torts (Interference with Goods) Act 1977, as these are the main remedies for interferences with property.[5]

Remedies in Property and Tort Law

As a general point, in this chapter, any reference to remedies means the relief that a person can obtain from the court.[6] As such, the term remedy does not denote the tort itself, rather the tort e.g., trespass to land, is the real-world event that causes trouble and as a result requires 'fixing' through a 'remedy',[7] typically damages or through some kind of specific performance action.

'Proprietary Remedies' and Remedies from a Property Perspective

Weir, in the introductory quote (some of which is spotlighted), explains at different points what a 'property remedy' would do in a specific scenario and contrasts this with (in his view) the poorly performing tort of conversion. However, English property law has no such 'property remedy'. This conception of a 'property remedy' must, therefore, be based either on i) what a property remedy, in

endrick, *Interests in Goods* (2nd edn, London: Lloyds of London Press, 1998); David Ibbetson, *A Historical Introduction to the Law of Obligations* (OUP 2001) 108.

5 Torts (Interference with Goods) Act 1977 (T(IWG)A).

6 This is a definition used in other works on remedies See Andrew Burrows, *Remedies for Torts and Breach of Contract and Equitable Wrongs* (4th edn, OUP 2019) 1. This chapter, therefore, will focus on remedies such as damages, injunctions, and return (under the Torts (Interference with Goods) Act) and not on self-help remedies.

7 ibid.

Weir's opinion, *should* do; or possibly, ii) what *rei vindicatio* did in Roman law (or what its modern descendants do in contemporary civil law systems). *Rei vindicatio* is (or was) an action an owner could bring to reclaim possession of their thing from another person who had possession of it, where their possession was a contradiction of the owner's rights. The claim is a direct assertion of the claimant's continuing ownership. The example that often appears in legal writing is that the claimant appears in court and argues 'That cow, Buttercup, is mine!' The result of a successful *rei vindicatio* claim was the return of the good or object;[8] so as in in the aforementioned example, the return of Buttercup the cow.[9] This paints a picture of *one* view of a proprietary remedy. In this sense, a proprietary remedy focuses on specific performance remedies of delivery up, injunctions, etc.

However, this is not the *only* way to define or think about proprietary remedies: The different possible conceptions of what it means for something to be a proprietary remedy raise a question about whether the problem Weir was elucidating was in the proprietary character and classification of the remedy/s or merely a concern for the lack of *return* as a possible remedy (or as the primary remedy). These propositions may have been confused and conflated and they are, in fact, not the same.

The authors of *Personal Property Law* elucidated a few of the alternative meanings of 'proprietary' remedies. These include: i) when the gist of the claim or action is to vindicate or to enforce an interest in property (focusing here on the substance rather than the form of the action); ii) when the rights protected or enforced persist against third parties, including a trustee in bankruptcy; iii) where the cause of action is proprietary in that specific relief is one of the available remedies, either as a matter of right or at least at the discretion of the courts.[10] It is proper and appropriate to describe a claim as proprietary if it satisfies *any* of these criteria.[11] The focus and operation of proprietary remedies, as they currently exist in English law, fall into the first two descriptions of proprietary remedies listed earlier, as opposed to the third.[12]

8 Barry Nicholas, *An Introduction to Roman Law* (OUP 1962) 99–101. It should be noted, however, that while return is the priority, the defendant can give damages as a substitute, this will be discussed shortly when comparisons are made to T(IWG)A and when comparisons are drawn between the real property torts and personal property torts.

9 This is a slight oversimplification; see previous note. This will be discussed later.

10 Michael Bridge, Louise Gullifer, Gerard McMeel, and Kevin FK Low, *The Law of Personal Property* (3rd edn, Sweet & Maxwell 2021) 1-054. Weir's conception of proprietary remedies would fall under the final of the three understandings which focuses on return. But it appears that even this definition may be wider than Weir's, as return only needs to be *available*, and can be discretionary.

11 ibid.

12 The important element in the classification of remedies as proprietary in English law seems to be their continuation in insolvency (see Craig Rotherham, *Proprietary Remedies in Context* [Hart 2002]. Also note, however, there is very little authority on remedies in conversion and conversion in general being used in insolvency. This is, however, an important element of a property right and an important element of a proprietary remedy. The lack of authority is likely because of the usefulness of equitable property remedies here), and the fact that the remedies are given in response to breaches of property rights. In contrast, other remedies that in English law are classified as proprietary are not akin to *rei vindicatio*, actions such as tracing, subrogation, and the remedial constructive trust do not

The role of damages (or monetary compensation) within a 'proprietary remedy' is an interesting question. Mattei argues that damages are, in fact, an important aspect of the protection of property rights. In certain cases, there are no alternatives to giving damages. Return is not possible if the item has been destroyed, or irreparably damaged.[13] So if, for example, A takes B's phone, but then drops it so that it is broken beyond repair, the only option is to award damages. Here the remedy of damages is the only possible protection for the right of ownership (or possession) that B had, and it would, therefore, be strange if we refused to label this kind of remedy as proprietary when it is attempting to vindicate a property right in the best (or only) way remaining. He argues, however, that to be seen as a property remedy, the structures and requisites of the damage award need to be outside the realm and structure of damages in tort.[14] For this to be the case, these damages awarded as a proprietary remedy should focus on B's property right at play and not on the defendant's (A's) faulty behaviour and the loss suffered by B, as would be typical in tort.

But is it only where there are no alternatives to awarding damages that they can be classed as proprietary? Or could there be other reasons for giving damages this label, for example, based on how they are quantified? If, as discussed in the previous paragraph, damages are quantified in a way that takes into account the proprietary character of the loss/harm, as opposed to being quantified in a 'tortious way', then this *should* be seen as a proprietary remedy (especially under the first of the alternative meanings put forward by the authors of *Personal Property Law)*.

The articulation of a potential role for damages within the concept of a 'proprietary remedy' raises an important point about what a remedy *should* be doing when property is interfered with from a property perspective. What does it mean, though, to 'vindicate/enforce property rights' or to 'take account of the proprietary character of the harm suffered'? What does a remedy need to do to ensure the action is properly protecting property? At this point, it is useful to recall some significant points regarding what is important about property and property rights from Chapter 2.

Here the work of Radin was employed to show the importance that some objects of property have to a person; some objects can be so important that they become intimately linked with a person's conception of themselves, and for these items (often things like wedding rings and other sentimental objects) it might seem that return, where possible, is extremely important when these kinds of objects of property are interfered with (stolen, etc.). The chapter, went on, however, to question the importance of property rights *per se*. Property rights are important, and this is because a property right is not just an interest in an object, but it also encompasses

rely on the return of the actual item, so this is not a fundamental element of what English law sees as a proprietary action/remedy. Or at least, this is not the yardstick that English law uses to determine the proprietary nature of remedies.

13 Ugo Mattei, *Basic Principles of Property Law: A Comparative, Legal and Economic Introduction* (Greenwood Press 2000) 81.

14 ibid 189–90.

an important interest in freedom in being able to control an element of one's environment.[15] The importance of protecting property rights derives from the protection of the freedom and control over the world that such a right gives to someone.[16] Remedies which enable a person to regain possession are important as they allow that person to regain control and freedom with regard to that aspect of their life.[17]

Remedies Viewed through Tort Law Theory

Weir presumes that the focus of tort law remedies is purely on loss and compensation, and this underlies his criticisms of using tort law to protect property. In his view, actions which have such a focus cannot *also* protect property (or at least do so well/fully). Property cannot be fully protected if the mechanisms that aim to protect it have little concern for the vindication of property rights and instead care solely about loss and compensation. As seen in the previous chapters, however, there are differing conceptions of tort law, giving different accounts of how tort should be viewed and what goal or aim tort law has. This has implications for how remedies are perceived and what remedies are seen to be doing.

Under the loss conception model, the focus of tort law is the compensation of loss and harm, just as Weir alludes to in his critique. This view, therefore, sees the role of damages, and tort in general, as compensatory – making up for the loss that has been caused to the claimant in the scenario.

This view can be contrasted with a rights-protection or corrective justice view of tort law. Advocates of these models of tort law see the role of remedies not simply as compensatory but rather as a way to vindicate rights[18] and to regain correlativity between the defendant and the claimant. A case has arisen between these two specific parties because one has suffered a wrongful loss and had a right violated, and one has violated that right and made a wrongful gain. The law seeks to correct this injustice by re-establishing the initial equality between the parties by removing the gain from the one party and restoring the loss of the other;[19] corrective justice in this sense has a rectificatory function. There are different views under this perspective, depending on whether the scholar advancing them adheres to a monist or

15 Joseph Raz, *Ethics in the Public Domain: Essays in the Morality of Law and Politics* (OUP 1995) 48.

16 Hanoch Dagan has made a similar claim in Hanoch Dagan, *A Liberal Theory of Property* (CUP 2020).

17 See discussion in Chapter 2, Section titled, What is the 'Property' That Needs Protecting through the Law? These ideas can be seen in works by Raz, see Raz (n 15); also in the ideas of scholars whose work is based on Kantian thought such as Ripstein and Beever, see Arthur Ripstein, *Force and Freedom: Kant's Legal and Political Philosophy* (Harvard University Press 2009) chapters 3 and 4; Allan Beever, *A Theory of Tort Liability* (Bloomsbury 2016).

18 Andrew Burrows, 'Damages and Rights' in Andrew Robertson and Donal Nolan (eds) *Rights and Private Law* (Hart 2011) 277.

19 Ernest Weinrib, *Corrective Justice* (OUP 2012) 16.

dualist conception of remedies.[20] Nevertheless, a connection is posited between the remedy and the wrong – the remedy responds to the injustice between the parties and tries to undo it.[21]

Some authors contend that the remedies (or damages) are substitutive; they are given in substitute to the right that has been infringed or lost in some way.[22] In many cases where the law of torts is concerned, by the time a case comes to court it is too late to purely enforce the primary right. After a priceless vase has been smashed, it is too late to enforce a primary right that no one interferes with it. However, this is not always the case, and some remedies in tort law do enforce the primary right, most obviously remedies that deal with specific performance such as injunctions and return.

If, however, it is too late, a new right exigible against the wrongdoer is generated.[23] Stevens refers to this as the 'secondary obligation'; this is usually an obligation to pay money and is the law's attempt to reach the next best position to the wrong not having been completed at all.[24] The starting point in valuing damages from this perspective is the value of the right. However, the defendant may also have to pay the claimant's consequential loss, or give up his own gain as well, as the law aims to return to the proximate position as if the event had never occurred.

20 The 'monist' view integrates the rights and the remedies. In Birks' words, the remedy is 'the same thing as the right, looked at from the other end'. See Peter Birks, 'Definition and Division: A Meditation on Institutes 3.13' in Peter Birks (eds) *The Classification of Obligations* (Clarendon 1997) 24. This view is adopted by scholars such as Ripstein and Weinrib. See Weinrib (n 19) Chapter 3 and Arthur Ripstein, *Private Wrongs* (Harvard University Press 2016) Chapter 8. They view the remedy as the continuation of the right. Rights survive their own violation. For example, if you had a property right in a vase, what you actually had was a right against others to constrain their behaviour in respect of the vase. The entitlement is to be the one who determines the use or what happens with the vase, and this continues after a violation. It survives, however, in a modified form, and Ripstein has said this modified form is 'in the form of your entitlement to have me do something that brings the object or a substitute under your control to the extent that it is possible to do so' (Ripstein, *Private Wrongs* [n 20] 243). The dualist approach, by contrast, recognises that rights and remedies are distinct and can be taken to greater or lesser degrees. Gardner, for example, advocates that a violation of a primary right gives rise to a secondary duty of repair. This secondary duty of repair is not a survival or continuation of the original duty that was breached. That first duty was 'discharged', but the reasons underlying that duty were not 'discharged' and so they continue and give rise to a secondary duty of repair. See John Gardner, 'What is Tort Law For? Part 1. The Place of Corrective Justice'. (2011) 30 L & Phil 1. Smith takes this further, he understands remedies as judicial rulings and as completely distinct from substantive laws. Substantive rules tell individuals how they should act in day-to-day life. Remedial rules are different in that they have distinct rules and are directed to courts, who then make orders, as opposed to being directed to citizens. The reasons that a person should act under these two distinct rules are also different. The reason to follow a court order, in Smith's eyes, are not the same as the reasons for the substantive rule that led to the situation. Court orders are commands and should be performed because of that. Under this idea, there is no real link or continuation of the right to the remedy. See Stephen Smith, 'Rights-Threats, Wrongs and Injustices: The Common Law's Causes of Action' (2017) 27 NZULR 1033, 1036–37.

21 Weinrib (n 19) Chapter 3.

22 Robert Stevens, *Torts and Rights* (OUP 2007) 59.

23 ibid.

24 ibid.

Ripstein similarly emphasises the link between the right/wrong and the remedy. He argues that the point of the remedy, in simple terms, is to 'make up for the wrong' – it is substitutive for the right that was infringed.[25] He suggests that this substitution is not perfect and not an equivalent because what it is making up for is the entitlement to constrain the defendant's behaviour and not merely the object that was interfered with.[26] Weinrib, in contrast to Stevens, argues that because what is rightfully the claimant's remains constant throughout, the remedy is just a continuation of the right. The duty of non-interference (which correlated with the right the claimant had) continues after the interference as a remedy in the form of a duty of restoration or reparation.[27] The right continues even if the physical item is destroyed or damaged and so, therefore, does the link between the claimant and the defendant.

As the remedy is seen as a continuation of the injured right in awarding the remedy, the law aims to remove the inconsistency with the claimant's rights by having the defendant restore what is rightfully the claimants.[28] This restoration can be both qualitative or quantitative (using Weinrib's terms here). The qualitative form restores the very thing that was the subject of the right, through specific performance, such as delivery up or injunctions; while the quantitative restores through an award of damages, the monetary equivalent to the injury.[29] In Weinrib's eyes, both forms of restoration represent the continuity of right and remedy.[30]

Thus, the understanding of remedies can vary depending on one's view of the purpose of tort law. As in the last chapter, there is a question of whether these underlying ideas concerning remedies may help alleviate some of the problems raised by Weir (and discussed in further sections). His critique in the passage quoted at the start of this chapter depicts remedies in tort as being solely focused on monetary compensation and compensating loss. This is not the only way to view tort law. And a view focused on protecting rights might allow the discussion to be shifted and reframed in a way that allows property rights to be respected in these remedies.

Proprietary and Tortious

Before considering the specific remedies available in the property torts, it is important to recall the role and nature of these actions. The property torts are actions which sit between property law and tort law; they are part of both property law and tort law and as such it is claimed that the torts have a hybrid nature.[31] The tortious

25 Ripstein (n 20) 4.
26 ibid.
27 Weinrib (n 19) 84.
28 ibid 94.
29 ibid.
30 ibid.
31 Sarah Green and John Randall, *The Tort of Conversion* (1st edn, Hart 2009) 169. This claim has been often made in relation to conversion.

role is often said to concentrate on loss and wrongdoing, although, as noted, the true role of the remedies depends on one's theoretical conception of tort law as a whole. The property aspect focuses on the protection of property rights. Some authors have suggested that when a tort performs a role in relation to rights, in our case property rights, it performs a 'vindicatory function'.[32] By this they mean the function of defining the scope and extent of the interest in question – the property right/interest – and protecting it.[33]

It is sometimes argued that because of this dual or hybrid role, the torts are not sufficiently vindicatory.[34] The implication of this is that they do not sufficiently focus on, or protect, property rights, and this may be exposed in the remedies provided in the torts.

Remedies in the Property Torts

The remedies available for interferences with property vary depending upon the action being claimed. In the real property torts, namely, private nuisance and trespass to land, the standard remedies are either damages or an injunction to stop the interference or intrusion, although the award of the latter is discretionary.[35] The personal property torts (conversion, trespass to goods, and negligence as far as it relates to damage to property) have their remedies (primarily) governed by the Torts (Interference with Goods) Act 1977 (T(IWG)A). The remedies here include damages and return (sometimes called delivery up).[36]

Due to the overlap and similarity in the remedies available in the different property torts, the discussion that follows will proceed remedy by remedy to avoid unnecessary repetition. To do so, the discussion will start with damages; it will then go on to consider the only two types of non-monetary remedies that have any significance in tort law, namely, injunctions and return under T(IWG)A.[37] The starting point can be that while the law of obligations is concerned with providing compensation, specific remedies 'are needed for the full protection of title' and proprietary interests; the use of tort law in this regard has generated a 'number of peculiar rules' explored herein.[38]

32 Peter Cane, *The Anatomy of Tort Law* (Hart 1997) 139.

33 ibid.

34 Shyamkrishna Balganesh, 'Property Along the Tort Spectrum: Trespass to Chattels and the Anglo-American Doctrinal Divergence' (2006) 35 CLWR 135, 136. The author here suggests that the torts are not fully focused on vindication.

35 Beever, *A Theory of Tort Liability* (n 17) 145.

36 These terms will be used interchangeably in this work.

37 Peter Cane, *The Anatomy of Tort Law* (Hart 1997) 98. Reference to damages will also be made in the latter two sections, specifically when talking about damages in lieu of injunctions and damages in lieu of return.

38 Peter Cane, *Tort Law and Economic Interests* (OUP 1991) 22.

Compensatory Damages

The usual function of damages is compensation,[39] and it is a fundamental principle in the law of torts that the basic aim of an award of compensatory damages is to provide a sum of money, which, as nearly as possible, will put the party who has suffered in the same position as she would have been in if she had not sustained the wrong for which she is now getting her compensation.[40] It is a monetary sum that, so far as possible, is equivalent to the claimant's loss.[41] How well a monetary sum can 'make up for the loss' will depend on the nature of the loss suffered. Distinctions are usually drawn between two different *types* of loss, namely, pecuniary and non-pecuniary loss.

The former is the loss of wealth, while the latter accounts for pain, suffering, loss of reputation, or mental distress.[42] Burrows argues that pecuniary losses can be well compensated with money, but non-pecuniary losses cannot, as they are not susceptible to monetary quantification.[43] In the words of Burrows, it's the distinction between losses which are of wealth and can, therefore, be readily translated into money and other losses.[44] Loss and damage to (and interference with) property appears to be viewed as pecuniary loss within the scheme, and so property here is viewed as nothing more than a holder of wealth freely exchanged for money or a substitution (seeing property here as fungible).

This focus on damages and monetary compensation as a remedy in the property torts, especially the torts which protect personal property, might be argued to be due to the nature of the goods which the torts seek to protect, namely, personal property. The common law distinguishes between personal and real property because of their differing characteristics, and this distinction roughly corresponds with the distinction drawn in the civilian system between moveable and immovable property. Real property, or realty, is land, and personal property is all other forms of property. While the reason for this distinction is historic, both types of property have differing characteristics which seem to justify the difference in treatment. Land is permanent, it is virtually indestructible and, as a major asset, it is expected to be passed on through successive generations.[45] Personalty (or personal property) does not share these characteristics. Instead, Mattei has suggested that for personalty, the most important transactions[46] are market transfers, the ability to

39 Andrew Burrows, 'Judicial Remedies' in Andrew Burrows (eds), *English Private Law* (3rd edn, OUP 2013) 21.75.

40 This is a sentiment taken from *Livingstone v Rawyards Coal Co* (1880) 5 App Cas 25 (HL) 38 and cited/repeated in Luke Rostill, 'Possession and Damages for Tortious Interferences with Chattels' (2021) OJLS 41(2) 459, 459.

41 Burrows, 'Judicial Remedies' (n 39) 21.75.

42 Burrows, *Remedies for Torts, Breach of Contract and Equitable Wrongs* (n 6) 35.

43 Burrows, 'Judicial Remedies' (n 39) 21.107.

44 Burrows, *Remedies for Torts, Breach of Contract and Equitable Wrongs* (n 6) 36.

45 See Andrew Bell, *Modern Law of Personal Property in England and Ireland* (Butterworths 1989) 19.

46 Transaction here meaning dealing with which the law is concerned and needs to regulate.

buy, sell, trade, or transfer. This he compares to realty (land) where the law is more concerned with *use*.[47] This distinction in the nature (and use) of property might suggest that damages would be sufficient as a remedy when dealing with the personal property torts. If the most important transactions are market transfers, and they are often held as a commodity or an investment,[48] then it would suggest that one of the most important factors in this kind of property is monetary value, thus being adequately protected by damages. A couple of points can be made to counter this.

First, this explanation does not seem to fully reflect that having property is more important than the object *per se*. The importance of property rights is not limited to possession of the physical thing but also includes the autonomy and decision-making ability that having property rights give to people. They enable you to make certain decisions with regard to the world around you and do things that you would be unable to do without rights in property. The compensation awarded needs to fully compensate for the interference with the right, as opposed to just focusing on the physical item. The primary aim of damages, one could claim, is not to compensate for loss but *should* be to substitute for the right infringed.[49] Though this interpretation of *what* damages are doing has been described as a 'radical, novel, and fascinating re-interpretation of the law', but one that doesn't stand up to scrutiny as to what the law currently *is*.[50] This is not to say that this should not be an aspiration of the law in this area or a way that the law can better accommodate the protection of property interests.

Second, the importance of property to personhood, as elucidated by Radin, counters the idea that *all* personal property can be seen just as wealth adequately compensated by money. Some objects have such sentimental value and importance that a person sees them almost as part of themselves, as constituting who they are as a person. Damages, especially when seen as purely making up for monetary loss, can never account for this. This is a point recognised by Ripstein. He says that while we talk of damages as putting a claimant into as good a position as if the wrong had not occurred, it is not being claimed that damages will make it that 'life can be just as enjoyable, or easy'.[51] He suggests that if an object is damaged or lost, the sentimental attachment to that property is not something that can be compensated, as it is not something that can be replaced[52] – suggesting that this 'making up' by damages alone will always be imperfect. In contrast, Descheemaeker has argued that tort law, in general, does already, at least sometimes, try to 'make up' for this 'moral loss'[53] or emotional harm, at least in relation to property. This can be seen in the property torts in *how* the damages are (sometimes) quantified.

47 Mattei (n 13) 88.
48 Cane, *Economic Interests* (n 38) 12.
49 Stevens (n 22).
50 Burrows, *Remedies for Torts, Breach of Contract and Equitable Wrongs* (n 6) 46.
51 Ripstein (n 17) 252.
52 ibid.
53 Eric Descheemaeker, 'Rationalising Recovery for Emotional Harm in Tort Law' (2018) 134 LQR 602, 602.

In general, when compensatory damages are awarded for claims relating to objects of personal property or land (things which are subject to a property relationship), there is a basic choice between whether to award: i) the diminution of the object/land or ii) the cost of cure.[54] Both aim to restore the claimant, as closely as possible, to their 'pre-wrong' position and make it as if the wrong had never occurred. The former does this by compensating the claimant for the loss of financial advantage in being deprived of the object or land (either completely or in a perfect condition). While the second compensates for the cost of putting the claimant back into the position she was, as if the object or land had not been damaged or taken.[55]

Awarding the diminution in value when the land or object is damaged is calculated by considering the normal market value of the undamaged good or land and then taking away the market value of the current object or land if it is still in existence. This is considered an appropriate award if the land or object was held purely as a speculation, not being occupied or used, but not if they intended to use or were using the land or good in a way that was not measurable in purely financial terms.[56] This type of award has also been given where the cost of cure or restatement was held to be unreasonable and the claimants had no actual intention of reinstating.

This can be seen in the case of *The Maersk Colombo,*[57] a case which concerned an irreparably damaged crane (destroyed by the negligence of the defendant). Here it was held that the cost of a replacement (which would be considered the cost of cure) would not be awarded as the price was unreasonable. The cost was so great as a new crane had to be modified and transported from the US, and this would have cost £2,359,484. Instead, the court awarded the resale value of the crane (the market value amounting to the diminution) which was £665,000. An important factor alongside (and adding to) the unreasonableness of this higher figure was that the claimant did not actually intend to replace the crane. They already had a larger crane on order waiting for delivery. In his leading judgment, Clarke LJ suggested that whether the diminution or cost of cure should be awarded 'will depend upon the circumstances of the particular case'[58] and laid down some general propositions to help the courts decide.[59] For the conclusion of this case, Clarke LJ suggested

54 Burrows, *Judicial Remedies* (n 39) 21.19.

55 ibid.

56 Donald Harris, David Campbell, and Rodger Halson, *Remedies in Contract and Tort* (2nd edn, Cambridge 2010) 524.

57 [2001] EWCA Civ 717.

58 ibid per Clarke LJ at [30].

59 They were; '1. The claimant will ordinarily be entitled to the diminution in value of the property unless the reasonable claimant would have reinstated the land at less cost. 2. The claimant who has in fact reinstated the property will ordinarily be entitled to recover the reasonable cost of doing so, even if the cost is greater than the diminution in value, unless he has acted unreasonably in reinstating the property. 3. Where the claimant has not in fact yet reinstated the property (subject to numbers 4 and 5 following), he will ordinarily be entitled to recover the reasonable cost of reasonable reinstatement, even if it is greater than the diminution in value. 4. In assessing what is the reasonable cost of reasonable reinstatement, the court will consider whether the amount awarded

that for reinstatement to be the appropriate basis for the assessment of damages, 'it must be both reasonable to reinstate and the amount awarded must be objectively fair as between the claimants and the defendants'.[60] In the present case, it was not. It was not reasonable to assess damages based on replacement cost where there was no intention to replace, especially as the figure was so out of proportion with the harm and the actual loss suffered. Cane has suggested that this decision in what to award shows a clash of obligation-based and property-based principles, which runs through much of the law here. Here, arguably, tort laws' 'concern with loss predominates over its concern with property'.[61] A theme raised numerous times and underlying the critique in this work

The other way to assess damages is to consider the cost of cure. This amounts to either the cost of replacing the object or repairing it, the latter being more common when the damage is to land. It has been said that in modern cases in relation to damage to goods, this has been the preferred measure.[62] Although these different ways to assess damages are actually quite similar in practice, as the reasonable cost of repair has been taken to amount to the diminution in value in *Coles v Hetherton*.[63]

While neither of the two methods seem to include any express mention of compensation for emotional harm or distress or moral loss, Descheemaeker has argued that English law does, in fact, compensate this. However, it does so in a disguised way, using labels that conceal the real nature of the harm being redressed or compensated.[64] He argues that while the normal way to quantify damages is based on the diminution, quantification is sometimes instead based on another measure, the cost of cure, as discussed earlier and seen in cases like *Bryant v Macklin*.[65] He further argues that when damages are awarded under this second option, the courts are awarding *more* than the financial loss, and that extra is, in fact, to make up for the moral loss.[66]

While Descheemaeker's argument does account for the moral losses that come from interference with property, this is done on an ad hoc basis by judges rather than through a system. The implication of this is that only in some cases will property rights be protected and recognised as the rights they are, including the autonomy and freedom they provide. There is also no clear reason given for why

---

is objectively fair; that is fair to both parties. In particular, the court will not award a sum which is out of proportion to the benefit conferred on the claimant. 5. In assessing what steps it is reasonable to take by way of reinstatement, the court will take account of the cost of the reinstatement. Thus, it may not be reasonable fully to reinstate the property because the cost of doing so may not be justified. All will depend on the circumstances of the particular case'. See ibid per Clarke LJ at [30–32].

60 ibid per Clarke LJ at [32].

61 Cane, *Tort Law and Economic Interests* (n 38) 33.

62 Burrows, *Remedies for Torts, Breach of Contract and Equitable Wrongs* (n 6) 237.

63 [2013] EWCA Civ 1704, [2015] 1 WLR 160.

64 Descheemaeker (n 53) 606.

65 [2005] EWCA Civ 762.

66 Descheemaeker (n 53) 609–10.

or when the courts will consider this type of award appropriate; instead, it appears to be based on the circumstances of the individual case or possibly just by chance. There is no design in place for when this 'extra' award is given, and, in fact, there is nothing obvious in the awarding of them, which signifies that this is to protect non-pecuniary value or moral loss. The courts do not seem to expressly state the reasons for changing the type of award, and so there is no real evidence to suggest that the courts are trying to compensate anything other than 'typical loss'.

Both of the mentioned methods are typical tortious ways of assessing compensatory damages. As such, normal rules also apply with regard to claims for consequential loss and making a claim for hiring, renting, or buying a substitute during the time you do not have access to your land/goods.[67] There is a question, however, of whether these property torts *should* just apply the typical tortious assessment of damages. In the fairly recent and important decision of *Kuwait Airways v Iraqi Airways,*[68] Lord Nicholls, commenting on conversion, made it clear that:

> [D]espite its proprietary base, this tort does not stand apart and command awards of damages measured by some special and artificial standard of its own. The fundamental object of an award of damages in respect of this tort, as with all wrongs, is to award just compensation for loss suffered.[69]

The problem is that conversion, and all of the torts which protect property, are not just typical torts: They have a dual role and focus that is (or should be) proprietary as well as tortious. This unique dual role of the property torts should be acknowledged, and it should be reflected in judicial reasoning and court decisions. With conversion in particular, it is often contended that it is only really classified as tortious due to its history and the lack of anywhere better to put it.[70] Conversion, for example, is really trying to complete three jobs:[71] First, standing as a substitute for *rei vindicatio* or a similar proprietary remedy and allowing the claimant, in some limited cases, to get redelivery of their thing or enforce their property rights; second, to compensate the owner's loss, a proper tort claim; and third, in some cases provide a restitutionary claim to reverse unjust enrichment. It would seem strange, then, that an action that is trying to complete all of these functions would focus purely on the rules in tort to quantify damages, rather than also acknowledging, in the remedies and damages provided, the proprietary or restitutionary goals of the action. While the other property torts might not have three roles, they are all of a

67 See *Dominion Mosaics Tile Co Ltd v Trafalgar Trucking Co Ltd* [1990] 2 All ER 246 and *Liesbosch Dredger v S.S. Edison* [1933] AC 449.

68 (Nos 4 and 5) [2002] UKHL 19, [2002] 2 AC 883.

69 ibid per Lord Nicholls [67].

70 Andrew Tettenborn, 'Conversion, Tort and Restitution' in Norman Palmer and Ewan McKendrick (eds), *Interests in Goods* (2nd edn, Lloyds of London Press 1998) 825.

71 ibid.

hybrid nature and have a role in tort law and in property law, compensating losses and protecting property.

In all of the property torts, despite their dual role, the remedies focus purely on the tortious element of the action. One can question whether this is appropriate or whether more attention should be paid to the dual nature of the torts in awarding damages and calculating the value of such. Some of the literature surrounding damages for interference with property talk of a 'clash of obligation-based and property-based principles',[72] or the rules being an 'amalgam of proprietary ideas and principles of the law of obligations'.[73] In practice, however, there does not seem to be this amalgamation of ideas. Instead, this highlights another example of the trend where the property torts' dual nature is disregarded, and this is problematic. Once again, the property element is ignored and dominance is given to *only* tort law.

However, there is a different way of assessing or quantifying damages that might show more respect for the property interest at play.

Negotiating Damages

Damages awarded for the property torts are not always compensatory, but instead, sometimes damages are awarded as user or negotiating damages (sometimes also called hypothetical negotiation damages,[74] licence-fee damages,[75] or 'Wrotham Park damages',[76] depending on the tort, and context in which they are awarded). This variation in terminology signals the existence of some debate about the true nature of this non-conventional method of assessing damages,[77] the two primary 'puzzles' relating to the award are: (i) what are the purpose of these awards?; and (ii) when can they be awarded?[78] In this chapter, they will be referred to merely as negotiating damages for ease of vocabulary. This aligns with the terminology used by the Supreme Court in the recent (and significant) case of *Morris-Garner v One Step (Support) Ltd*.[79]

The literature surrounding these types of damages is vast, and the nature or focus of these damages is not yet fully agreed upon, though the Supreme Court decision of *Morris-Garner* has helped elucidate some aspects or at least has provided a

72 Cane, *Economic Interests* (n 38) 33.

73 ibid 44.

74 *Bocardo SA v Star Energy UK Onshore Ltd* [2010] UKSC 35, [2011] 1 AC 380.

75 This is the terminology used by Peter Jaffey, *Private Law and Property Claims* (Hart 2007) 100. This also appears in Nicholas McBride and Roderick Bagshaw, *Tort Law* (5th edn, Pearsons 2015) 771.

76 Named after the breach of restrictive covenant case of *Wrotham Park Estate Co Ltd v Parkside Homes Ltd* [1974] 1 WLR 798. This was arguably the best-known cases in which damages were assessed in this way. See Burrows, *Remedies for Torts, Breach of Contract and Equitable Wrongs* (n 6) 322.

77 Andrew Burrows, 'One Step Forward?' (2018) 134 LQR 515, 515.

78 Burrows, *Remedies for Torts, Breach of Contract and Equitable Wrongs* (n 6) 322.

79 *Morris-Garner v One Step (Support) Ltd* [2018] UKSC 20, [2018] 2 WLR 1353.

clear view of how the Supreme Court views these damages. The basic idea, in practice, is that the defendant is made to pay the price that would have been reasonably negotiated for a licence (or permission) to do the thing done; the defendant is made to pay 'a reasonable sum for the fact that he has committed a tort'.[80] For example, in an action of trespass for crossing land, the defendant will pay the fee that a reasonable claimant would have charged to have granted such permission or to give a licence or easement of access. Or in a case of conversion, the defendant will be made to pay the price that a reasonable claimant would have sold the good for in a hypothetical sale. An example, borrowed from Bagshaw and McBride in a previous version of their textbook, helps show how negotiating damages are used:

> *C* goes for a ride on *O's* horse without *O's* permission, and brings the horse back to *O* in good condition.[81]

In negotiating damages (or licence fee damages as the authors refer to them) *O* can sue *C* for a reasonable sum for the use he has made of the horse. Before *Morris-Garner*, different scholars had argued this was because these damages focused on disgorgement or restitution, making C give up the gain he made (by riding the horse for free),[82] or they were the law's attempt to 'vindicate' the claimant's property right by providing a substitute for this infringement of rights,[83] or that they were compensatory damages, either compensating for the material and tangible loss that the owner of the horse has suffered – and that loss is the loss of a chance to charge for the ride[84] – or compensating for a different *type* of loss.[85] Under the last conception, while normal compensatory damages compensate for some material tangible loss that has been suffered as a result of a tort, licence fee damages compensate the victim for an immaterial intangible loss that they have suffered. This includes the ability to determine what should happen to her and the things under her control.[86] In the example just discussed, the negotiating damages are supposed to compensate for the fact that the owner has been deprived of the power to decide whether or not her horse should be taken out – loss of the ability to determine how her item of property was to be used, when it was to be used, and by whom; this

80 McBride and Bagshaw, *Tort Law* 5th edn, (n 75) 770. This discussion is not replicated in the newer version of this text.

81 ibid 771.

82 Burrows, R*emedies for Torts, Breach of Contract and Equitable Wrongs* (n 6). James Edelman, *Gain-Based Damages* (Bloomsbury 2002). See also, Andrew Burrows, 'Are Damages on the Wrotham Park Basis' Compensatory, Restitutionary or Neither?' in Djackhongir Saidov and Ralph Cunnington (eds.), *Contract Damages: Domestic and International* (OUP 2008).

83 Stevens (n 22) ch 4.

84 Robert Sharpe and Stephen Waddams 'Damages for Lost Opportunity to Bargain' (1982) 2 OJLS 290. See also, to the same effect, Francesco Giglio, *The Foundations of Restitution for Wrongs* (Hart 2007); *WWF v WWF* [2006] EWHC 184 (QB) at [137] per Peter Smith J; *Devenish Nutrition* v *Sanofi-Aventis* [2009] Ch 390, at [40]–[41] per Arden LJ.

85 McBride and Bagshaw, *Tort Law* 5th edn, (n 75) 770. This discussion is not replicated in the newer version of this text.

86 ibid 771.

is often the real 'loss' suffered for invasions of property rights.[87] This view was adopted by both judges and scholars.[88]

The use and idea of negotiating damages in the property torts, when they are seen on the basis of this last interpretation as making up for intangible loss, aligns closely with the conception of what is important about property discussed in this work. The importance of property lies not just in the tangible object or thing but rather in the freedom or autonomy that having property gives a person. When compensatory damages compensate merely for the pecuniary value of the thing, this ignores this important intangible aspect of property rights and of having rights in property, namely, that property enables a person to be the author of their own life. While Descheemaeker has argued that compensatory damages are *sometimes* awarded in a way that makes up for some kind of 'moral loss' and loss of choice/autonomy that comes with interference to property, this is done in an ad hoc way. Negotiating damages, understood in this way, shows respect for this. The focus is on compensating for the interference with a right, a property right, and the things that this property right encompasses. This method, then, comes very close to compensating and valuing the property right infringed.[89] This implies that these kinds of damages are closely connected with the concept of property and are particularly apt at protecting property, as the remedy reflects the underlying importance of property right.

The Supreme Court, in *Morris-Garner*, confirmed that the purpose of negotiating damages are to compensate the claimant for loss.

> In these cases, the courts have treated user damages as providing compensation for loss, albeit not loss of a conventional kind. Where property is damaged, the loss suffered can be measured in terms of the cost of repair or the diminution in value, and damages can be assessed accordingly. Where on the other hand an unlawful use is made of property, and the right to control such use is a valuable asset, the owner suffers a loss of a different kind, which calls for a different method of assessing damages. In such circumstances, the person who makes wrongful use of the property prevents the owner from exercising his right to obtain the economic value of the use in question, and should therefore compensate him for the consequent loss.[90]

87 Josias Senu, 'Negotiating Damages and the Compensatory Principle' (2020) 40 OJLS 110, 117. Arguing that '[b]y looking at the bargain itself, we miss the real loss suffered by the claimant, namely the claimant's choices over his property (which sits behind the infringement of the right). When the defendant promises not to breach a restrictive covenant and then does so, there is a difference between the claimant's position before and after the breach. Before the defendant's invasion of the claimant's right, the claimant had several choices available to him; after the breach, the claimant has fewer choices available'.

88 See discussion in Charles Mitchell and Luke Rostill, 'Making Sense of Mesne Profits: Remedies' (2021) 80(3) CLJ 552, 556.

89 Burrows, R*emedies for Torts, Breach of Contract and Equitable Wrongs* (n 6) 48.

90 *Morris-Garner* (n 79) [30].

Andrew Burrows's extra-judicial analysis of the court's opinion suggested that 'Lord Reed effectively says that the relevant loss is the loss of the opportunity to obtain value or is the value of the right/asset of which the claimant has been deprived'.[91] For Burrows, the former equates to the 'loss of opportunity to bargain' analysis previously put forward by scholars such as Robert Sharpe and Stephen Waddams,[92] and the latter seems close to valuing the right infringed. The dicta of Lord Reed accords with the analysis of seeing these damages as compensatory, which fits within this idea of valuing the right where the right is seen as including aspects of freedom and autonomy. Or to put another way, the relevant loss being compensated is the right to control the use of the thing, an aspect of the property right itself.[93]

As well as being apt at protecting property, these types of damages seem to have a special role in protecting property. Negotiating damages have been held to be available in conversion,[94] trespass to land,[95] and private nuisance,[96] and previous case law has doubted whether they can be awarded for any non-proprietary tort.[97] In *Morris-Garner*, Lord Reed concluded that negotiating damages were available for cases concerning invasions of rights to tangible, movable, or immovable property; infringement of intellectual property rights; damages in substitution for an injunction based on the economic value of the right which the court has refused to enforce; and contract cases, but only where the loss suffered is represented by the value of an asset of which the claimant has been deprived, such as the right to control the use of land or intellectual property or a confidentiality agreement.[98] As such, these types of awards are linked to property rights or claims relating to property (or closely analogous rights[99]) and could represent a more property-like way of assessing and quantifying damages as previously suggested. Lord Reed also confirmed a specific role for this method of assessing damages when damages are given in lieu of an injunction under section 50 of the Supreme Court Act 1981.

There are, however, some criticisms of these types of damages, the most relevant for this purpose being: (i) how accurately the figures awarded can be assessed; and (ii) what being awarded these damages amounts to in practical terms. There is literature questioning how accurately this figure of how much a person would have charged to grant a licence, in the case of real property rights or for a negotiated sale, in the case of personal property, can be determined. Arguably this often

91 Burrows, One Step (n 77) 518.
92 Sharpe and Waddams (n 84).
93 Eric Descheemaeker, 'The Standardisation of Tort Damages' (2021) 84(1) MLR 1, 18.
94 *Kuwait Airways Corpn* v *Iraqi Airways Co* (n 68) at [87] (per Lord Nicholls).
95 Roderick Bagshaw and Nicholas McBride, *Tort Law* (6th edn, Pearsons 2018) 781.
96 The Court of Appeal decision in *Forsyth-Grant* v *Allen* [2008] EWCA Civ 505 seems to indicate that in an 'exceptional' case (Patten J, with Mummery LJ agreeing at [31]–[32]) or an 'appropriate' case (Toulson LJ at [38]) licence fee damages may be awarded against a defendant who commits the tort of private nuisance.
97 *Devenish Nutrition* (n 84).
98 *Morris-Garner* (n 79) per Lord Reed at [95].
99 Burrows, One Step (n 77) 520.

undervalues the claimant's position; it is the claimant that holds the bargaining power.[100] The claimant, *without the interference*, would have had the power to decide if they wanted to grant a sale or licence, and might, then, have been able to charge a premium for doing so. The case law has made clear, however, that the quantification must be based on what a reasonable person in the claimant's position would have accepted[101] and that the licence or release should be calculated only for the period that the trespass occurred.[102] This appears to be quite an artificial notion of negotiation, because were the claimant not to bring proceedings to end to the interference, for example in *Eaton Mansions*, this was the removal of air-conditioning units from a roof, the trespass would have continued and any negotiation which happened, in reality, would not have been for this hypothetical arbitrary period. *Bocardo SA v Star Energy UK Onshore Ltd*[103] is an example of devaluing the claimant's bargaining position. Here, the Supreme Court quantified the damages based on the cost of compulsory acquisition of land, amounting to only £1,000 for all past and future trespasses. It is unlikely that had a licence been negotiated, such a figure would have been reached and the defendant would have been able to negotiate such a favourable release, which is in line with government's compulsory acquisition, as a private company. While there are some issues with the quantification of negotiating damages, they nonetheless do seem to recognise the importance of the property right and focus on that as the primary issue in these cases. They are also able to create a better situation for the claimant in some scenarios, as some claimants may have previously had to settle for purely nominal damages if no damage had been caused.[104]

However, there are still criticisms of this type of remedy and what the award amounts to in *practice*. Two different points are raised here; the first is that as Peter Devonshire has argued, this way to quantify damages does not impose any real sanction on the defendant because the defendant is no worse off as a result of the judgment.[105] In the end, all he is required to do is pay the fee he should have paid before he started the trespass or nuisance. This could create a situation where people (possible defendants) may feel that it is worth 'chancing it', in not gaining a licence before the trespass, because the worst-case scenario is that they pay after (unless, of course, an injunction is awarded instead, but as we will see they are discretionary and not available as of right).

This type of remedy has been claimed to, in effect, result in a forced bargain – a forced judicial sale or a forced judicial licence/easement;[106] the granting of a right

100 Peter Devonshire, 'The Hypothetical Negotiation Measure: An Untenable Fiction?' (2012) 3 LMCLQ 394, 411.

101 *Morris-Garner* (n 79).

102 See *Eaton Mansions (Westminster) Ltd v Stinger Compania de Inversion SA* [2013] EWCA Civ 1308, [2014] HLR 4.

103 [2011] 1 AC 380.

104 Devonshire (n 100) 393.

105 ibid 401.

106 ibid 401.

or the transfer of the thing that the claimant never wanted to give or be departed from. While a forced licence, or forced sale, would be deeply problematic and would go against the idea of protecting property rights, it is important to remember that the licence fee damages *do not* physically remove property; instead, a previous act has already done that. The defendant, in committing the tort, has interfered with some right already, they have damaged or taken or interfered with some right in property. The licence fee damages, now, after the act, step in and 'corrects the wrong'. Depending on one's view of tort law, the role of damages is to either enforce the original right and duty or to enforce a secondary obligation in substitution of the right already interfered with. This remedy does that and does it in a way that respects and quantifies the fact that a property right has been lost.

Injunctions

An injunction is a coercive order backed up by a threat of contempt proceedings[107] instructing a defendant to either: 1) stop doing something, a prohibitory injunction; or, 2) do or fix something, a mandatory injunction. The latter involves the defendant taking positive action(s) to, for example, restore land or property; while the former normally acts negatively.[108] Injunctions are mainly sought[109] in torts which seek to protect the claimant's real property rights, namely, private nuisance and trespass to land.[110] They can be seen as examples of enforcing the primary right

107 Harris, Campbell, and Halson (n 56) 473.

108 Burrows, R*emedies for Torts, Breach of Contract and Equitable Wrongs* (n 6) 511.

109 Do note, however, that injunctions are also available in trespass to goods and potentially negligence. While these actions fall under the 'wrongful interference' actions in the Torts (Interference with Goods) Act 1977 (T(IWG)A) (discussed more shortly) unlike conversion, the remedies are not completely guided by the act and the remedies that were available in these actions prior to the introduction of the T(IWG)A still apply. This allows a claimant to claim damages or an injunction. See Andrew Tettenborn (eds), *Clerk & Lindsell on Torts* (24th edn, Sweet & Maxwell 2024) 16–140. There is a question of whether injunctions are available for negligence. The courts have the power to grant an injunction whenever it appears to be 'just and convenient' to do so, in effect allowing the court to grant an injunction where the court of equity would have done so (see Senior Courts Act 1981 s.37(1); County Courts Act 1984 s.38) and signifying that (in appropriate cases, at least) injunctions may be granted in relation to any form of tortious conduct. In practice, however, there is no English precedent where an injunction has been awarded against a defendant to stop him breaching a duty of care (see Bagshaw and McBride (n 75) 78; *Miller v Jackson* [1977] QB 966 at 980 where Lord Denning said 'The books are full of cases where an injunction has been granted to restrain the continuance of a nuisance. But there is no case, so far as I know, where it has been granted so as to stop a man being negligent'; and, *CBS Songs Plc v Amstra*d [1988] AC 1013, 'damages and an injunction for negligence [were] sought' (ibid, at 1060) against the defendants, but no duty of care was found to be owed in that case.) While some authors suggest this is because duties of care are rarely breached on a continuing basis, leaving no space for injunctions, as it is too late by the time the claimant finds out about the breach (see Bagshaw and McBride (n 75) 78), others argue that there could (and should) be space for injunctions in negligence (John Murphy, 'Rethinking Injunctions in Tort Law' (2007) 27 OJLS 509 and, Rachael Mulheron *Principles of Tort Law* (CUP 2020) 543 saying that injunctive relief may also be sought for the tort of negligence).

110 Burrows, R*emedies for Torts, Breach of Contract and Equitable Wrongs* (n 6) 514.

of the claimant not to be interfered with: The injunction is merely enforcing the claimant's right to be free from interference in the example of a trespass or the right to be free from unreasonable interference in the case of a nuisance. Injunctions are considered to be one of the primary remedies in both private nuisance and trespass to land actions.[111] In fact, Cane argues that there is something special about the torts which protect 'property' interests which justifies this focus of injunctive relief. He maintains that the availability of injunctions in these torts 'reflects the high value that tort law puts on interests classified as 'property' interests'. For him, the ideological underpinning for this type of protection is clear enough: 'Private property forms the bedrock of our economic and social life, and real property is one of the most important forms of private property'.[112] As such, there is almost a correlation between rights seen as important and the availability of injunctions or specific performance remedies. More recently, John Murphy (and others) have shown that no such hierarchy of protected rights in tort exists,[113] or at least the hierarchy is not perfect, as some non-proprietary rights are protected by injunctions (etc.),[114] and so it cannot safely be asserted that the free availability of injunctions in tort law is linked to the high-ranking status of certain interests.[115] It cannot be denied that there is *some kind of* correlation between torts that have a focus on property rights and specific performance style remedies like injunctions, even if this is not a perfect mirror or correlation, and for the real property torts, injunctions are the primary remedy.

Despite being one of the primary remedies in the real property torts, injunctions are not available 'as of right' (as damages are) but are instead a form of equitable remedy[116] which is discretionary.[117] The basic principle is that if the claimant can show actionable damage (or merely an interference in trespass to land[118]) flowing from the interference, then she will automatically be entitled to damages. She may not, however, be automatically entitled to an injunction. The court has a discretion when awarding an injunction to instead award damages in lieu, and this applies *even if* the interference is ongoing.[119] Regardless of this discretion, especially in cases concerning continuing interference, injunctions are commonly the remedy of choice for the real property torts, as most claimants would prefer that the interference be brought to an end, rather than to receive damages for the annoyance or

111 Kevin Gray and Susan Francis Gray, *Elements of Land Law* (5th edn, OUP 2009) 10-012. The alternative to awarding an injunction is the award of damages, see *Clerk* (n 111) 10-131.

112 Cane, *Anatomy* (n 32) 140.

113 John Murphy, 'Torts Hierarchy of Protected Interests' (2022) 81(2) CLJ 356, 377.

114 ibid 375.

115 ibid 377. Arguing 'Injunctions may be obtained with relative ease in various torts that overwhelmingly protect our most lowly interests; while, at the same time, they may also be denied where our most highly cherished interest (i.e. bodily integrity) is in jeopardy'.

116 Burrows, *Remedies for Torts, Breach of Contract and Equitable Wrongs* (n 6) 510.

117 Some authors have expressed their disapproval over this terminology, see Allan Beever, *The Law of Private Nuisance* (Hart 2013) 145.

118 As trespass is actionable *per se* without proof of damage.

119 Beever, *The Law of Private Nuisance* (n 117) 145.

harm that has been caused previously and that may continue into the future.[120] This applies in both nuisance and trespass cases.

The cardinal principle underpinning the award of an injunction is that compensatory damages are not an adequate remedy.[121] Damages are (sometimes) considered inadequate to compensate for continuing trespasses or nuisances, because damages can only operate retrospectively and cover past interferences or intrusions.[122] An example is the well-known private nuisance case of *Sturges v Bridgman*.[123] Here, damages would not adequately compensate for the ongoing interference caused by the noise and vibrations of the confectionary machines used in the property neighbouring the (at the time of the case) doctor's private practice. Damages may also be seen as inadequate where the compensation value is low. For example, in the case of *Anchor Brewhouse Developments Ltd v Berkley House (Docklands Developments) Ltd*,[124] an injunction was awarded where cranes had been allowed to invade the neighbouring airspace. As no damage had been suffered in the 'technical' trespass, the damages (or compensation) would be minimal, which would not sufficiently compensate the claimant for the interference they had suffered.

The question of when an injunction is likely to be granted, or conversely refused, is an important one, especially as some authors have raised concerns about whether a claimant's property right would have been adequately vindicated where damages in lieu are awarded.[125] As a remedy for trespass to land and nuisance, injunctions serve to protect property rights. They do so by ensuring that there is no further interference with the possession or enjoyment of their property in the future or that the damage is 'put back right'. The same is not necessarily true for damages.[126]

In his work on nuisance, Beever suggests that the essence of nuisance is prioritising property rights. Nuisance, in effect, creates a hierarchy of property rights which it then uses to settle conflicts between land uses/users.[127] So in theory, a more fundamental property right should trump a less fundamental property right, indicating who will win a nuisance claim. For Beever, then, damages in lieu of an injunction should only be awarded when 'issuing an injunction would result in allowing the defendant's more fundamental right to be trumped by the less fundamental right of the claimant'.[128]

In practice, however, this is not what underlies the exercise of discretion in this area. Judges do not decide whether to grant an injunction based purely on the

120 John Murphy, *The Law of Nuisance* (OUP 2010) 6.02.

121 ibid 6.07.

122 Gray (n 111) 10-011.

123 [1877] S 223, (1879) 11 Ch D 852.

124 (1988) 4 Const LJ 29.

125 Devonshire (n 100) 394.

126 This is subject to the discussion in the previous part of this chapter which looked at when/how damages might be sufficiently property-like.

127 Beever *The Law of Private Nuisance* (n 117) 15.

128 ibid 149–50.

strength of the relative property right. Instead, historically, judicial guidelines were developed to help the court determine when damages should be given in lieu of an injunction, in other words, when an injunction should not be granted. This can be seen in the decision of *Shelfer*.[129] In this case, Smith LJ sought to lay down a general rule (a good working rule) concerning when damages should be awarded in lieu of an injunction. This stated:

> (1) If the injury to the plaintiff's legal rights is small, (2) And is one which is capable of being estimated in money, (3) And is one which can be adequately compensated by a small money payment, (4) And the case is one in which it would be oppressive to the defendant to grant an injunction: then damages in substitution for an injunction may be given.[130]

In practice, the conditions noted can be seen in the decision in *Jaggard v Sawyer*,[131] a case which concerned building in breach of a covenant that required the defendants to leave a private road clear for use. While the court recognised that damages would not be able to compensate the ongoing trespass, the court still granted damages in lieu because an injunction would be oppressive when the harm was minimal. The court stressed, in this decision, that injunctions should be the normal remedy in a restrictive covenant case unless the four conditions are made out, giving a strict reading to the test advocated in *Shelfer*. In fact, prior to *Lawrence v Fen Tigers* discussed in the next paragraph, the general approach of the courts was to *rarely* deny a prohibitory injunction in relation to trespass to land or private nuisance.[132]

But more recently the Supreme Court has taken a step back from this suggestion and held that instead the courts have an unfettered discretion[133] where they are able to take into account a range of factors including the terms of any planning permission, public interest, and the effect on other persons.[134] Thus, *Lawrence v Fen Tigers* indicates that a more flexible approach is likely to be applied when considering whether damages in lieu of an injunction will be awarded. The comments from the Justices suggest that it will be harder to obtain an injunction where the development is of public benefit and has planning permission.[135] This suggests that were cases similar to *Anchor Brewhouse* (cited previously) to come to court today, an injunction would be less likely to be awarded, and instead, damages in lieu would be given because of the planning permission and public benefit of the activity.

129 *Shelfer v City of London Electric Lighting Company. Meux's Brewery Company v City of London Electric Lighting Company* [1895] 1 Ch 287.
130 ibid per Smith LJ at 322–23.
131 [1995] 1 WLR 269.
132 Burrows, *Remedies for Torts, Breach of Contract and Equitable Wrongs* (n 6) 444.
133 *Lawrence and another v Fen Tigers Ltd and Others* [2014] UKSC 13, [2014] AC 822.
134 ibid.
135 ibid.

The Supreme Court, even more recently, reinforced this idea in its dicta in *Fearn*.[136] While remedies were not decided by the Supreme Court as they were not raised in the appeal,[137] Lord Leggatt implied that the public interest and balancing the rights of the parties were more appropriately dealt with at the remedies stage of the proceedings. Confirming, again, that external influences and public benefit might factor into the exercise of discretion in awarding an injunction (or not). This is particularly interesting, as it has been said that a very important feature of the traditional approach to granting injunctions was that the courts were not prepared to deny a prohibitory injunction on the ground that the public interest was more important than the claimant's private right or property interest.[138] *Lawrence*, and potentially even more so *Fearn*, undermines and moves away from this traditional approach. In doing so it also weakened the primacy of the injunction.[139]

The discussed 'test' for when a judge should use their discretion and not award an injunction seems totally void of any property right style analysis, and instead focuses purely on external factors such as how easily it is compensated in money, whether the defendant will be unduly affected by ordering an injunction, or the public benefit of the activity. As such, the strength or importance of the property right does not seem to determine the availability of a property-style remedy enforcing specific performance, but instead we seem to retreat to fairness and tort law ideals.

This links back with Beever's claim that an injunction should only not be awarded when it would mean trumping a more fundamental property right with a less fundamental one. This calculation does not seem to come into play in the judge's discretion, at least as it used to be articulated in the *Shelfer* test or with the increased flexibility introduced in *Lawrence* and confirmed in *Fearn*. While it is a remedy that protects property rights more sufficiently than damages, it is not governed by property style principles, instead being governed completely by tort law ideals.

The caveat here is that the property right forms the basis of these remedies – without a property right, the claim for the remedy does not even get off the ground. The factors from *Shelfer* and the wider remit of the discretion developed in *Lawrence* and *Fearn* are the countervailing considerations that weigh up against the property right; they are the other side of the scales. Obviously in this situation, the court has to consider factors such as the administration of justice, the interests of the other party, and the need to avoid oppressive court orders. But the analysis completed and the discussion of discretion seems to 'forget' about the property right that they are balancing against. Surely the right at play should be more of a feature in the balancing exercise. This shows once again how tort law prevails, and the property concerns and property rights importance is ignored due to their

136 *Fearn v Tate Gallery* [2023] UKSC 4, [2023] 2 WLR 339.
137 ibid [131].
138 Burrows, *Remedies for Torts, Breach of Contract and Equitable Wrongs* (n 6) 446.
139 ibid 449.

tortious classification. This implies a failure to recognise the specifically property-protecting role of these actions and the importance of property within these torts.

Along with the decision of whether or not to grant damages in lieu of an injunction are questions concerning what, from a practical perspective, the refusal to grant an injunction (and awarding of damages instead) means for the claimant. Peter Devonshire has suggested that in practical terms this refusal means that that the unauthorised acts or state of affairs can continue indefinitely (if damages are awarded that are supposed to account for past and future trespasses or nuisances), and as such, the damages that are given here are effectively amounting to compulsory acquisition of a right.[140] When damages are given in lieu of an injunction, the court is granting a forced permission or grant of a licence, which the claimant may never have wanted to give. Damages in lieu of an injunction have the effect of legitimising an interference with property rights by reducing them to a monetary payment in return for their discharge.[141] The strength of this concern, however, turns on whether in practice injunctions are only exceptionally awarded or instead are usually awarded. The former would suggest an issue, while the latter would not.[142]

Remedies Under the Torts (Interference with Goods) Act (T(IWG)A) – Return

Imagine the following scenario: X has his bike stolen. X is upset by this situation. A few days later X sees a person (Y) with their bike, X knows it is their bike as it is easily distinguishable (for example, it could have a label on it which means that X knows it to be theirs). X, knowing this to be their bike, goes up to Y and takes the bike back (peacefully), telling them, 'this is my bike and if you have an issue to seek redress'. The end result here pleases X, X has regained possession of their bike.

If, however, X is unable to catch up to the person, but X does manage to follow Y home and find out their address, and then, knowing that Y is the person in possession of their bike (whether Y was the person who took it or someone who purchased it from the wrongdoer), sought to bring an action in conversion, the end result may differ.

The remedies available for the 'wrongful interference' torts, namely, conversion, trespass to goods, and negligence as far as it relates to damage to property,[143]

140 Devonshire (n 100) 402.

141 David Sawtell, 'Injunctions, Land and the Cynical Breach' (2022) 42 LS 649, 651.

142 The second caveat to this is that it is not the award that *actually* transfers the property, the 'wrong' has already occurred. As discussed in the Damages section previously.

143 While the discussion of return and the remedies under T(IWG)A technically applies to *all* of the wrongful interference actions (conversion, trespass to goods, and negligence), the main focus is on conversion. This is because the remedy of return is unlikely to be awarded, or actually requested, in trespass to goods or negligence, despite the remedies for these actions being guided by s3(2) of the T(IWG)A. This is because trespass and negligence do not normally deal with interferences where the claimant has lost possession and so return is not relevant or required.

are specified in the Torts (Interference with Goods) Act 1977 (T(IWG)A).[144] Under this legislation, there are three potential remedies available. These are, an order for delivery up of the goods, an order for delivery up *with* the option to pay damages in substitute, or an award of damages.[145] In practice, the latter is the most commonly awarded and ordering delivery up of the goods under the T(IWG)A is not available *as of right* in tort; instead, it is discretionary,[146] and, in fact, orders under s3(2)(a) for delivery up, without the option of paying damages in lieu, occurs relatively infrequently.[147] These types of orders can be granted, nonetheless, in certain situations, which include: (1) where the goods are unique and sentimental; (2) where the goods are of particular value to the claimant; (3) where they are not easily replaceable; or, (4) where the replacement would take considerable time and effort.[148]

The primary principle underlying the choice between delivery up and ordering damages is that delivery up should *not* be ordered if damages would be adequate, and, hence, the noted exceptions are examples of situations where damages will not be seen as sufficient.[149] Delivery up, then, would not normally be ordered for most 'ordinary' goods, on the basis that damages will enable a substitute to be bought on the market and, therefore, damages will be adequate and compensate the claimant sufficiently.[150]

So in this scenario, even though X knows that Y has their bike and X has rightfully brought a claim against them, X is likely to end up without their bike, but instead, with damages. Does it not seem peculiar that the redress available in law through tort, which is specifically in place to deal with this situation, results in a less claimant-friendly result than if X were just to physically take back possession when they saw Y in the street with their bike? When thinking about this, comparisons are often drawn with *rei vindicatio* in the Roman tradition, because in conversion, unlike in *rei vindicatio*, the claimant is unlikely to automatically receive his goods back.[151] And this, for scholars such as Weir, is problematic; as for him (and others who stress the need for a remedy which focuses on return) the remedy that best protects a person's property interest in a thing is *return*. The property interest that a claimant has is best protected when the claimant has a chance to have the item returned. And arguably if protection against misappropriation were seen as

144 Torts (Interference with Goods) Act 1977, (T(IWG)A) 1997.

145 (T(IWG)A) 1977, s3(2). This section, however, focuses most predominantly on the remedy of return under T(IWG)A. In doing so damages, as they specifically relate to T(IWG)A, will also be considered.

146 Steele, *Tort Law: Text, Cases and Materials* (4th edn, OUP 2017) 892.

147 *Clerk & Lindsell* (n 109) 16–91.

148 ibid.

149 Burrows, R*emedies for Torts, Breach of Contract and Equitable Wrongs* (n 6) 578. See also *Blue Sky One Ltd v Blue Airways LLC* [2009] EWHC 3314 (Comm) [309].

150 Green and Randall (n 31).

151 The situation in *rei vindicatio* is less black and white than often stated when considering the remedy. While return is the primary remedy, there is an alternative of damages if the defendant does not want to return the thing.

part of the law of property, there could be no doubt that specific return would be the prime remedy, just as it was/is in the Roman law tradition.[152]

It does need to be acknowledged here that there are other factors at play in the second scenario when the law of torts and the courts are involved that simply do not arise if X finds the bike in the street. Once the court is involved, the property right in the thing can obviously no longer be the only thing that matters; issues pertaining to the administration of justice such as the efficiency and cost of litigation as well as the cost and ease of enforcement are all considerations which arise here. As such, the law and the rules within T(IWG)A need to strike a balance between these competing considerations. Comparisons to the factors relevant in awarding an injunction above could be raised here. The balance T(IWG)A strikes favours damages and relegates return to exceptional scenarios, this is the opposite balance/position to the one made in *rei vindicatio*. The question is whether this is the correct way to strike the balance.

The damages given in this scenario (when return is not granted) are supposed to adequately compensate the loss, but there is a question of whether they always will and a question of whether it is the same. Should the claimant in the hypothetical scenario not have a say in whether they get their bike back, just because they want the bike back, rather than the hassle of getting compensation and then having to use that in order to buy a new bike to put them back into the position before the unfortunate circumstances began? The question of whether the claimant gets a say in wanting their actual thing back is also particularly poignant when we consider the importance of property for autonomy and freedom. This issue raises particularly interesting points about whether the property rights at play here are being sufficiently protected when property is protected through tort law.

It might be suggested that the focus on damages (and the infrequency of return) in the personal property torts, with which the T(IWG)A is concerned, is because of the nature of the goods. Two different claims are made; the first is that with regards to personal property, the most important transactions for these types of goods are market transfers.[153] If the most important transactions are market transfers, then it would suggest that one of the most important factors in this kind of property is monetary value, thus being adequately protected by damages. The second claim is that chattels, or personal property, are not typically unique or of special value to their owner;[154] 'tangible property is very often treated by its owner simply as a commodity or an investment'.[155] Obviously, there are some types of objects which have *more than* economic value and have some kind of sentimental factor or are otherwise rare and special, but in the scheme of remedies under the T(IWG)A, as previously explained, you would be able to try to recover the actual property in this case. For example, delivery up can be awarded where goods are physically unique.

152 Cane, *Economic Interests* (n 38) 33.
153 Mattei (n 13) 88.
154 Cane, *Anatomy* (n 32) 145.
155 Cane, *Economic Interests* (n 38) 12.

In the case of *García v De Aldama*,[156] the court held that a manuscript comprising a collection of poems of the Spanish poet and playwright Federico Garcia Lorca could, and would, have been eligible for the remedy of delivery up to the claimants if they successfully proved their case. Similarly, though in a very different context, delivery up was awarded in *Howard Perry Ltd v British Railway Board*,[157] where the defendants refused to deliver steel or allow the claimants to collect their steel (through fear of retaliations by those striking) during a strike of steel workers. As such, the court found that the defendants were retaining or detaining the claimant's steal. The court here granted a s3(2)(a) delivery up of the steel being detained because, due to the steel strike, steel was not readily available on the open market and thus was not easily replaceable. So, while the goods here were not physically unique, they were 'commercially unique' and, thus, rare and special.[158]

The position of tort law, then, is to start with the assumption that interests in tangible property are purely economic interests, and then in limited cases modify that assumption.[159] Not everyone, however, sees all other personal property that falls outside the limited exceptions where return is likely to be granted simply as 'value', in the monetary sense. The value gained from a car is that it provides transport, not just that it can be sold for a sum; the value gained from a phone is that it can be used to stay connected. On a basic human level, people have attachments and relationships with their possessions which are of a completely different kind to just appreciating their market transfer value. A person might want to have their phone returned because they want that specific phone back, they do not want to have the money's worth and have to repurchase a similar phone. But is this desire to get that specific phone back for personal reasons enough to reach the level of 'sentimental value' that is needed to satisfy for delivery up under T(IWG)A? If not, then by only allowing damages, the protection of property under T(IWG)A is limited.

There are links here with personhood theory as it was explained by Radin.[160] There are two separate points to make relating to personhood theory and T(IWG)A. The first are the parallels between the ideas, and the second is the issue concerning where the line is drawn between what counts as personal property and how this relates to the exceptions in T(IWG)A.

Parallels can be seen between the formulation of remedies under the T(IWG)A and personhood theory. Specifically, in how the personhood theory explains the relationship that people have with objects and whether these objects are seen as 'personal property' or 'fungibles'. Personal here means property that is seen as valuable 'in itself' and that the holder sees almost as part of who they are. This could be things such as wedding rings or things which have sentimental value.

156 [2002] EWHC 2087, [2003] ECDR CN1.

157 [1980] 1 WLR 1375.

158 This term was used in *Blue Sky One Ltd v Blue Airways LLC* [2009] EWHC 3314 (Comm) [314].

159 Cane, *Economic Interests* (n 38) 12.

160 Margaret Radin, 'Property and Personhood' (1982) 34 Stan L Rev 957, 961.

In contrast, fungible goods are goods which are not valuable in themselves, and instead are those goods or things which are seen as wealth holders which are happily exchanged for money's worth. This distinction was drawn on in the property chapter to explore how the objects of property rights are perceived. The premise of Weir's argument is that remedies which do not allow return (as of right) do not sufficiently protect property. The idea of personhood suggests something different, however. It suggests that while return is necessary for some items, for others, compensation or money equivalent would adequately remedy the loss – those goods that are seen purely as wealth holders, for example. This scheme *is* replicated in the T(IWG)A. Here the basic idea is that compensation is available as of right, but the judge can decide *instead* to order for the delivery up/return of the item. This is particularly the case when the item has sentimental value. The parallels are clear to see.

The issue is that *if* personhood is the basis for the requirement of return, the theory fails to explain why return is always necessary. In fact, the personhood theory suggests that the current law of remedies is framed correctly for interferences with personal property. T(IWG)A allows return when return is necessary because of a personal and close connection with an object or thing but allows monetary compensation when things are not seen as important in themselves. On this basis, the T(IWG)A remedies seem well thought through and highly appropriate. This does not, however, explain Weir's focus on return.

In Chapter 2, different justifications for the focus on return were considered, this primarily centred on Raz and Kantian thought concerning the importance of property rights *per se*. The importance of property rights is not just the importance of the *object* of the right but also the autonomy and decision-making that having rights allows someone to have. The importance of having an object of property is not just the importance of the object, but the importance of also being able to decide what you do with the object and whether you want to keep the object or sell the object, etc. This then goes further than personhood in suggesting when return is important. From this perspective, return is not only important when the object is valuable in itself, but return is always important as it is only through return of the taken item that a person regains the autonomy to decide what they do with the objects in which they have rights. From this perspective, T(IWG)A does not have the same appeal. In fact, any mechanisms which do not have return as a focus seems to disregard the importance of property rights.

The second point is that there may be a discrepancy between the exceptions (which justify return) and things or items that people feel are important and part of themselves (when they would *want* return). What people *see* as personal property (in the personhood sense) varies,[161] and while this special relationship may be accommodated by the sentimental attachment provision, it is also likely that it may not be *fully respected* by the provision of sentimental attachment. While things like wedding bands might fall under this categorisation, as many have special

161 Radin suggests that what counts will vary from person to person, ibid 961.

relationships with those items, other things with such value to a particular claimant might not fall into this category.

The sentimental attachment felt by some, and importance of that item to them, may sometimes be less obvious. For example, a 'standard clock' might nonetheless hold special value to the person because of who bought it. Here damages are likely to be awarded because on the face of it a clock is easily replaceable on the open market, but it would fail to account for the sentiment and close relationship that the particular claimant has to the clock.

A Comparison between the Protection of Real and Personal Property

As the only two types of non-monetary remedies to have any significance in tort law,[162] comparisons are often drawn between return (in personal property) and injunctions (in real property). There has been a lot of critique within academic commentary of the remedies available for conversion and the personal property torts, and specifically the availability (or lack) of return, but this has not been replicated in the real property actions in the same way.

The torts that deal with real property are well known at this point, but alongside these actions sit ejectment, or now, to use the modern terminology, an order for possession.[163] Through the use of an order for possession, or through an injunction in the torts, a claimant is much more likely to be able to compel 'return' of land. The exercise of discretion in the land-based torts seems to work in the opposite way to the personal property torts. In the real property actions, injunctions are seen as the primary remedy for many interferences, and while it is acknowledged that they are discretionary, in practice, damages in lieu are given less frequently. Here historically damages will be awarded only if the injury to the right is small, capable of being quantified in a small amount of money, and an injunction would be oppressive. *Lawrence* and *Fearn* have added flexibility to this and confirmed that the court does, in fact, have an 'unfettered discretion' and should not feel bound to grant an injunction simply because all four of the *Shelfer* conditions are not satisfied. The result still being that, in practice, an injunction will be the norm unless the criteria are satisfied or the courts otherwise feel an injunction is not necessary and damages are deemed adequate. While this position can still be (and was) critiqued, nonetheless, the situation seems to reverse for conversion and the claimant in personal property law cases, as in the personal property torts, damages are the norm unless some extra criteria are satisfied and then a property-style remedy of return will be considered.

The prioritisation in these two scenarios is different. The former, the real property actions, prioritise the specific performance style remedy; the remedy that returns property. If this is then deemed inappropriate, the law falls back to damages instead. In the latter, the damages are considered the standard and appropriate

162 Cane, *Anatomy* (n 32) 98.

163 See RSC ORDER 113 – Summary proceedings for possession of land.

remedy. Then, if the claimant can show some special attachment or that the thing or item is unique, they can ask for a specific performance style remedy of return (and this then falls to the discretion of the judge). It would seem, therefore, that the prioritisation in personal property torts is not towards a property remedy, and this is the opposite to how the torts which deal with real property work.

The same can be said with *rei vindicatio*, the action Weir seeks to draw a comparison with. While in the quote spotlighted at the start of this chapter Weir implies that a property remedy (and *rei vindicatio)* means return, the reality is less black and white. While 'the defendant was asked, in the first place, to return the object; if he refused to do so, he was condemned to pay "*quanti ea res erit, tantam pecuniam*"'.[164] Meaning that return was the first option, with damages as an alternative. In *rei vindicatio*, and in the real property torts, then the prioritisation is reversed when compared to the remedies under the T(IWG)A. The specific performance style remedy had priority with damages as an alternative.

Some of the factors that cause such a distinction were dealt with prior and they relate to the history of the actions and the difference in importance and treatment of land and other goods (this accounts for the different prioritisation in land). But this distinction and the difference in the exercise of discretion and prioritisation and the relative frequency of awarding a specific performance-type action is what has created such a level of critique around conversion. The result is that T(IWG) A fails to prioritise property rights and remedies in a way which seems to respect the property right that has been interfered with. Allowing return so infrequently does not respect the right underlying the tort and fails to protect the freedom and autonomy that is encompassed by property rights.

What Does All This Suggest?

One of the core themes running through this work is the influence of tort law ideals on how the property torts protect property interests. This can *also* be seen in the remedies available. The property torts sit (or *should* be seen to sit) in between property and tort law; the foregoing discussion, however, shows that the focus of these actions is very much based on tort law ideals. There seems to be little (or sometimes no) attempt to temper this with property law. The exercise of discretion in injunctions, and also specific return, is devoid of any 'property' elements and thus the strength of the property right does not play a part in the analysis when deciding whether specific performance or damages are given. Instead, these remedies are governed only by tort law ideals.

When tort law is viewed from the perspective of loss and compensation, the loss that compensatory damages are trying to compensate is purely pecuniary, making up for value and the tangible. This fails to acknowledge that from other perspectives, particularly from the rights-based or corrective justice perspective,

164 Reinhard Zimmermann, *The Law of Obligations: Roman Foundations of the Civilian Tradition* (OUP 1996).

the property torts *should* be compensating not merely for the physical loss, but for the interference with the property right. Property rights encompass more than the value of the physical thing; they encompass freedom and autonomy that having such a right gives to a person. Failure to recognise this fails to fully compensate the claimant (do note this is sometimes achieved, according to Descheemaeker, through varying how compensation is calculated, but this is ad hoc and doesn't fully alleviate the criticism). The failure to fully compensate and further the failure to respect what is deemed important about property rights may be alleviated by a change in perception of the view of tort law. Viewing tort law from a rights-based perspective ensures the focus is on the underlying right, which is a property right in this incident. This then prompts attention to the whole property right and why that is important. Negotiating damages, as an alternative way to assess damages, in contrast do seem to compensate for the loss or interference with the *right* (*the property right*) rather than merely the loss of value in the object. They compensate for the loss of freedom of choice, caused by someone else making decisions about an object or land that you had a right in. These damages focus more on the right underlying the action, and specifically the property right in these actions, aligning more with the view of tort law held by the rights/corrective justice theorists

This suggests that in trying to temper the remedies with tort law ideals, the remedies do not recognise the view of property law and also does not respect the importance of the property right at play, and what these actions, from a property law perspective, at least, should be protecting. As such, Weir is correct in arguing that unfortunate consequences ensue when tort law tries to fill the role of property. The next chapter explores the implications of the critique raised here and in the previous chapter, and the final chapter puts forward a solution to combat the issues raised thus far.

PART III

A New Solution for the Tortious Protection of Property

6 Implications and a Suggestion Already Made

The principal argument thus far is that issues arise from the common law's choice to protect property interests through mechanisms provided by the law of tort. Property rights are protected by a group of claims rooted in an area of law that, as a whole, is informed by a set of concerns that have little to do with the vindication of property rights. This causes the property element of these torts to often be ignored, and the resulting judicial decisions move the actions away from their property roots. Put another way, because the property torts are classified and thought of as tortious, this leads to a lack of protection and a lack of respect for the property aspects and nature of these types of actions. Furthermore, the remedies available do not focus on what is important about 'property'. Altogether, this leads to a failure to properly protect property rights.

The focus of this chapter is to further elucidate and explore the implications of these issues and to discuss a suggestion for change that has already been made to alleviate these. The chapter considers the reform suggestions made by Tony Weir and Nick Curwen but argues that these ideas do not fully rectify this overarching problem and are not practical. Instead, the next chapter of Part III sets forth a new proposal focused on a different way of thinking about these actions.

Issues and Implications

The foregoing chapters have raised a number of issues that are caused by the common law's reliance on tort law for the protection of property. One such issue is that the demarcation of those able to bring a claim has been unduly influenced by loss-thinking. Rather than focusing on the property rights underlying the actions, the torts have been extended, through judicial decisions, to assist anyone who has suffered some loss and who judges feel deserves some compensation. Another issue concerns the remedies available, which have similarly been influenced by the tortious classification, resulting in remedies which do not fully protect the rights underlying the actions or what is deemed important about these rights.

Underlying these issues is the tension between what property law *should* be protecting and how tort law *chooses* to protect it. These tensions flow from how the English common law uses tort law to protect property. While most systems rely on tort law to some extent to protect things that belong to people, the English common law is unique in its reliance on tort law, as opposed to property law, for the

DOI: 10.4324/9781032692098-9

protection of proprietary rights or a person's rights in things. Because these actions are tortious, the perception and view of tort law shape the actions – although it does so without fully respecting the importance to property law that these actions have – and this has implications for the protection of property. Property is, therefore, protected by a group of claims and remedies that are rooted in an area of law that is informed by a completely different set of concerns. Arguably the existence of any perceived difficulty associated with this combination of proprietary and tortious concerns depends upon (i) the assumption that these issues require separate treatment and (ii) an interpretation of tort, which does not allow in and of itself the protection of property rights.[1] The analysis thus far has shown this latter aspect to be the case. The concerns of tort law, as evidenced in the case law and shown in the foregoing, are focused on remedying loss instead of the protection of property rights. This leads to profound and fundamental problems since the protection of property through tort is simultaneously too broad and too narrow and the decisions undermine the category of property rights and the balance struck by the law by both showing a lack of respect for the proprietary nature of these interests and resulting in a lack of protection.

This can be seen in the discussion in Chapter 4 regarding the question of who can bring a claim. The role of property law in determining the rights underlying these actions has been ignored, and extensions and exceptions have been created, allowing more people to bring a tort action (for example, *Dutton* in trespass to land).[2] This artificially extends the actions and causes them to lose their property focus. It also undermines the balance of what rights are seen as proprietary and what rights have implications for third parties. As property rights have implications for third parties, those rights that can be considered proprietary are closed in number; there is a *numerus clausus*. This balance struck by property law ensures that people can make use of things but do not have so much control over external things as to hinder other people's lives (this is why personal rights are not binding on third parties). For property to be properly protected, this boundary needs to be respected for the sake of property holders and the population at large. This might mean that the torts in this area look 'complex', but the complexity is caused by the complexity of the institution of property and the numerous social functions that the concept performs and balances.[3] The balance that the law has sought to achieve limits those affected by such rights, but cases like *Dutton*, and even more recently *Fearn*,[4] nevertheless, alter this balance by allowing these rights to bind third parties.

Similarly, the classification of these actions as tortious, and in turn the application of tortious ideas, also causes a lack of protection of property. This can be seen through the remedies available in the property torts. Injunctions and return are only

1 Sarah Green, 'Understanding the Wrongful Interference Actions' (2010) 1 Conv 15, 15.

2 *Manchester Airport Plc v Dutton* [2000] 1 QB 133, [1999] 3 WLR 524.

3 Peter Cane, *The Anatomy of Tort Law* (Hart 1997) 149.

4 *Fearn v Tate Gallery* [2023] UKSC 4, [2024] AC 1.

discretionary remedies, with the latter in particular being awarded less frequently, and the quantification of damages does not always give full respect to the right that has been interfered with, as discussed in Chapter 5. What is important about property rights is not just the thing in which the right subsists but rather the control and freedom given by that right. The property right in a thing enables a person to control an aspect of their life and make decisions about it. Any remedies need to protect and compensate for the loss of the right, rather than merely the loss of the thing or object of property.

Both of these issues flow from the same foundational problem. The problem is that tort law ideas inform and change the property torts in ways that are not acceptable from a property law perspective. Property protection is rooted in an area of law that is informed by a completely different set of concerns. Tort law ideas are dominant, and property is ignored because the actions are classified and thought of as purely tortious actions.

This has been recognised by other scholars in the past, though usually this discussion is fairly confined to conversion or the personal property torts as a category. For example, Sarah Green, speaking of the wrongful interference actions, argued that one of the major difficulties with this area of law is how the actions are regarded as 'attempting *uncomfortably* to accommodate the concerns of both property and tort law'.[5] Within that same paper, Green argued that any difficulty (perceived or real) associated with the combination and amalgamation of tortious and proprietary ideas depend upon an interpretation of tort law that does not allow, or cannot allow, for the protection of property rights in and of itself.[6] This is what has been found thus far in the book. The problems with the amalgamation of tort and property are, in fact, compounded because the view of tort law that prevails is one based on loss (in the broad sense described in Chapter 4), rather than one based on rights or corrective justice.

This shows the importance of classification, and in particular, the *appropriate* classification of actions. There cannot be actions which appear 'wrongly placed', since classification, when seen as dispositive, shapes and influences judicial decision-making.[7] As this discussion and the previous chapters have shown, the classification of these remedies as tortious influences judicial development of the law, and this suggests that the classification of the property torts needs to be rethought, or at least re-justified,[8] and implies that reform is necessary.

5 Green, 'Understanding the Wrongful Interference Actions' (n 1) 15–16. Emphasis added.

6 ibid 16.

7 Charlie Webb, 'Treating Like Cases Alike: Principle and Classification in Private Law' in Andrew Robertson and Hang Wu Tang (eds), *Goals of Private Law* (Hart 2009) 215; Chapter 4 of this book.

8 This is further reinforced if one considers why these actions are classified as tortious – because of their history. The torts developed from the forms of actions, and once forms were abolished, it was necessary to classify and group actions into substantive law areas. Actions such as trespass, conversion, and nuisance fell into the classification of tort law. It is often said that the forms of action still rule from the grave, and this, rather than conscious decisions regarding what the actions were protecting, determined how they were classified. See Frederic Maitland, *Maitland's The Forms of Action at Common Law: A Course of Lectures* (WJ Whittaker and AH Chaytor ed, CUP 1910) 295.

A Suggestion Already Made: The Introduction of a Proprietary Mechanism

Reform suggestions are not new, especially reform which advocates for the introduction of a proprietary mechanism for the common law. This has been suggested by many scholars, notably by Tony Weir and by Nick Curwen[9] as a response to some of the criticisms discussed thus far, specifically in relation to conversion.[10] There remain questions, however, as to how this might work in the English common law tradition and whether this type of solution could be extended across all of the property torts which protect tangible property and land to deal with the problems elucidated earlier.

Rei Vindicatio

There are different responses of the law to interferences with property,[11] and three different areas of private law that may afford protection to property rights.[12] These three areas are property law, tort law, and the law of unjust enrichment.[13] The methods provided by these areas, as Birks has indicated, are:

> i. the direct assertion of the pre-existing proprietary right; ii. the assertion of an obligation arising from a wrong; iii. the assertion of a new property right arising from a wrong; iv. the assertion of an obligation arising from unjust enrichment; and v. the assertion of a new property right arising from unjust enrichment.[14]

While the tortious mechanisms dealt with so far fall into the second category – although some authors would argue that conversion is actually trying to complete all of these roles simultaneously[15] – *rei vindicatio* falls into the first, as it is a *true* proprietary claim.

Rei vindicatio is a classical Roman law action where a claimant could go to court and make a direct assertion of his ownership to the asset in question.[16] The example typically given is that the claimant appears in court and argues: 'That cow, Buttercup, is mine!'[17] This claim was the *vindicatio*. It relies on the survival of the

9 Nick Curwen, 'The Remedy in Conversion: Confusing Property and Obligation' (2006) 26 LS 570.

10 Other authors have also advocated for this approach. See, for example, David Ibbetson, *A Historical Introduction to the Law of Obligations* (OUP 2001) 108; Andrew Tettenborn, 'Conversion, Tort and Restitution' in N Palmer and E McKendrick, *Interests in Goods* (2nd edn, London: Lloyds of London Press, 1998).

11 Peter Birks, 'Personal Property: Proprietary Rights and Remedies' (2000) 11 KCLJ 1, 3.

12 Simon Douglas, *Liability for Wrongful Interferences with Chattels* (1st edn, Hart 2011), 1–2. The concentration here is on property rights in things/chattels as opposed to real property rights.

13 ibid.

14 Birks (n 11) 3.

15 Tettenborn (n 10) 825.

16 Birks (n 11) 4.

17 ibid.

old right *in rem*, or property right (in this example, the property right in the cow), which survives the loss of possession and can then simply be reasserted against the defendant.[18] *Rei vindicatio* as an action was only available to be claimed by the owner of the good, and thus ownership needed to be proven to maintain this action. Furthermore, a claim could only be brought against the subsequent possessor of the good where that possessor was still in possession of the good. Even though *rei vindicatio* is often thought of as an action focused on return, and, indeed, this is how Weir portrays it in the introductory quote, in reality, it is less clear cut. While 'the defendant was asked, in the first place to return the object, if he refused to do so he was condemned to pay "quanti ea res erit, tantam pecuniam,"'[19] meaning that return was the first option with damages as an alternative. When this is appreciated, the remedy seems more similar to conversion, but this element of the story is often ignored by proponents of the introduction of a *rei vindicatio* action in the common law.

To show the differences between the remedies the common law currently has (i.e. conversion) and a *rei vindicatio* action, the following example may be useful. Imagine that A is the owner (and possessor) of a ring. B takes this ring. If English law recognised a *rei vindicatio* style remedy, then A would go to court and assert that the ring that is now in the possession of B is actually theirs. A would prove ownership with receipts or insurance documents, etc. and the court would then order return of the ring. This is very different from how a claim in conversion works.

In conversion, A would go to court and claim that B has converted the ring to their own use and, therefore, has wronged the claimant. The action is strict liability, and all the claimant needs to prove is an intentional interference with the ring that was in the possession of A and that the interference amounts to an act of dominion. If this is proven, which in these circumstances is likely, then the court will decide either to award damages or to order return. Return is ordered only if the goods are special or unique in some way, such as if they have sentimental value. For this reason, return is relatively uncommon and, instead, an award of damages is often considered the primary remedy and would likely be awarded here.

Criticisms of a **Rei Vindicatio** *Style Action in English Common Law*

There has been criticism of any suggested introduction of a *rei vindicatio* style of remedy in the common law. The critique contends that *rei vindicatio* is less sophisticated[20] and more limited[21] than conversion and the property torts; although this is often because the critique of *rei vindicatio* focuses purely on the action itself

18 Peter Birks, *Unjust Enrichment*, (2nd edn, OUP 2005) 29.

19 Reinhard Zimmermann, *The Law of Obligations: Roman Foundations of the Civilian Tradition* (OUP 1996).

20 Sarah Green and John Randall, *The Tort of Conversion* (1st edn, Hart 2009) 55.

21 Douglas (n 12) 2.

without looking at the wider law surrounding and supporting it historically and within other jurisdictions. This critique, then, paints a skewed picture of the action and its possible usefulness in the common law. This critique can nevertheless be understood by slightly varying the example given to see the potential limits of the action.

The first variation concerns who now has the asset. As noted, B steals the ring from A but having stolen the ring, B sells it to C. A *rei vindicatio* style action can only be brought against someone in possession of the asset and so A does not have an action against B, but will have one against C (if C can be found). In conversion, however, the answer is different. In conversion, both B and C have intentionally interfered with the asset and thus A can bring an action against either party, although they will only be able to seek return from C who is now in possession of the ring, and this will depend on whether the goods are deemed to be unique. If not, then A's claim will be in damages.

The situation is different again if, instead of B selling it on, the ring is lost. In this example, A does not have a *rei vindicatio* style claim that could be successful against anyone, as the current possessor is unknown. The situation is better for a person bringing a claim in conversion, as conversion depends on some 'wrong'; the interference with the property right is sufficient without B still possessing the item interfered with. A can, therefore, still bring a claim against B, but this will be limited to damages. This variation exemplifies the criticism that *rei vindicatio* is actually *more limited* in scope than conversion and the property torts, because it is necessary that A is bringing a claim against someone still in possession of the asset.[22] Because of this requirement, in some situations, despite an interference and a loss of a property right, the claimant is left without a *rei vindicatio* style remedy, and this does not seem to fully protect the rights that it set out to do. This critique, however, ignores the other actions in Roman law that would typically have dealt with such a scenario. For example, the *actio furti*, which was an action against thieves that straddles the modern division between torts and criminal law, with the thief being liable for either double (or quadruple) the value of the asset taken.[23] Most reformers would not suggest that conversion needs to be removed and replaced with a *rei vindicatio* style remedy, but rather conversion should be more limited in scope and a *rei vindicatio* style remedy should then sit alongside it. This would be more akin to Roman law, with its actions for the differing scenarios, rather than conversion, which 'rolls up' the possible scenarios into one action.

A different variation in the scenario shows another deficiency that is often alleged in the literature. Imagine this time that A is not the owner of the ring, but instead just has possession of it. When B then takes/steals the ring, A cannot bring a *rei vindicatio* claim as she cannot prove ownership. In conversion, again the story

22 ibid.

23 Reinhard Zimmermann, 'Theft, Roman' in *Oxford Classical Dictionary* (Online publication March 2016) <https://oxfordre.com/classics/view/10.1093/acrefore/9780199381135.001.0001/acrefore-9780199381135-e-6335> Accessed 07/10/2024.

is better, since to bring a claim, A only needs to show possession or an immediate right to possess, which she is able to show. Conversion can, therefore, provide protection to a far greater range of people.[24] Once again, however, this critique applies only if other elements of the Roman law tradition are ignored. While *rei vindicatio* does not protect possession, possession is protected through the *interdicts*, which are orders forbidding the disturbance of possession or restoring it once disturbed,[25] or again, through the *actio furti*.

The critiques explored herein are often brought forward to counter the argument that the common law has failed by not having a proprietary-style remedy. Green and Randall, and Douglas, for example, all make these points. Green and Randall, however, also recognise that comparisons of *rei vindicatio* and conversion are not true or fair comparisons, as the aims of the actions are different.[26] Conversion focuses on possession, while *rei vindicatio* focuses on ownership. The comparison often made between *rei vindicatio* and conversion thus ignores that the Roman law tradition has remedies focused on possession which align more closely to conversion, namely, the Roman *possessory interdicts*,[27] as well as the *actio furti* discussed previously.

It seems, therefore, that the criticism waged against *rei vindicatio* is founded on a straw man argument. No adequately informed suggestion for a *rei vindicatio* style remedy in the common law would suggest its inclusion and the total removal of conversion. This would ignore the background of the action in the Roman law tradition and the other mechanisms which are in place to complement it. Any proposal seeking to introduce a *rei vindicatio* style action would need also to consider the surrounding law and how the benefits of the current property torts (in terms of the protection of possession and an action that still allows a claim when the items are lost or sold on) can be replicated.

A Proprietary Mechanism for English Common Law?

The Roman law *rei vindicatio*, or any proprietary mechanism, cannot simply be imported into the common law tradition without considering how proprietary mechanisms work in the common law. Curwen articulates a way that the common law could introduce a proprietary mechanism without the omissions which have concerned some of the authors mentioned prior.[28] He gains inspiration from the

24 Green and Randall (n 20) 55.

25 Barry Nicholas and Alan Rodger 'Possession, Legal' in *Oxford Classical Dictionary* (Online publication March 2016) <https://oxfordre.com/classics/view/10.1093/acrefore/9780199381135.001.0001/acrefore-9780199381135-e-5276?rskey=4vhJGv&result=1> Accessed 07/10/2024.

26 Green and Randall (n 20) 55.

27 ibid.

28 This iteration of the introduction of a proprietary mechanism has been chosen as the focus here, as it deals most closely with how this kind of action could be introduced in the common law, arguing by analogy with equitable proprietary mechanisms and actions aimed at the protection of land, rather than merely suggesting an importation of *rei vindicatio*. That is not to say this is the only sugges-

use of equitable proprietary mechanisms and mechanisms used in the protection of land in order to fashion a proprietary remedy for the common law, rather than merely transplanting *rei vindicatio*. This can serve as a good starting point.

Curwen argues that rather than simply replacing conversion with a proprietary mechanism, conversion should be split into two actions; a proprietary action and a tortious one. Conversion, because of its development and its consumption of what used to be the realm of detinue, has a dual focus, attempting to be a tort and a substitute for a proprietary remedy at the same time.[29] Some authors have gone further and suggested that conversion is actually trying to do three jobs; be a surrogate for *rei vindicatio*, compensate losses as a tort proper, and on occasion reversing unjust enrichment.[30] Regardless of how many jobs it is trying to complete, the amalgamation of tort and property has been shown in this work, and Curwen suggests this makes the action confused and unfair.[31] The solution he offers is to revive a detinue-style action but also to reinvent this action as a purely proprietary action.[32] This proprietary remedy would be available only against those who are still in possession of the goods; the defendant would not normally have an option to pay damages in lieu of return, and the liability would be strict.[33] Alongside this proprietary action, however, a normal tort law action would remain. This action would be available against all past converters, and damages would be the appropriate remedy. Because Curwen sees this as a tort claim proper, he suggests that fault should be introduced and that this should not be a strict liability action.[34]

Curwen makes this suggestion despite the Law Reform Committee having considered and rejected a similar approach when the 1977 Torts (Interference with Goods) Act was being debated.[35] This type of proposal would bring the protection of property in the common law closer to the protection offered in Roman systems, consisting of a property mechanism complemented by other mechanisms similar to the *actio furti* and a tort claim proper to ensure all interferences are dealt with.[36] Curwen, however, develops his proposal by considering how this would assimilate and mirror the land position and would align better with the protection afforded by equity, rather than any attempt to transplant or 'copy' *rei vindicatio*.

In terms of the protection of land, Curwen highlights how there is both tortious protection – in the form of trespass to land, which in his words is 'remediable at

tion of a proprietary mechanism in the literature, other authors making this suggestion have been mentioned in Note 10.

29 It is sometimes claimed that conversion is trying to complete three jobs: a proprietary role, a tortious role, and standing in for unjust enrichment. See discussion in Chapter 5.

30 Tettenborn (n 10) 825.

31 Curwen (n 9) 570.

32 ibid 582.

33 ibid.

34 ibid.

35 Law Reform Committee, *Conversion and Detinue* (Law Reform Com No Cmd 4774, 1971) para 11.

36 It would not be identical to the Roman solution, however, as it would replace the latter's monetary order in lieu of return (see 6.2.2. and in particular reference Note 19) and other actions that sit alongside *rei vidicatio* with a fault-based tort remedy.

common law by an award of damages'[37] and a 'personal remedy'[38] – and also an action for recovery, the modern equivalent of ejectment. This account is problematic, as it ignores the fact that trespass, like conversion, occupies a position straddling the personal and proprietary divide. While damages are available, injunctions are also available in trespass to land, which are used to regain and recover land in the form that it was before some intrusion or interference. It also seems to suggest that the order for possession and trespass are two distinct actions, while, in fact, they are actually much more intertwined and linked.[39] Leaving these points aside, however, it is true that there are both remedies more centred on damages and a more proprietary remedy to regain possession, and this does mirror Curwen's suggestions for personal property.

Curwen also considers the remedies available to a beneficiary through equity and uses these to argue that there should be a proprietary remedy for the legal owner. He argues that it does not make sense for a beneficial owner to be in a better position and to have access to a proprietary remedy, if the legal owner would not have access to such a remedy. If goods were held under a trust for the benefit of X, X has an equitable property right in them. If Y then interferes, Curwen points out that X has access to two types of action; either (1) he can bring a claim for 'knowing receipt', and this will afford him compensation and a personal remedy or (2) he can bring an action in equity for the return of the trust goods (as long as the defendant is not a *bona fide* purchaser without notice).[40] This, Curwen says, is a proprietary action involving the return of the goods.[41] The result, if the claimant was a beneficiary in equity, then varies in resolution from conversion, where the legal owner is unlikely to get return unless the goods are special. He argues that common law needs to move closer to equity in order to achieve effective protection and fairness and thus recommends that common law should provide a proprietary remedy alongside a tortious one (that is, changed to being fault-based).

This solution would counteract some of the common critiques of having a *rei vindicatio* style remedy. It would, for example, address the comments by Green and Douglas explored previously. Here the concerns about only being able to bring a claim against those that are still in possession are reduced, since, if no one can be found who is still in possession, the tort action remains and can be used to claim damages. This solution would also bring the protection more in line with the Roman law system, if the system is considered as a whole, rather than taking *rei vindicatio* in isolation.

This proposal to split and refine conversion into a property element and a tortious element is a sophisticated solution. However, the obvious negative aspect is that it was considered and rejected by the Law Reform Committee prior to the 1977

37 Curwen (n 9) 575.

38 ibid.

39 *Dutton* (n 2), for example, was a case about an order for possession, but it is widely held to have changed the rules for bringing a claim in trespass to land.

40 Curwen (n 9) 576.

41 ibid.

legislation. There is a question, therefore, about whether there is impetus or desire for this kind of solution. The Law Reform Committee, in their report, used the French law system as a comparison point, which is similar (though not identical) to Curwen's proposal. The Committee explained this option as retaining detinue as a purely restitutionary remedy (standing as a substitute for *rei vindicatio*) where return would be the remedy and abolishing conversion as a strict liability action and allowing negligence to fill the gap and provide fault-based protection.[42] The difference between the two proposals is merely that Curwen transforms conversion into a fault-based action, while the Law Reform Committee extends negligence to fill this gap. The Committee saw this as a radical change in the law that was unjustified and unconvincing.[43] The strong history of protection of property through *in personam* mechanisms in the common law and the historical importance of the strict liability action, gave the Committee 'sound practical reasons' for rejecting this new approach and maintaining conversion as a strict liability action.[44] The Committee also felt any change along these lines would have been inconsistent with the Twelfth Report, which aimed to balance the sanctity of property with the commercial importance of transfers of chattels.[45]

It is argued, however, that if there was a desire to have a proprietary-style remedy, this is how it would have to be implemented and provides a good example of such reform.

Does This Solve All the Issues Underlying the Protection of Property in the Common Law?

Both of the core problems explored in this book were connected to, and stemmed from, the tort law classification of these actions, and specifically a view of tort law (either intentionally or unintentionally) as loss-based. This classification, and the perception of what that means, has influenced and caused the actions to move away from their property roots. While the introduction of a proprietary remedy would appear to help mitigate the critiques and mean that the actions charged with the protection of property concentrate on the underlying property right, there are still some issues to consider. The main issues that require comment and discussion are: (1) the scope of the proposals with regard to personal property; (2) the practicality of the proposals; and (3) how much they solve *all* the issues identified in *all* the torts.

Firstly, the new property remedy for personal property would still need to be supplemented with a tortious action (a limited version of conversion) because of the scope of the proprietary remedy. This means that although this proposal may provide the necessary protection to owners, it does not protect other property rights,

42 Eighteenth Report of the Law Reform Committee (n 35) para 12.
43 ibid para 13.
44 ibid.
45 ibid.

notably the rights of a possessor.[46] So, while the concerns would be alleviated in the case of A's ring being taken by B who is still in possession of it (because the proprietary remedy is now available), if the case between A and B were more complex, some of the problems identified would still remain. For example, if instead A has a ring, that she has a possessory right in, or which is in her possession (giving her some right), and this is taken by B, she is left without a claim in the new proprietary action and instead must fall back to the tort that remains alongside it. This tort, it can be assumed, will suffer from the deficiencies that are found in conversion currently and discussed earlier and in Chapters 4 and 5.

Further, consider what happens if B takes the ring from A but it is then lost. A only has the option to bring a claim in the tortious mechanism that remains alongside the proprietary one. Here, the same issues regarding the suitability and quantification of damages exist and the same issues about who can sue. Further, this new action, being a 'tort claim proper', might mean that the action is over-extended because of the loss-focused thinking that frequently influences reasoning in tort cases. If B takes the ring and then sells it to C, A will be able to use the proprietary mechanism to ensure return from C. In this scenario, like the standard scenario presented previously, the solution is better for A, who will be able to regain possession of their ring.

Consequently, in two of the four scenarios, 'better' results for A are achieved, while the others contain the same issues as the solution provided by conversion, since the claimant is forced to fall back on a tort action that suffers the same issues identified throughout this book (or, indeed, even more extreme issues, it now being a tort claim proper rather than a mixed or hybrid action).

It is also possible, however, to imagine other scenarios which are less advantageous for A. Imagine that B takes the ring and sells to C, but then C has the ring stolen by D. In this scenario, B and D cannot be found. A's only option, then, is to bring a tort claim against C who has been in possession of the ring. The problem is that, in the new formulation of 'conversion' as elucidated by Curwen, this would now be a fault-based action; and because C is not at fault, since they simply bought a ring without knowing it was stolen, A is left without a remedy.

This solution, therefore, does not fully rectify the issues with the personal property torts. This is primarily because – while the introduction of a proprietary remedy for the personal property torts would reduce many of the issues surrounding the remedies available in the torts (as discussed in Chapter 5) by increasing those able to get return or specific performance – the application of the proprietary mechanism is only partial. In the formulation put forward by Curwen and supported here alongside this proprietary mechanism there would remain a conversion-like action to ensure protection for those that fall outside the property mechanism. However, this is reformulated as a purely tortious conversion action. As such, the remedy is damages, and those are likely to be calculated in a tortious way, it being a 'tort claim proper' (and not having the dual focus that we currently associate with

46 This was found to be proprietary in Chapter 2.

conversion). This means that some of those that suffer interference will still have the same issues with remedies, as detailed in Chapter 5, although these may be more extreme because there is even less emphasis on the importance to property now, as this is seen as a proper tort. Issues might also arise around the question of who can bring a claim and the slide into loss-thinking – especially as this is now a fully tortious claim. There will be less impetus to consider the new conversion claim as being a property tort or centring on the property right underlying the action, and the stretching of those entitled to bring a claim is likely to continue.

The second problem concerns practicality. Curwen's solution to split and refine conversion into a property element and a tortious element is a sophisticated one. However, this type of suggestion has already been considered, and rejected, by the Law Reform Committee. Furthermore, despite much discussion in the academic literature over the years about the usefulness of a proprietary mechanism, this has never been taken seriously by law reformers. This would suggest that while such a change might be welcomed within academic circles, it is unlikely to get the support needed to enable such a suggestion to become law.

A final objection to the proposal derives from asking how much it solves *all* the issues identified in *all* the torts. This solution is most appropriate for dealing with the problems identified in conversion – that is their aim. It has been shown, however, that *all* the property torts suffer from the *same* problems and that these problems are associated with the use of tortious mechanisms to protect property. Curwen's proposal suggests replicating the protection that is given to land through trespass and an action for possession. However, Chapters 4 and 5 have identified flaws in the protection that is provided in this way, and Curwen's solution would not resolve these. The underlying problem is that tort law is used to protect property and that loss thinking prevails in tort law. While changing some actions into proprietary actions will relieve the specific issues connected with those actions, this approach will not eradicate the fundamental issue. This will persist as long as property is protected through actions classified as tortious and while these actions are thought of only as tortious. This is a fundamental tenet of Curwen's proposals.

Consequently, this is not a workable solution for the English common law on a practical level or indeed a solution that will rectify all the concerns raised in this book. Instead, a less radical solution would be favourable – but one that targets the core problem identified, which is the use of tort law to protect property and the tortious classification and predominance of loss thinking that comes with this. The next chapter sets out a new proposal for achieving this.

7 A New Proposal

Following on from the previous chapter, which outlined the failure of previous reform suggestions to target the underlying problems caused by relying on tort law to protect property, this chapter sets out a new suggestion for reform. This new proposal is based on radically rethinking the property torts' current grouping. It advocates reclassifying the actions so that the special place they have, and their unique role spanning property and tort law, is recognised and respected. These actions are fundamentally part of both property law and tort law, and if it can be ensured that the actions are thought of as such, then these incremental changes (as decided in each new case) which move the torts away from property and lead to a lack of protection (or indeed over-protection) can be halted and reversed. This thinking can and will result in changes in outcomes in the cases (as well as different reasoning being employed). Evidence of this can be seen in the recent Court of Appeal nuisance cases[1] of *Network Rail Infrastructure Ltd v Williams*[2] and *Fearn v the Board of Trustees of the Tate Gallery*.[3]

Proposal: Overview

Property is currently protected by a group of claims and remedies that are rooted in an area of law that is informed by a completely different set of concerns. The role (and concerns) of tort law have been discussed at length thus far in this book, and at its most basic level tort law can be seen either to protect rights (from a rights-protection or corrective justice model) or to protect losses. While many would argue that tort law has moved on from the strong pull of the loss model that preoccupied tort law judges (and judgments) in the 1980s–1990s, this work has shown that there is still an implicit link and appeal to remedying loss in tort law.[4] Tort law

1 See discussion of these cases in ‘A Change in Perception Seen in Practice’ of this chapter and also in Chapter 4.

2 [2018] EWCA Civ 1514.

3 [2020] EWCA Civ 104. Note this decision has since been heard by the Supreme Court and the reasoning and decision has since changed and will be discussed following as an example of the importance of focusing on property in property tort cases.

4 For scholars who argue that the loss model no longer holds true for tort law, see Nicholas McBride and Roderick Bagshaw, *Tort Law* (7th edn, Pearsons 2024). The work has shown that loss remains a factor in Chapter 4.

DOI: 10.4324/9781032692098-10

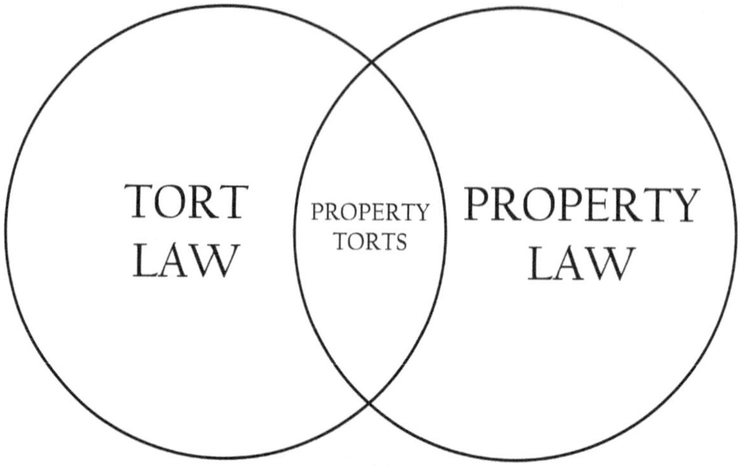

Figure 1 Venn diagram showing the position of the property torts

should not, however, protect *all* losses. Tort law should *only* be concerned with losses that involve some interest or right that tort law relates to or a loss that is caused by a person who has a connection to another through a right or duty of care, i.e. 'normative losses' in Weinrib's vocabulary,[5] at least from the rights-protection or corrective justice perspective. It is clear from the analysis made in this work that this is not always the case in practice.

In the case of the property torts, those rights (or losses) that *should* be focused on are property rights. The rights are the creation of property law, but they are given protection through tort law.[6] The property torts, therefore, should be seen as part of *both* tort law and property law. The importance and influence of property law in these mechanisms should not (and cannot) be forgotten or ignored. In fact, when talking of conversion, Andrew Tettenborn has gone as far as saying that the action is 'not really tort' but personal property law.[7] This work suggests that instead it should be seen as an amalgamation or combination of ideas, a hybrid action.

This view has been supported by Bagshaw and McBride,[8] who suggest that in a Venn diagram the property torts would sit in the intersection between property and tort, as shown in Figure 1.

5 See Ernest Weinrib, 'Corrective Justice in a Nutshell' (2002) 52 UTLJ 349; Ernest Weinrib, *The Idea of Private Law* (OUP 2012).

6 Peter Cane, *Anatomy of Tort Law* (Hart 1997) 75.

7 Andrew Tettenborn, 'Damages in Conversion – The Exception or the Anomaly' (1993) 52(1) CLJ 128, 129.

8 Roderick Bagshaw and Nicholas McBride, *Tort Law* (6th edn, Pearsons 2018) 30. This idea is not repeated in the more recent edition of this text.

The proposal set out here is that there needs to be a rethinking and, more specifically, a shift in the perception of the property torts, which should be viewed as both part of property law and part of tort law. Their dual or hybrid role needs to be acknowledged and respected in order to stop tort law (influenced by loss-focused ideas and thinking in the broad sense) from overly influencing decisions and continuing the shift away from property law ideals. Alongside this, the role of tort law needs to be understood as rights-based or through a corrective justice model to ensure that sufficient attention is paid to the property right underlying the actions (and to prevent extensions caused by loss-based thinking). The two changes are interlinked; the latter helps ensure the former and both are required.

Focusing on the rights that tort law protects, and the rights-protection role of tort law, facilitates giving attention to the property rights at stake in the property torts and their role in property law. The prominence that a rights-based perspective, when applied to a property tort, gives to the right that is being protected helps to ensure that the nature of that right – the fact that it is specifically a property right – is given due attention. This link is a facilitative one. Focusing on the right facilitates paying attention to the nature of the right, which in the case of a property tort is a property right. The success of such an approach can be seen recently in the nuisance cases of *Network Rail Infrastructure Ltd v Williams* and the Court of Appeal decision in *Fearn v the Board of Trustees of the Tate Gallery*, discussed in Chapter 4.[9] These proposals show how such an approach can be continued in this and the other torts, and, hence, indicates a way forward for practitioners and judges who are grappling with the problems in these actions. Moreover, the chapter also shows how this approach is founded in both theory and logic, giving those practitioners a firm footing for changing the perceptions of these actions and making radical changes to the torts.

This approach of rethinking and reclassifying these actions, so that both the tort law and the property law background are recognised and respected, will result in a change in the law. Such deeper change is, in fact, the aim. The proposal will lead not only to different reasoning within the cases and a different view of the actions but in practice also to different outcomes and conclusions. This is shown below through a re-analysis of existing case law in the light of these proposals.

This approach of rethinking the mechanisms the common law currently has can be opposed and contrasted with the far-reaching proposals made by Curwen (and others), discussed in the previous chapter. There are two reasons for this preference. The first is practical and the other is based on principle. As to the first, it was stated earlier that the law surrounding the property torts has already been considered by the Law Reform Committee. When considering the changes brought in by the Torts (Interference with Goods) Act 1977, the Law Reform Committee expressly considered whether, and rejected, the proposal that the law should have a proprietary mechanism. It seems unlikely, therefore, that large-scale changes would be successful in this area, especially those that have already been discussed

9 See Chapter 4, 'Protecting Property Rights - Private Nuisance'

extensively in the literature and considered and rejected by reformers. The recent Law Commission work on Digital Assets further implies that such a move is *still* unlikely to be favoured. When considering how the Common Law should adapt in light of the increased prevalence of digital assets, the Law Commission suggested that judges should develop a new tort, or 'new tortious liability', by analogy with, or drawing on some elements of, the tort of conversion to deal with wrongful interference with third-category things (digital assets).[10] There was no discussion or consideration of a proprietary mechanism to fill this gap, despite the critique of conversion as a substitute for a proprietary mechanism; suggesting once again that there is no impetus for the creation of a proprietary mechanism.

Further, from a practical perspective, even the large-scale changes proposed (such as the introduction of a proprietary mechanism) do not seem to alleviate all the problems raised and, therefore, seem inadequate as a response to the criticisms raised.[11] Such a radical reform can only be championed if it is likely to solve all of the issues discussed previously. Finally, from a practical standpoint, thinking of these actions as property torts and maintaining a focus on the proprietary nature of the actions has recently been seen to be successful in some Court of Appeal nuisance cases, as will be discussed shortly. The success of this approach in nuisance implies that it is worth considering as a solution to the problems that run throughout the property torts. Practitioners and judges have been grappling with the problems in the property torts for many years, and this accounts for some of the differences in reasoning between individual judges and different courts.[12] These proposals suggest a way to solve the problems troubling judges and to solve them in a way that judges (and practitioners) can implement through the reasoning and decisions in cases, as is a unique feature of the common law.

From a more principled standpoint, the question needs to be asked about how the law *should* be structured and how these rules *should* be thought of. While historically these actions were classified as tortious, the structure of the law should be based on reason and logic and not history (or lack of anywhere else better to 'put' the actions).[13] This might suggest a need to reclassify these actions as purely part of

10 See Law Commission, *Digital Assets: Final Report* (Law Com No 412, 2023). Discussed in Victoria Evans, 'Conversion and its Future (Reflecting on the Law Commission's work on Digital Assets)' (2024) 88(3) Conv 267.

11 This is because alongside a proprietary mechanism, a tortious mechanism will have to remain to catch the interferences that do not fall within the new action. This tort is likely to suffer from the same deficiencies as I have explored thus far because, once again, the law is using tort to protect property without sufficient weight or emphasis on the property rights underlying the action. See discussion in Chaper 6, 'A Propriety Mechanism for the Common Law'.

12 The differences in the opinions of different judges in the same case can be seen in *Dutton*, and the differences in different courts in the same case can be seen in *Fearn* and *Williams*. See *Manchester Airport Plc v Dutton* [2000] 1 QB 133, *Williams* (n 2), and *Fearn* (n 3).

13 Andrew Tettenborn 'Conversion, Tort and Restitution' in N Palmer and E McKendrick, *Interests in Goods* (2nd ed, London: Lloyds of London Press, 1998) 825; Peter Birks, 'Personal Property: Proprietary Rights and Remedies' (2000) 11 KCLJ 1, 3.

property law; after all, some would argue that this is what the actions really are,[14] and to some extent this is what the proposals of Curwen advocate. This would, however, split the classification of actions which protect property, because some actions would be left as tortious and those 'more proprietary' would be reclassified into property. For example, negligence has an important role to play in the protection of property, but it is also the 'typical tort' so it cannot ever be classified as anything other than tortious (or predominantly tortious). Actions such as conversion or trespass, however, might be able to be reclassified and thought of as proprietary. But actions which fit together to provide full protection to personal and real property[15] would then be split across different classifications, and this does not make sense.

Instead, if the function of these property torts are considered (using a function-based classification idea), they need to be classified and grouped together based on their shared function in the protection of property. The function of these actions, however, is dual or hybrid. They protect property but do so in a unique way because of their tortious heritage. The problem is that the tort element, when seen purely on its own terms, is overwhelming and over-influencing these actions. This is something explored throughout the work but also recognised by other authors previously. Sarah Green, for example, argued that conversion has a tendency to focus on what the claimant has lost as opposed to what they are entitled to (or what they have rights in) because of the tortious nature of the action.[16]

The suggestions made here do not deny that historically, or even now, tort is *capable* of protecting property rights. Indeed, '[t]he protection of property has always been one of the prime functions of the law of tort'.[17] But rather, the argument here is that tort law has developed in such a way that judges often forget or at least do not think about tort law in this way. And so tort law has developed a reputation which creates a perception that the torts that protect property sit uncomfortably within tort law as they are unable to accommodate the concerns of both property and tort law.[18] But this reputation and perception is dependant on a view that holds that tort and property require separate legal treatment and an interpretation of the law of torts which does not allow, in and of itself, for the protection of property rights.[19] The proposals set out here try to argue that this is not the only way to view tort law – and the key to solving many of the issues identified stems from understanding and classifying these actions based on the importance of both property and tort law and advocating a view of tort law that respects this and their

14 See Tettenborn, ibid.

15 See Sarah Green, 'Understanding the Wrongful Interference Actions' (2010) 1 Conv 1, 16.

16 Sarah Green, 'Can a Digitized Product be the Subject of Conversion?' (2006) 4(Nov) LMCLQ 2006 568, 570.

17 Peter Cane, *Tort Law and Economic Interests* (OUP 1991) 21.

18 Green, 'Understanding the Wrongful Interference Actions' (n 15) 15–16.

19 This is argued here as well as in my previous work, see Victoria Ball, 'The Influence of Loss in the Property Torts'. (2020) 31(3) King's Law Journal 426. This is also something said by Green, 'Understanding the Wrongful Interference Actions' (n 15) 15–16.

special function in the law. For this reason, it is important to think of them, and classify them, as the property torts, overlapping and spanning the two categories of property and tort, as shown in Figure 1.

Proposal: A Change in Perception

This proposal, therefore, focuses primarily on the need for a shift in the perception of the property torts so that they are viewed as both part of property and part of tort law. This would mean a development in legal reasoning, so that the property torts are not thought of only (or primarily) as part of tort law but their importance to property law is also recognised. In practice, this would mean that in cases concerning the property torts, their dual nature should be acknowledged and express reference made to the property and tort dimensions of a given decision. This should not be controversial, as this has already become more common in cases concerning private nuisance (which has resulted in some positive decisions as discussed in Chapter 4) and thus could be replicated across the property torts. The changes proposed will not, however, simply result in modification in judicial reasoning but more importantly will lead to different outcomes. They will ensure that the category of those entitled to sue is restricted in line with property principles as well as ensuring a focus on what is important about property rights when damages are awarded. The way in which this would work is demonstrated in the following example.

Tort Law's Protection of Property

Curwen (an advocate for the introduction of a proprietary mechanism into the common law) suggests that there is historic confusion; confusing proprietary claims with claims in tort. He links this to the quasi-property position of detinue and conversion's eventual assumption of detinue-type cases which have turned conversion semi-proprietary. Nevertheless, he strongly argues, like Weir and other scholars, that tort law is not the place for this type of property protection.[20] In his words: 'Tort, being a wrong-based system, concentrates heavily on the defendant's conduct, whereas property law, being a rights-based scheme, concentrates on the claimant's interest in an asset'.[21] While this approach can be seen in the case law,[22] there is a question of whether this is inescapable and whether tort law *must* be viewed in this way. While some conceptions of tort law are focused on the defendant's actions (as, for example, the causer of loss), not all are so focused. Some alternative conceptions might help to find a solution to this problem. If tort law, or at least the property torts, can be thought of not as focused on loss (the cause of the

20 This has also been suggested by Andrew Tettenborn, who argues that conversion is only really tortious because of a lack of anywhere better to put it. See Tettenborn (n 13).

21 Nick Curwen, 'The Remedy in Conversion: Confusing Property and Obligation' (2006) 26 LS 570, 578.

22 See Chapter 4.

decisions which move the torts from their property focus) but instead on a different conception of tort law, then respect for and appreciation of the dual nature or the quasi-property element of these actions can be ensured. Recall that tort law has always had as one of its prime functions the protection of property. As such, it must be possible to view tort law in a way that respects this role and function of the law.

It is useful to recall the different conceptions of tort law.[23] The predominant conceptions were: (1) the idea that tort law is the law's response to loss, under the loss conception; or (2) that tort law follows a rights-based or corrective justice approach.[24] The first suggests that the role of tort law is to respond to loss, to hold one person liable where they cause loss to another. The prominence of this idea (with the growth of negligence) has caused a shift from protecting property interests in the property torts to providing a remedy to all those who have suffered loss (broadly confined). Loss-focused thinking arguably also lies behind the extension of protection to rights other than property rights, as all rights violations could be seen as similarly involving normative loss.[25] Much of this work has already sought to show this to be the case. But this tendency towards a loss-focus has also been discussed by numerous authors. Green, for example, has referenced the tortious focus on what has been 'lost' in the actions as opposed to concentrating on rights or entitlements;[26] and Cane has similarly suggested that the prime focus of tort law is on 'loss' and making good a loss suffered with compensation.[27] It was shown in Chapter 4 how this focus on loss can be implicit and potentially even unintentional. Rather this unspoken idea of loss (and negligence) in tort law is cross-influencing the whole category of actions.

The rights-based or corrective justice conception suggests that instead of focusing on loss, tort law should focus on rights. To bring a claim in tort law the claimant needs to show that they had a right exercisable against the defendant and that this right has been infringed by the defendant. A remedy is given because one party has made a gain and one has made a loss; there is a single liability that links the defendant and the claimant. This express focus and attention on rights can help break down and deconstruct the innate ideas about what torts that deal with property should do and what they should or should not focus on (e.g., loss).

A shift in thinking from the first conception (which was found in Chapter 4 to have prevalence and influence in the property torts) to the second would help these torts to retain their important position in between property and tort law and keep respect for the property aspect of the action. The discussion of the recent (Court of Appeal level) nuisance cases in Chapter 4 illustrates this point. By maintaining an approach that focused on the underlying right, the Court of Appeal in both cases

23 See discussion in Chapter 3, 'The Role of Tort Law' B.

24 Note that other conceptions were discussed and prevalent in the wider literature, but these were the two conceptions focused on for this work because of the usefulness for this argument and relevance to the cases discussed thus far.

25 See Chapter 4.

26 See, for example, Sarah Green, Digitized Asset (n 16).

27 Cane (n 6) 103.

resisted the urge to extend the actions beyond their remit. This is because concentrating on the right in the property torts facilitates keeping the focus on property law, since the rights in question are created by property law. This, then, is another important aspect of the shift in perception that needs to occur. The property torts need to be seen as both part of tort law and as part of property law and, in order to achieve this, we should think of tort law not as a response to loss but as the response to right infringements or based on corrective justice. The proposal has two facets, but the two are linked.

Facet one suggests that we need to think about tort law as rights-based or from a corrective justice approach. This does two things: (1) it ensures that the loss thinking explored in Chapter 4 that is infiltrating the torts is minimised, and (2) it maintains a focus on rights in the property torts which facilitates the achievement of the second facet, i.e. the recognition of the property torts as part both of property law and tort law.

A Change in Perception as Seen in Practice

This proposal has the potential to rectify some of the slide into loss-thinking that has been identified, as can be seen in a couple of recent Court of Appeal decisions in nuisance. In nuisance, there has been less of a shift away from property rights and respecting the property aspect of the decision or, perhaps more accurately, after a flirtation in *Khorasandjian v Bush*[28] with the loss model or with an approach to tort law that seems to revolve around remedying 'losses', there has been a (re-) assertion of a rights-based understanding. So there has not been such a shift as in the other torts or this has at least been true up until the recent decision in *Fearn* in the Supreme Court. This is because there are strong dicta and emphasis in nuisance about the action's role as a tort based on land/property. This can be seen in *Hunter v Canary Wharf*[29] and the more recent Court of Appeal cases in nuisance of *Williams* and *Fearn*. In all these cases, a strong judicial focus on the property element of the tort prevented a potential slide into negligence or loss-thinking. It is useful to recap them briefly here.[30]

Williams concerned the question of whether encroachment of Japanese knotweed without physical damage was sufficient for an actionable nuisance or in the alternative, whether the presence of knotweed interfered with the quiet enjoyment and amenity value of the land by affecting the market value. While the recorder found that the second element was satisfied, the Court of Appeal held that the amenity of the property in nuisance does not include the right to realise the value of the property. The claimants, however, still had a case because the Court of Appeal held that the mere presence of the knotweed interfered with amenity without need for physical damage because of the immediate burden of increased difficulty and

28 [1993] QB 727.
29 [1997] AC 655.
30 But see Chapter 4, 'Protecting Property Rights - Private Nuisance' for the full discussion.

cost of development. Sir Terence Etherton MR was clear that the decision of the recorder was wrong in principle because the purpose of nuisance is not to protect the value of property as a financial asset. Its purpose is to protect the owner of land and their use and enjoyment, which is a facet of ownership or exclusive possession; enjoyment being part of the property right that the 'owner' has. The recorder's decision would have extended the remit of nuisance and meant that it was available for pure economic loss, which in turn would move the tort away from the rights it should be protecting. Sir Terence Etherton MR, in his reasoning, made express reference to nuisance as a property tort[31] and to its role in the protection of real property rights. While the outcome was not changed here because of the particular facts of the case, the reasoning was. If the original reasoning had been upheld, in future cases remedies might have been given for pure economic loss, which from a property perspective would have been wrong. In those future cases there would not have been an interference with a recognised aspect of a property right, and nuisance would once again have been moved away from its property roots. This change in perspective and a respect for the property aspect of the decision halted such future developments.

There was a similar focus in *Fearn* in the Court of Appeal, where the classification of nuisance as a property tort and a strong emphasis on this in the decision helped maintain the tort's proper focus. This case concerned whether overlooking (or an invasion of privacy) could be considered an actionable nuisance. While Mann J, in the first instance, held that there was no nuisance on the facts, he found that overlooking could, in principle, amount to a nuisance. The Court of Appeal, however, disagreed and stated that overlooking could not be a nuisance. They based this on the idea that nuisance was a tort that protected real property rights, and as per *Victoria Park Racing,*[32] 'English law is, rightly or wrongly, clear that the natural rights of an occupier do not include freedom from the view and inspection of neighbouring occupiers or of other persons'. As a property tort, the tort should concentrate on the underlying property rights to give them direction. As there is no right not to be overlooked, and this is not an element of ownership, there had been no breach, and the 'law does not always provide a remedy for every annoyance to a neighbour, however considerable that annoyance may be'.[33]

These decisions show how a strong emphasis on property rights and the role that the torts have in the protection of property can stop the slide into 'loss-thinking'. This emphasis appears to be easier to sustain if we think of tort law as rights-based. This is because the rights-based (or corrective justice) model directs attention to the underlying right that is being protected, which in the case of these torts (including negligence when it is being used to protect a property interest) is a property right. This link between rights-based thinking and recognition of the specifically property-protecting role of a property tort can be seen in these decisions. The cases

31 *Williams* (n 2) para 40.

32 *Victoria Park Racing & Recreation Grounds Co Ltd v Taylor* (1937) 58 CLR 479.

33 *Williams* (n 2) [79].

show the prominence that a rights-based perspective on a property tort gives to the right that is being protected or served. It further shows how this ensures that the nature of that right – the fact that it is specifically a property right – is given due attention. The link between rights-based thinking and such recognition shown in these cases is not a necessary one resulting from a logical or conceptual connection between the two (after all, torts can and do also protect rights to other interests). Rather, it is what one could call a facilitative one; focusing on the right facilitates paying attention to the nature of the right, which, in the case of a property tort is a property right.

The very recent Supreme Court decision in *Fearn*,[34] however, shows that words alone are not enough to maintain a focus on the property underlying the decision, and the sentiment behind those words needs to be followed through. This is because the Supreme Court reversed the decision of the Court of Appeal, but it did so while simultaneously paying lip service to the idea that the action is a property tort.[35] Both the majority decision, given by Lord Leggatt, and the minority decision, delivered by Lord Sales, acknowledged that private nuisance was a 'tort against land'. However, note that the majority here framed the idea of a property tort in a broader way than the Court of Appeal (and in a broader way than framed in this work), which previously focused on the need for a violation of property rights. The majority of the Supreme Court talked of the need for there to be a wrongful interference with claimant's enjoyment of rights over land for it to constitute a tort against land. Lord Sales' discussion in the minority does provide a fuller articulation of the land-based tort nature of private nuisance in line with what has previously been discussed in the Court of Appeal and previously in this work. The result of this was that while the majority attempted, to some extent, to recognise the property tort nature of the action, they did so in a limited way and in words only, which allowed the actual decision to undermine the property dimension of the case. This is because they accepted that the action still relates to interests in land, but now can be founded on the basis of visual intrusion, this reshaped the concept of property so that the protection from visual intrusion is now part of a property right that the law protects. And this is a significant change in the scope of nuisance but also potentially significant *beyond that* for 'property'. And this latter aspect of the discussion is often forgotten, but this is the implication of the dual nature of the property torts.

This Supreme Court judgment shows that more than mere words are needed to respect the dual nature of the property torts. There needs to be a focus on the *rights* that are being protected, the property rights, through these actions. While mentioning the property basis of the action, the court failed to identify or discuss the *right* that the action was protecting. In doing so, they actually extended the right beyond the scope of the previous understanding, implying that the right protected was not an exclusionary right but rather a 'right to use and enjoy' that, nonetheless, had

34 *Fearn v Trustees of the Tate Gallery* [2023] UKSC 4.

35 Victoria Ball, 'The "Property" in [Tate] Modern Nuisance: Case Comment on *Fearn v Trustees of the Tate Gallery*'. (2023) 87(2) Conveyancer and Property Lawyer 205.

'claim-right' characteristics making it binding on third parties – this is treading new ground, especially for those that advocate that property is about exclusion, and this is the element that has implications on third parties. As such, the Supreme Court judgment is another example of how a failure to *properly* recognise the property dimension in a property tort case can extend and re-shape property in an unacceptable way.

The difference in result from when the underlying right is the focus of the inquiry and when it is not, is clear. And when the property in the property torts is given sufficient weighting, this resulted in decisions which respect the underlying property right. As such, a small change in perception advocating the importance of the property in the property torts has the power to change the outcomes of decisions, and, therefore, to alter the development of the actions themselves. This suggests a way forward for the other torts as well, and this can be shown through examples as well as through recognising the difference between the Court of Appeal and Supreme Court's approaches in *Fearn*.

A New Illustration

As a new illustration, a decision from Chapter 4 will be re-analysed to show how a change in perception might translate into a different decision, one which better respects 'property' concerns. *Manchester Airport v Dutton*[36] would be a useful decision to discuss first because it provides a clear example of how the judges failed to concentrate on the rights underlying the action and instead fashioned a remedy based on some normative loss suffered by the claimant. We should recall that in *Dutton*, a claimant was able to bring a claim for an order for possession (and, hence, a trespass action) on the basis of a licence to occupy and without actual possession. In this case, the judges seem to have concentrated on the loss that the claimant had suffered. This loss was a normative loss, as a loss of a right, but not one exercisable against the defendant. The judges wanted to remedy that loss or protect that personal right. As a result, they awarded a remedy (which would normally only be available to someone with a property right) to someone who had no property right in the land or even a right that was enforceable against the defendants. The claimants had a personal right to occupy, and this was enforceable only against the person that granted the licence and not the defendants (who were protestors).

When thinking about this case, and tort law in general, from a protection of rights or corrective justice standpoint, the focus of tort law is about infringement of rights. To make a claim under this perspective, the claimant needs to show that he had a right exercisable against the claimant, and that this right was infringed. Stevens has said that where a tort claim concerns a thing or land, the claimant needs to show a right in that thing or land which is exercisable against the defendant,[37]

36 [2000] 1 QB 133.
37 Robert Stevens, *Torts and Rights* (OUP 2007) 120.

and this is normally done by showing a property right. This is because property rights are exercisable against the whole world; they are rights *in rem*.[38] This is important, as Stevens argues, because if, instead, we allowed all those who suffer a loss as a result of damage to any property to have a claim in tort, we would live in a legal system where all of us had rights in relation to all things or land.[39] Yet this seems to have been what happened in the *Dutton* decision, as the claimants were allowed to bring a tort claim without having a right exercisable against the defendants. If, however, this decision is 're-written' or re-analysed so that the hypothetical judges' reasoning corresponds with the idea that trespass is a property tort (and thus that both the property and tort aspects need to be respected), the outcome would change. In this new decision, the judges would concentrate on the dual or hybrid nature of the property torts; on the right(s) that the claimant had (or did not have) against the defendant and on whether that right was infringed.

When starting to analyse such a case, it is proposed that the judges should start with reference to the tort in question. They might state, for example, that this case concerns a question of trespass to land and relates to whether an order of possession can be given in circumstances where the claimant lacks any property right in the land and merely has a licence instead. A statement such as that '[T]respass to land is a property tort and involves the violation of real property rights' would be appropriate to make at the outset. This can, indeed, already be found in recent Court of Appeal nuisance cases.[40] Such statements and considerations ensure at the outset that the focus is kept on the dual nature of the action and that the importance of property law to such a decision is not overlooked.

The first substantive question to ask in such a decision, in line with a rights-based approach, is whether the claimants have a right. The answer here is yes, that they do. The claimants have a licence, which gives them a right (albeit a personal one as opposed to a right *in rem*) to enter and occupy the land. This personal right to enter and occupy is only enforceable against the other contracting party, namely, the National Trust. The second question is whether that right has been infringed, and again the answer is yes, that it has. The claimant was entitled to occupy the woods for the purpose of felling trees, and they are unable to do so because of the defendants, and, therefore, their right has been infringed. The final question that should be asked is whether the right that has been infringed was exercisable against the defendant – is it a property right?, as should be the case in the property torts. Here the answer is no. The personal right that the claimants had was only enforceable against the party who granted it, in this case the National Trust (who own the woods where the trees needed felling), but not the defendants who were protestors. Therefore, the decision, when we respect the role of tort law as protecting rights, should be that the claimants do not have a claim against the defendants and do not have standing to bring an order of possession or a trespass to land claim.

38 See Chapter 2, 'What is the Property that needs Protecting Through the Law'.
39 Stevens (n 37) 120.
40 See *Fearn* (n 3) [31].

While this means that the claimants here do not have a remedy, it does not follow that they are now powerless to remedy the situation and unable to stop the actions of the protestors. What should have happened was that the National Trust should have made the claim, as they had both possession and ownership at the time. This possession and ownership of the land gave them a right *in rem*, a property right, enforceable against everyone, against interference with the land. The court could then have made an order to remove the trespassers, and the claimants in the case could then have occupied the woods on the basis of their licence and felled the trees. This approach would not have undermined the role of the tort or the distinction between personal and property rights, unlike the original decision (discussed in Chapter 4).[41]

This shows how concentrating on the property tort nature combined with a rights conception view of tort law can ensure that the property torts, in this case specifically trespass to land, are stopped from inappropriate expansion and retain a focus on the property rights, which should be the core of the action. This prevents the slip into negligence or loss thinking. Thinking of tort law as rights-based or from a corrective justice-based approach, along with a recognition of where it sits between property and tort law, could help retain the emphasis of the property torts and ensure that they protect property interests appropriately. This is in direct contrast to the original decision, which, through a focus on loss and loss thinking, extended the conception of property and gave a remedy to someone who should have been without one. This is the difference that thinking of trespass (and all the property torts) from a different theoretical perspective which focuses on rights can have. It can change the outcome of the decision.

The results of other cases discussed in Chapter 4 can similarly be changed as a result of this proposal and by maintaining a focus on the dual nature of the rights. For example, it was suggested that cases succeeded in conversion where a claimant merely had a contractual right to possess.[42] If the proposals made here were to be taken up in these decisions, the dual property-tort nature of the rights would similarly be advanced at the outset. Through a rights-based focus, the courts in such cases would direct their attention first, to whether there has been an interference with a right; and second, to whether that right was enforceable against the defendant. Here, as in *Dutton*, the answer to the second question is no. The contractual right is merely enforceable against the other party to the contract, not against anyone else. Therefore, once again, there is not a right enforceable against the defendant. The result would be that a claim in conversion could not succeed here. Instead, the claimant would have contractual claims against the other party to the contract, and that party could potentially have a separate claim against the interferer.

41 See Chapter 4, 'The Property Torts, Entitlement to Sue, and the Concept of Loss 'as a Necessary and Sufficient Criterion'.

42 See Chapter 4, 'Use of Possession - Conversion and Trespass to Goods'.

Fixing the Remedies with a Change in Perception

While these small changes in thinking are useful to ensure the focus remains correct in the property torts, Chapter 5 also recognised that there were problems concerning the remedies available in the torts. Specifically, that chapter questioned whether the remedies available, and those commonly given, adequately protected property interests. Part of this problem can, once again, be corrected by thinking about tort law in terms of rights protection or as achieving corrective justice as mentioned earlier.

Part of the criticisms of the remedies given when monetary compensation was awarded, was how it was quantified and whether this adequately respected the property right that had been interfered with or lost as a result. Part of the importance of property rights is the freedom and control that having such rights provide. They enable you to control elements of your environment and allow you to have a degree of autonomy and control over decisions.[43] When property is interfered with, destroyed, or taken away from the rightful owner/possessor, the remedy needs to respect that what is lost is not just the physical object but this freedom also. And when damages are awarded, the loss they should be compensating for should account for this loss of control and autonomy or freedom, as well as the loss of the physical asset. When tort law is viewed as the law's response to loss, this idea is obscured. It creates a perception that loss is the core of the action and that loss is physical and can be remedied simply by paying the value of the item, if physically lost, or the cost of returning it to the previous condition, if it is land or cannot be easily replaced.

A change in the way that tort law is viewed is likely to help here, once again. If tort law is not viewed as society's response to loss but instead is concerned with rights and the vindication of rights, then the understanding of what damages should be doing is slightly altered. They are, then, not simply compensating for physical harm but vindicating or compensating also for the interference with the right, which allows this loss of autonomy to be considered in the monetary award. This seems to happen when damages are awarded on the basis of negotiating damages and could also account for the decisions which seem to award a higher figure, which accounts for this 'moral loss', as discussed by Descheemaeker.[44]

The quantification and perception of how damages should be awarded and what they are compensating for is only part of the problem with the remedies for the torts discussed thus far. A large problem, and one of the main concerns of Weir and many authors,[45] is the lack of specific performance remedies and, more specifically, the lack of return available for interference with personal property. This is often the motivator for any calls for reform. There is a discrepancy between how

43 This brief 'conclusion' of the importance of property rights is subject of a fuller discussion in Chapter 2 of this work. See 2, 'What is the Property that needs Protecting Through the Law'.

44 See, for example, Eric Descheemaeker, 'Rationalising Recovery for Emotional Harm in Tort Law' (2018) 134 LQR 602.

45 See, for example, Curwen (n 21).

often injunctions are awarded in the real property torts and how often return is awarded in the personal property torts. Although both are labelled as discretionary, in the former it is acknowledged that they should be awarded in cases of ongoing interferences, and, in these cases, damages should be awarded in lieu only in more exceptional circumstances (although post-*Lawrence* and *Fearn* it does seem that this trend is changing). In the personal property torts, however, damages are the norm, and return is discretionary and exceptional, to be applied only if the asset is special or irreplaceable. This difference in treatment leads to criticism of the protection in personal property torts. Return is an important remedy and should be available in a wider range of circumstances and not as exceptionally as it currently is. This can be done within the role and format of a tortious mechanism and is done in the real property actions.

While it is advocated that the correct approach to the problems raised here is through changes in perception of these torts, it is worth also having a closer look at the Torts (Interference with Goods) Act (T(IWG)A) 1977, the legislation that deals with the personal property torts and interferences with personal property. This legislation governs the remedies available for wrongful interference with property, and this is contained in section three of the Act. Here the relief granted should be: (a) an order for delivery of the goods; (b) an order for delivery of the goods but giving the defendant the alternative of paying damages by reference to the value of the goods; or (c) damages.[46] The granting of delivery up without the option of paying damages in substitute is discretionary[47] and likely to only be awarded where the goods are unique or special or are of particular value to the claimant, or they are difficult to replace. However, delivery up as a remedy only occurs relatively infrequently, in reality.[48] The exercise of discretion, then, seems to work in the opposite way in the personal property torts when compared to the real property torts. In the real property actions, injunctions are often seen as the primary remedy for many interferences, and, while it is acknowledged that they are discretionary (with the exercise of discretion in awarding damages in lieu governed by the *Shelfer*[49] principles with flexibility added more recently in *Lawrencer v Fen Tigers Ltd*[50]),[50] in practice damages in lieu are given less frequently. Here, damages will be awarded only if the injury to the right is small, capable of being quantified in a small amount of money, and an injunction would be oppressive. It, therefore, seems in practice that an injunction will be the norm unless the criteria for damages are satisfied, and damages are deemed adequate.

In the real property torts, the property-type remedy is the norm, and then if some criteria are satisfied and this is deemed unnecessary, the law falls back to damages. On the other hand, in the personal property torts, damages are the norm unless

46 Torts (Interference with Goods) Act 1977 (T(IWG)A) s3(2).

47 ibid s3(3).

48 Andrew Tettenborn (eds) *Clerk & Lindsell on Torts* (24th edn, Sweet & Maxwell 2024) 16–91.

49 *Shelfer v City of London Electric Lighting Company. Meux's Brewery Company v City of London Electric Lighting Company [1895] 1 Ch 287.*

50 [2014] UKSC 13, [2014] AC 822.

some extra criteria are satisfied and then a property-style remedy of return will be considered. If the exercise of discretion in the personal property torts was treated more in line with how it works in the real property torts, then the actions would arguably focus more on property and the criticisms discussed in the previous chapter would be reduced. This seems to be the case in the real property torts, as there is less criticism of the remedies in trespass to land and nuisance than there is in the personal property torts. While on paper the actions are similar, with the property-type remedies being discretionary, the practice in the real property torts and how the discretion works in practice has yielded better results in terms of property protection and could, therefore, help us to describe a route forward for the other torts which protect property. This would again mean that the torts better protect property and would also show greater respect for the dual nature of these actions and where they sit between property and tort law.

Some authors, Cane in particular, have sought to explain why a distinction exists between the protection of real and personal property. This was dealt with fully in Chapter 5, so only a brief discussion is needed here. Cane has argued that the difference in treatment and difference in prioritisation between the 'proprietary-style' remedy and damages is accounted for by the fact that chattels or personal property are not normally unique or of special value to their owner.[51] Respectfully, while this is often rehearsed as the reason, this does not necessarily accord with real life, and neither do people always have sentimental attachments to real property. Rather, this is a simplified generalisation – something that Cane recognised.[52] This work, instead, proceeds on the basis that the importance of property *per se* comes from the freedom it grants the holder, and the ability that one has, with property, to control aspects of one's life. When viewed in this way, the ability to regain control is always important. Further, the sentimental value and personhood-related arguments concerning personal property were already recited and discussed in Chapter 5.

To show the difference in prioritisation in practice, we can recall the bicycle example used in Chapter 5. Here, the prioritisation in the personal property torts was questioned by explaining the likely solution to a bicycle theft. The chapter argued that in conversion it was highly unlikely that return would be awarded, unless the claimant bridged the additional obstacles and succeeded in showing that the bicycle had special sentimental value or was in some way unique. The chapter questioned whether this was the correct approach. In doing so, comparisons can be drawn to injunctions where the discretion works in the opposite way. If this approach was taken, the preference would be for awarding return, unless the claimant (or defendant) could show that it was unnecessary or inappropriate and that damages would be sufficient.

51 Cane (n 6) 145.
52 Peter Cane, *Tort Law and Economic Interests* (OUP 1991) 12.

Proposal: Conclusion

The suggestions here centre around the need for a change in how we view or perceive the property-protecting torts, and they advance a novel way of thinking about this group of actions. Changes such as recognising the importance that these actions have to property and tort law and a change in how we view the role of tort law in these actions can solve the problems raised. These actions are fundamentally part of both property law and tort law, and if it can be ensured that the actions are thought of as such, then these incremental changes (as decided in each new case) which move the torts away from property and lead to a lack of protection, can be halted and reversed. This thinking can, and will, result in changes in outcomes in the cases. This proposal, therefore, points a way forward, backed in theory and logic, which can be used by judges and practitioners who are grappling with these problems in the case law, as evidenced in the first instance and Court of Appeal cases of *Fearn v Board of the Trustees of the Tate Gallery* and *Williams v Network Rail*.

8 Conclusion

Cane, writing in 1997, said that one of the 'most important products' of the analysis he completed in *The Anatomy of Tort Law* was a 'greater recognition of the central role of tort law in protecting property'.[1] Almost three decades later this work has shown that there remain problems within the torts that have been tasked with protecting property. Specifically, there is a failure to recognise the importance and role of *property* within the *property torts*.

The common law's lack of any true proprietary action (in terms of a mechanism that is proprietary in both substance *and* form) and its subsequent reliance on the law of torts for the protection of tangible property interests and land has invoked criticism.[2] And indeed, it has been shown that issues do arise when the protection of property interests is left to mechanisms that are rooted in an area of law that, as a whole, is informed by a set of concerns that have little to do with the vindication of property rights. Much of this previous critique comes from consideration of the tort of conversion, and this can be seen in the quoted segments spotlighted at the outset of each chapter. These criticisms hold true, however, for all of the torts, not just conversion, and a consideration of *all* of the torts elucidates previously unnoticed patterns and similarities. Two core issues were addressed in this work.

The first issue was that the demarcation of those able to bring a claim has been unduly influenced by loss-thinking. Rather than focusing on the property rights underlying the actions, the torts have been extended through judicial decisions to assist anyone who has suffered some loss (be that physical or normative loss) and whom judges feel deserves some compensation. The second issue concerns the remedies available, which have similarly been influenced by the tortious classification, resulting in remedies which do not fully protect the rights underlying the actions or what is deemed important about these rights.

Underlying these issues is the tension between what property law *should* be protecting and how tort law *chooses* to protect it. Because these actions are tortious,

1 Peter Cane, *The Anatomy of Tort Law* (Hart, 1997).

2 See, for example, Andrew Tettenborn, 'Damages in Conversion – The Exception or the Anomaly?' (1993) 52 CLJ 128; Andrew Tettenborn, 'Conversion, Tort and Restitution' in Norman Palmer and Ewan McKendrick (eds), *Interests in Goods* (2nd edn, Lloyds of London Press 1998); Alison Clarke and Paul Kohler, *Property Law: Commentary and Materials* (CUP 2005); Nick Curwen, 'The Remedy in Conversion: Confusing Property and Obligation' (2006) 26 LS 570.

DOI: 10.4324/9781032692098-11

the perception and view of tort law shapes the actions – although it does so without fully respecting the importance to property law that these actions have – and this has implications for the protection of property. Green has previously argued that any perceived difficulty that flows or is associated with this combination of proprietary and tortious ideas rests on the assumption that (i) these two areas require separate treatment and (ii) on an interpretation of tort law that does not allow, in and of itself, the protection of property. This work has shown that as things stand, the latter is true. As the law is *currently* working, in practice, tort law fails to properly protect property and fails to consider property ideals. Property is, therefore, protected by a group of claims and remedies that are rooted in an area of law that is informed by a completely different set of concerns. The concerns of tort law, as evidenced in the case law, are focused on remedying loss instead of the protection of property rights, and this leads to profound and fundamental problems since the protection of property through tort is simultaneously too broad and too narrow and undermines the category of property rights and the balance struck by the law by both showing a lack of respect for the proprietary nature of these interests and resulting in a lack of protection.

This can be seen regarding who is entitled to bring a claim. The role of property law in determining the rights underlying these actions has been ignored, and extensions and exceptions have been created, allowing more people to bring a tort action (for example, *Dutton*[3] in trespass to land). This artificially extends the actions and causes them to lose their property focus. It also undermines the balance of what rights are seen as proprietary and what rights have implications for third parties.

Similarly, the classification of these actions as tortious, and, in turn, the application of tortious ideas also causes a lack of protection of property. This can be seen through the remedies available in the property torts. Injunctions and return are only discretionary remedies, with the latter in particular being awarded less frequently, and the quantification of damages does not always give full respect to the right that has been interfered with. What is important about property rights is not just the thing in which the right subsists but rather the control and freedom given by that right. The property right in a thing enables a person to control an aspect of their life and make decisions about it. Any remedies need to protect and compensate for the loss of the right rather than merely the loss of the thing or object of property.[4]

Both of these issues flow from the same foundational problem. The problem is that tort law ideas inform and change the property torts in ways that are not acceptable from a property law perspective. Property protection is rooted in an area of law that is informed by a completely different set of concerns. Tort law ideas are

3 *Manchester Airport Plc v Dutton* [2000] 1 QB 133.

4 This idea has been discussed fully in Chapter 5, including the opposing ideas of Peter Cane and the arguments about *why* real property is given 'greater' protection to personal property. See Chapter 5, 'Remedies in the Property Torts'.

dominant, and property is ignored because the actions are classified and thought of as purely tortious actions. Because they are classified and thought of purely as tortious, the inherent 'propertiness' of the actions are ignored or forgotten. As mechanisms aimed at the protection of property, this is a key flaw. This shows the importance of classification, and in particular, the *appropriate* classification of actions. There cannot be actions which appear 'wrongly placed', since classification shapes and influences judicial decision-making.[5]

The rectification of these issues, however, does not need great legislative change but rather a change in how these actions are thought about and how they are perceived. If these actions are thought of as property torts, with a foot in both property and tort law, some of the implications identified can be minimised. Greater recognition needs to be given to the special place that these actions have, as they have a unique role spanning both property and tort law. If this is done, and in conjunction that we think of tort law in a way that respects the underlying rights it serves to safeguard, property can be better respected and protected by tortious actions. For this to be successful, it is also useful for tort law to be perceived not as loss-based but rather as rights-based or based on corrective justice. This is because the rights-based or corrective justice model directs attention to the underlying right that is being protected, which in the case of these torts (including negligence when it is being used to protect a property interest) is a property right. This facilitative link between rights-based thinking and recognition of the specifically property-protecting role of a property tort can be seen in these decisions. They show how the prominence that a rights-based perspective on a property tort gives to the right that is being protected or served to ensure that the nature of that right – the fact that it is specifically a property right – is given due attention.

These changes will ensure better protection of property and will respect the role and aim of the actions. While the courts have already shown willingness to respect the importance of the 'property-tort' classification in recent Court of Appeal nuisance cases, ultimately, judges and the decisions and dicta from the highest courts will determine the success of these proposals.

5 Charlie Webb, 'Treating Like Cases Alike: Principle and Classification in Private law' in Andrew Robertson and Hang Wu Tang (eds), *Goals of Private Law* (Hart 2009) 215; Chapter 4 of this book, 'Loss and Tort Law - Classification'.

Bibliography

Books

Alexander G and Penalver E, *An Introduction to Property Theory* (CUP 2012)
Austin J, *Lectures on Jurisprudence or the Philosophy of Positive Law* (Robert Campbell ed, 5th edn, The Law Book Exchange 1885)
Baker J, *An Introduction to English Legal History* (4th edn, Butterworths 2002)
Beever A, *A Theory of Tort Liability* (Hart 2016)
Beever A, *The Law of Private Nuisance* (Hart 2013)
Bell AP, *Modern Law of Personal Property in England and Ireland* (Butterworths 1989)
Birks P, *Unjust Enrichment* (2nd edn, OUP 2005)
Bridge M, *Personal Property Law* (4th edn, OUP 2015)
Bridge M, Gullifer L, McMeel G, and Low K, *The Law of Personal Property* (3rd edn, Sweet & Maxwell 2021)
Burrows A, *English Private Law* (3rd edn, OUP 2013)
Burrows A, *Remedies for Torts and Breach of Contract and Equitable Wrongs* (4th edn, OUP 2019)
Cane P, *Key Ideas in Law: Tort Law* (Hart 2017)
Cane P, *The Anatomy of Tort Law* (Hart 1997)
Cane P, *Tort Law and Economic Interests* (OUP 1991)
Clarke A and Kohler P, *Property Law: Commentary and Materials* (CUP 2005)
Dagan H, *A Liberal Theory of Property* (CUP 2020)
Dixon M, *Modern Land Law* (11th edn, Routledge 2018)
Douglas S, *Liability for Wrongful Interferences with Chattels* (1st edn, Hart 2011)
Edelman J, *Gain-Based Damages* (Bloomsbury 2002)
Elvin D and Karas J, *Unlawful Interference with Land* (2nd edn, Sweet & Maxwell 2002)
Fifoot, *History and Sources of the Common Law: Tort and Contract* (Stevens & Sons, 1949)
Giglio F, *The Foundations of Restitution for Wrongs* (Hart 2007)
Giliker P, *Tort* (8th edn, Sweet & Maxwell 2023)
Goudkamp J and Nolan D (eds), *Winfield & Jolowicz Tort* (20th edn, Sweet & Maxwell 2020)
Gray K and Gray SF, *Elements of Land Law* (5th edn, OUP 2009)
Gray K and Gray SF, *Land Law* (7th edn, OUP 2011)
Green S and Randall J, *The Tort of Conversion* (1st edn, Hart 2009)
Harris D, Campbell D and Halson R, *Remedies in Contract and Tort* (2nd edn, Butterworths 2010)
Hegel GWF, *Hegel's Philosophy of Right* (Knox TM, tr, Clarendon Press 1952)
Ibbetson D, *A Historical Introduction to the Law of Obligations* (OUP 1999)
Jaffey P, *Private Law and Property Claims* (Hart 2007)
Maitland FW, *The Forms of Action at Common Law: A Course of Lectures* (Whittaker WJ and Chaytor AH ed, CUP 1910)

DOI: 10.4324/9781032692098-12

Mattei U, *Basic Principles of Property Law: A Comparative, Legal and Economic Introduction* (Greenwood Press 2000)
McBride N and Bagshaw R, *Tort Law* (5th edn, Pearsons 2015)
McBride N and Bagshaw R, *Tort Law* (6th edn, Pearsons 2018)
McBride N and Bagshaw R, *Tort Law* (7th edn, Pearsons 2024)
Mulheron R, *Principles of Tort Law* (CUP 2020)
Murphy J, *The Law of Nuisance* (OUP 2010)
Nicholas B, *An Introduction to Roman Law* (OUP 1962)
Penner JE, *The Idea of Property in Law* (OUP 2003)
Pretto-Sakmann A, *Boundaries of Personal Property: Shares and Sub-Shares* (Hart 2005)
Raz J, *Ethics in the Public Domain: Essays in the Morality of Law and Politics* (OUP 1995)
Ripstein A, *Force and Freedom: Kant's Legal and Political Philosophy* (Harvard University Press 2009)
Ripstein A, *Private Wrongs* (Harvard University Press 2016)
Rostill L, *Possession, Relative Title, and Ownership in English Law* (OUP 2021)
Rotherham C, *Proprietary Remedies in Context* (Hart 2002)
Smith R, *Property Law* (8th edn, Pearson 2014)
Steele J, *Tort Law: Text, Cases and Materials* (4th edn, OUP 2017)
Stevens R, *Torts and Rights* (OUP 2007)
Tettenborn A (eds) *Clerk & Lindsell on Torts* (24th edn, Sweet & Maxwell 2024)
Vaines C, *Personal Property* (1st edn, Butterworths 1954)
Weinrib E, *Corrective Justice* (OUP 2012)
Weinrib E, *The Idea of Private Law* (OUP 2012)
Weir T, *A Casebook on Tort*, (10th edn, Sweet & Maxwell 2004)
Zimmermann R, *The Law of Obligations: Roman Foundations of the Civilian Tradition* (OUP 1996)

Official Publications

The Eighteenth Report of the Law Reform Committee (Conversion and Detinue) Cmnd. 4774, 1971
Law Commission, *Digital Assets: Final Report* (Law Com No 412, 2023)
Law Commission, *Digital Assets: Consultation Paper* (Law Com No 256, 2022)

Book Chapters

Birks P, 'Definition and Division: A Meditation on Institutes 3.13' in Birks P (ed), *The Classification of Obligations* (Clarendon 1997)
Burrows A, 'Are "Damages on the Wrotham Park Basis" Compensatory, Restitutionary or Neither?' in Saidov D and Cunnington R (ed), *Contract Damages: Domestic and International* (OUP 2008)
Burrows A, 'Damages and Rights' in Robertson A and Nolan D (ed), *Rights and Private Law* (Hart 2011)
Burrows A, 'Judicial Remedies' in Burrows A (ed), *English Private Law* (3rd edn, OUP 2013)
Lady Carr, 'Torts Borderlines' in William Day and Julius Gower (ed), *Borderline in Private Law* (OUP 2024) 63.
Douglas S and McFarlane B, 'Defining Property Rights' in Penner J and Smith H (ed), *Philosophical Foundations of Property Law* (OUP 2013)
Lord Fancourt, 'Property's Borderline' in William Day and Julius Grower (ed), *Borderlines in Private Law* (OUP 2024)

Giliker P, 'Marking the Boundary: The Relationship between Private Nuisance, Negligence and Fault', in Lowry J and Edmunds R (ed), *Environmental Protection and the Common Law* (Hart 2000) 177.

Giliker P, 'The Relationship between Property Law and Tort Law' in Hudson A (ed), *New Perspectives on Property Law: Obligations and Restitution* (Taylor and Francis 2003)

Gray K and Gray SF, 'The Idea of Property in Land' in Bright S and Dewar JK (ed), *Land Law: Themes and Perspectives* (OUP 1998)

Harris D, 'Concept of Possession in English Law' in Guest A (ed), *Oxford Essays in Jurisprudence* (OUP 1961)

Honoré A, 'Ownership' in Guest A (ed), *Oxford Essays in Jurisprudence* (OUP 1961)

Hudson A, 'Trespass to Goods' in Palmer N and McKendrick E (ed), *Interests in Goods* (2nd edn, Lloyds of London Press 1998)

McBride N, 'Rights and the Basis of Tort Law' in Robertson A and Nolan D (ed), *Rights and Private Law* (Hart 2011)

Nolan D and Davis J, 'Torts and Equitable Wrongs' in Burrows A (ed), *English Private Law* (3rd edn, OUP 2013)

Nolan D, '"A Tort Against Land": Private Nuisance as a Property Tort' in Robertson A and Nolan D (ed), *Rights and Private Law* (Hart 2011)

Nolan D, 'The Essence of Private Nuisance' in Ben McFarlane and Sinead Agnew (ed), *Modern Studies in Property Law, Volume 10* (Bloomsbury 2019)

Lord Sales, 'Borderline in Private Law: An Introduction' in William Day and Julius Gower (ed), *Borderlines in Private Law* (OUP 2024)

Scott A, 'The Scope of Non-Contractual Obligations' in Ahern J and Binchy W (ed), *The Rome II Regulation on the Law Applicable to Non-Contractual Obligations: A New International Litigation Regime* (Martinus Nijhoff 2009)

Stevens R, 'Rights and Other Things' in Robertson A and Nolan D (ed), *Rights and Private Law* (Hart 2011)

Tettenborn A, 'Conversion, Tort and Restitution' in Palmer N and McKendrick E (ed), *Interests in Goods* (2nd edn, Lloyds of London Press 1998)

Webb C, 'Treating Like Cases Alike: Principle and Classification in Private Law' in Robertson A and Tang HW (ed), *The Goals of Private Law* (Hart 2009)

Weir A, 'Staggering March of Negligence' in Cane P and Stapleton J (ed) *The Law of Obligations: Essays in Celebration of John Fleming* (Clarendon Press OUP 1998)

Journal Articles

Atmaz Al-Sibaie J, 'Possession and Using Land as an Owner Would' (2024) 88(2) Conv 176

Balganesh S,' Property Along the Tort Spectrum: Trespass to Chattels and the Anglo-American Doctrinal Divergence' (2006) 35 CLWR 135

Ball V, 'Looking Back on *Dutton*: The Precedent Set, the Accounts Given and the Problems Caused' (2023) 87(2) Conv 181

Ball V, 'The Influence of Loss in the Property Torts' (2020) 31(3) King's Law Journal 426

Ball V, 'The "Property" in [Tate] Modern Nuisance: Case comment on *Fearn v Trustees of the Tate Gallery*' (2023) 87(2) Conv 205

Beever A, 'What Does Tort Law Protect?' (2015) 27 SAcLJ, 626

Birks P, 'Personal Property: Proprietary Rights and Remedies' (2000) 11(1) KCLJ 1

Burrows B, 'One Step Forward?' (2018) 134 LQR 515

Calabresi G and Melamed D, 'Property Rules, Liability Rules, and Inalienability: One View of the Cathedral' (1972) 85 Harv L Rev 1089

Cane P, 'Justice and Justifications for Tort Liability' (1982) 2 OJLS 30

Cane P, 'The Anatomy of Private Law Theory: A 25th Anniversary Essay' (2005) 25 OJLS 203

Cane P, 'What a Nuisance!' (1997) 113 LQR 515
Clarke A, 'Use, Time and Entitlement' (2004) 57 CLP 239
Cohen F, 'Dialogue on Private Property' (1954) 9 Rutgers L Rev 357
Curwen N, 'The Remedy in Conversion: Confusing Property and Obligation' (2006) 26 LS 570
Descheemaeker E, 'Rationalising Recovery for Emotional Harm in Tort Law' (2018) 134 LQR 602
Descheemaeker E, 'The Standardisation of Tort Damages' (2021) 84(1) MLR 1, 18
Devonshire P, 'The Hypothetical Negotiation Measure: An Untenable Fiction?' (2012) 3 LMCLQ 393
Dobbs A, 'Possession and Occupation – Two Sides of the Same Coin?' (1999) 10 KCLJ 226
Douglas S, 'The Nature of Conversion' (2009) 68 CLJ 198
Eekelaar JM, 'Nuisance and Strict Liability' (1973) 8 IJ 191
Epstein R, 'Nuisance Law: Corrective Justice and its Utilitarian Constraints' (1979) 8 JLS 49
Essert C, 'Nuisance and the Normative Boundaries of Ownership' (2016) 52 Tulsa Law Review 85
Evans V, 'Conversion and its Future (Reflecting on the Law Commission's work on Digital Assets)' (2024) 88(3) Conv 267
Fox D, 'Relativity of Title at Law and in Equity' (2006) 65(2) CLJ 330
Gardner J, 'What is Tort Law for? Part 1. The Place of Corrective Justice' (2011) 30 L&Phil 1
Goode RM, 'The Right to Trace and its Impact on Commercial Transactions – I' (1976) 93 LQR 360, 364
Green S, 'Can a Digitized Product be the Subject of Conversion?' (2006) 4 LMCLQ 568
Green S, 'To Have and to Hold? Conversion and Intangible Property' (2008) 71 MLR 114
Green S, 'Understanding the Wrongful Interference Actions' (2010) 73(1) Conv 15
Hohfeld W, 'Fundamental Legal Conceptions as Applied in Judicial Reasoning' (1916–1917) 26 Yale LJ 710
Hohfeld W, 'Some Fundamental Legal Conceptions as Applied to Judicial Reasoning' (1913–1914) 23 Yale LJ 16
Johnson DR, 'Reflections on the Bundle of Rights' (2007) 32 Vermont LR 247
Lee J, 'Different Views of Nuisance' (2023) 139 LQR 535
Lee M, 'What is Private Nuisance?' (2003) 119 LQR 298
Lochery E, 'Pushing the Boundaries of Dutton?' (2011) 74(1) Conv 74
Macklam N, 'Colour Quest Ltd v Total Downstream UK Plc: The Nature of a Beneficiary's Interest Under a Trust' (2010) 73(3) Conv 265
Merrill T, 'Property and the Right to Exclude' (1998) 77 Neb L Rev 730
Mitchell C and Rostill L, 'Making Sense of Mesne Profits: Remedies' (2021) 80(3) CLJ 552
Murphy J, 'Hybrid Torts and Explanatory Tort Theory' (2018) 64(1) McGill Law Journal 1
Murphy J, 'Rethinking Injunctions in Tort law' (2007) 27(3) OJLS 509
Murphy J, 'Torts Hierarchy of Protected Interests' (2022) 81(2) CLJ 356
Nolan D, 'The Distinctiveness of *Rylands v Fletcher*' (2005) 121 LQR 421
Panesar S, 'The Importance of Possession in the Common Law Tradition' (2003) 8(1) Cov LJ 1
Paton E and Seabourne G, 'Unchained Remedy: Recovery of Land by Licensees' (1999) 63 Conv 535
Posner R and Landes W, 'The Positive Economic Theory of Tort Law' (1980) 15 Ga L Rev 851
Radin MJ, 'Property and Personhood' (1982) 34 STAN L REV 957
Ramaekers E, 'What is Property Law' (2017) 37(3) OJLS 588
Rostill L, 'Possession and Damages for Tortious Interferences with Chattels' (2021) 41(2) OJLS 459
Rudden B, 'Things as Thing and Things as Wealth' (1994) 14(1) OJLS 81

Sawtell D, 'Injunctions, Land and the Cynical Breach' (2022) 42 LS 649
Scott A and Rushworth A, 'Rome II Regulation: Choice of Law for Non-contractual Obligations' (2008) 3 LMCLQ 274
Scott A, 'Total Chaos?' (2010) 4 LMCLQ 536
Senu J, 'Negotiating Damages and the Compensatory Principle' (2020) 40 OJLS 110
Sharpe R and Waddams S, 'Damages for Lost Opportunity to Bargain' (1982) 2 OJLS 290
Smith H, 'Property as the Law of Things' (2012) 125 Harv L Rev 1691
Smith H, 'Property is Not Just a Bundle of Rights' (2011) 8 Econ Journal Watch 279
Smith S, 'Rights-Threats, Wrongs and Injustices: The Common Law's Causes of Action' (2017) 27 NZULR 1033
Swadling W, 'Opening the Numerus Clausus' (2000) 116 LQR 354
Tettenborn A, 'Damages in Conversion – The Exception or the Anomaly?' (1993) 52(1) CLJ 128
Tettenborn A, 'Trust Property and Conversion: An Equitable Confusion' (1996) 55(1) CLJ 36
Weinrib E, 'Corrective Justice in a Nutshell' (2002) 52 UTLJ 349
Winfield PH, 'Nuisance as a Tort' (1931) 4(2) CLJ 189

Online Sources

Nicholas B and Rodger A, 'Possession, Legal' in *Oxford Classical Dictionary* (Online publication March 2016) <https://oxfordre.com/classics/view/10.1093/acrefore/9780199381135.001.0001/acrefore-9780199381135-e-5276?rskey=4vhJGv&result=1>
Zimmermann R, 'Theft, Roman' in *Oxford Classical Dictionary* (Online publication March 2016) <https://oxfordre.com/classics/view/10.1093/acrefore/9780199381135.001.0001/acrefore-9780199381135-e-6335>

Index

Note: Page numbers followed by 'n' indicate note numbers

FSC
www.fsc.org
MIX
Papier | Fördert
gute Waldnutzung
FSC® C083411

Kolibri 360 GmbH
Ferdinand-Jühlke-Straße 7
99095 Erfurt, Deutschland
produktsicherheit@kolibri360.de